BALLROOM

A PEOPLE'S HISTORY OF DANCING

HILARY FRENCH

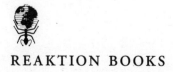

REAKTION BOOKS

Published by
REAKTION BOOKS LTD
Unit 32, Waterside
44–48 Wharf Road
London N1 7UX, UK
www.reaktionbooks.co.uk

First published 2022
First published in paperback 2025
Copyright © Hilary French 2022

Printed and bound in Great Britain
by CPI Group (UK) Ltd, Croydon CR0 4YY

A catalogue record for this book is available from the British Library

ISBN 978 1 78914 999 9

'Have you ever watched *Strictly Come Dancing* and wondered about the history of ballroom and Latin dancing? If so, Hilary French has provided an authoritative and accessible introduction . . . French's richly detailed book is thoroughly recommended for anyone intrigued by the social history of dancing.'

BBC History magazine

'French's fascinating people's history of dancing is also a cultural history of social space: those cathedral-sized palaces created to meet the enormous demand for dancing at the turn of the twentieth century.'
Morning Star

'Fascinating . . . tells the history of dance from the very beginning . . . an essential read. It explores the dances, lavish venues, competitions and influential instructors. It also traces the decline of partner dancing and it resurgence in recent years with the hugely popular TV shows *Strictly Come Dancing* and *Dancing with the Stars*.'

Dance News

'*Strictly* fans will love Hilary French's *Ballroom*, a "people's history" of dancing that tells how American ragtime and Parisian tango fuelled a dancing craze in Britain in the early part of the last century. The book also charts the emergence of Latin dance, and the rise, fall and rise again of ballroom dancing.'

Choice Magazine, UK

'A MUST read for anyone curious and interested in the special origins and developments of Ballroom and Latin American dancing.'
Marcus Hilton MBE, President of the British DanceSport Association, and with Karen Hilton MBE nine times World Professional Ballroom champion

'A fascinating book. Hilary French tells the history of dance from the very beginning. I learnt a lot and found it immensely interesting and insightful. If you are interested in dance and how we have got to where we are today, this is an essential read. Enjoy!'

Matthew Cutler, British, UK and World's Latin champion,
Strictly Come Dancing champion and owner, Matico Dance Studio

'Given the global popularity of *Strictly Come Dancing* and spin-offs, and the renaissance of partner dancing, it is amazing that no-one has written a cultural history of *Ballroom* before. Hilary French's pioneering book – written from the perspective of someone who combines a deep commitment to ballroom dancing with acknowledged expertise in design – combines social history, economics, fashion, music, dance technique *and* architecture and design in an engaging mix. At one level, this is the story of a very British phenomenon influenced by Hollywood, Latin America and Europe. At another, it is the story of a privileged pastime which morphed into working class culture. At yet another, it celebrates couple dancing over the solo variety. *Ballroom* has mapped out a rich area of study, and it blends scholarship with infectious enthusiasm.'

Professor Sir Christopher Frayling, Cultural Historian,
Broadcaster and Former Rector of the Royal College of Art

CONTENTS

'Dancing is marvellous – it's our whole life. It isn't just the physical pleasure. It's the dressing up, the competing and even the worries and disappointments that drive us.'

Vicky Green and Michael Barr (World Champions 1981–5),
interviewed in the *Daily Mirror*, 12 May 1971

A typical mid-twentieth-century image of ballroom dancers Bob Burgess and Doreen Freeman, May 1962, successful competitors, teachers and proprietors of the Grafton Dance Centre, London.

Introduction

The BBC launched *Strictly Come Dancing* in 2004. Very quickly, it became one of its most popular broadcasts, with spin-off versions sold worldwide and growing audience figures. In 2022 Blackpool's Showtown Museum is scheduled to open with a section dedicated to 'how Blackpool became the spiritual home of ballroom dance and continues to host the biggest international dance festival in the world'.[1] Ballroom dancing, once the privilege of the wealthy leisured classes in their private houses, became the most popular working-class pastime during most of the twentieth century, rivalled only by cinema until its demise in the face of other demands on leisure time and a rapidly changing music scene. Dancesport, the competitive version that has continued unabated, together with its reinvented social form, share a stubborn refusal to give up their relationship with a more glamorous past. Yet the history of ballroom, from its early days at the beginning of the twentieth century to the razzmatazz of *Strictly*, is a little-known subject. This book sets out to tell the story – its places, its people and its dances.

Ballroom: A People's History of Dancing focuses on what was originally termed modern dancing and became the 'English style' or standard: the waltz, foxtrot, Viennese waltz, ballroom tango and quickstep, and on the Latin American dances: the rumba, samba, jive, paso doble and cha-cha-cha. These are a series of dances that were codified in the mid-twentieth century; today they remain the ten International Style dances. The story in this book begins with the surge in popularity of dancing among the working classes that resulted in the construction of Britain's first public ballrooms in Blackpool. The growing demand led to the professionalization of teachers of dancing and their decisions to organize and codify modern dancing. Dancing remained a popular pastime and, through its depictions in Hollywood musicals, established its association with new European design ideas that helped to reinforce the idea that it represented glamour and luxury. This lifestyle was emulated by the company Mecca in its Palais de Danse – dance palaces – and at holiday camps where dancing was the perfect indoor activity. The early days of radio and then television consolidated ballroom dancing's position as the most popular leisure time activity in Britain, and it figured in the daily press on a regular basis. Ballroom was a part of everyday life – a people's passion.

In the second half of the twentieth century the exotic Latin dances arrived; the modern dances or the English dances began to be regarded as outdated and old-fashioned. Eventually, with rapid changes in leisure activities, new music styles, recorded music, television and beach holidays, ballrooms, or palais, became redundant and dance halls closed down. In most social situations, partner dancing came to an end and dancing solo without physical contact became the norm. Competition dancing continued, however, rebranded as Dancesport to distinguish it from dancing as a leisure activity. More recently Ballroom and Latin dancing has seen a renewed interest; devoted social dancers all over the country have taken charge of the repertoire and explored other forms of dancing too. Social dancers are happy to enjoy party dances, to mix sequence and line dances with Ballroom and Latin dancing, authentic or club dances and alternative rhythms, and to demand their own kinds of competitions often ignoring the professional associations' regulations.

The story of ballroom is primarily a British one. What were to become the agreed international styles for Ballroom and Latin dances were codified in Britain before being spread across the world by British champions. It is at the same time a story of adoption, appropriation and reinvention, as the dances originated elsewhere. Influences from America are particularly important, as many new styles of music and dancing originated there. Early forms of jazz and ragtime were followed by the Charleston, jitterbug, rock'n'roll and twist. In Britain, the dancing teachers' associations, aiming to create a standard that could be taught and learnt by everyone everywhere, took the basic form of the imported dances and re-designed them into new forms that suited their taste and could be easily assimilated.

Ballroom explores the codification of the dances and the growth of dancing competitions, but this is primarily a cultural history. It therefore necessarily intersects with other aspects of twentieth-century history. In design terms, new public ballrooms either imitated the theatrical Neoclassical styles of the upper-class private ballrooms or the glamorous Art Deco set designs of 1930s Hollywood movies. In the first decades of the twentieth century ballrooms and dance halls were just one of a growing number of other new kinds of interior space: department stores, hotels, restaurants and cinemas – all buildings that contributed to new forms of public life experienced by women in particular. The growing numbers of entertainment and leisure companies such as Mecca or Rank who ran ballrooms made a significant contribution to Britain's economic history.

This story is written from the perspective of a committed social dancer and occasional competitor. It is one step into this charismatic world and takes a very broad view but one which has touched upon many other aspects of dancing to be explored in more detail – the multitude of traditional and folk dances; the design history of the many ballrooms and dance halls; the costumes, and how they have responded to changing fashions yet have remained untouched by the external world; music and its role in the history of dancing; the institutions that run ballroom; and ballroom's relationship with sport.

Ballroom dancing occupies a space unlike other forms of dance. Classical ballet and its related forms of dancing has a set of rules to follow and training to hone the skills needed – the results are for performance. Social dancing, the vernacular, is participatory and has many different forms that have emerged in every culture; easy to pick up and dance either with or without a partner, alone or in groups. Ballroom and Latin dancing sits between the two, requiring studied and acquired technique beyond the level of other partner dances alongside its social participatory purpose. In its most developed form this is a unique type of dance, which beyond the glitzy costumes and make-up requires the energy and cooperation of two people to create a performance and experience together.

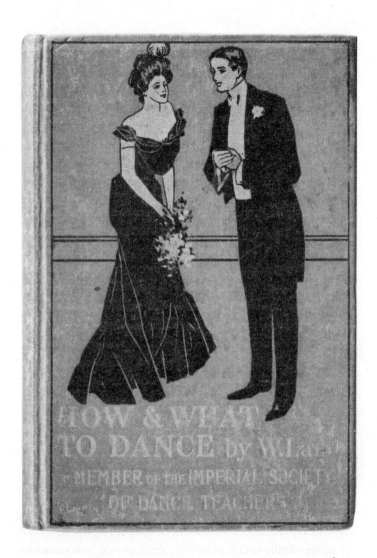

Cover of *How and What to Dance* by William Lamb (1906). The book included chapters on 'Round Dances', 'Square Dances' and 'Miscellaneous Dances' and an introductory section on subjects such as etiquette, deportment and hints for managing a dance.

ONE

'A Flood of Splendour':
Blackpool's New Ballrooms

The sight of the Blackpool Tower has stood for the loss of inhibitions, the encouragement of pleasure and for several generations, the chance of uninterrupted Tango and cha-cha.

The Observer, 1994[1]

Any ballroom dancer would agree that Blackpool should be at the centre of a history of modern ballroom dancing. The Blackpool Dance Festival, or simply 'Blackpool' for dance devotees, was launched in 1920, has been held every year since (apart from 1940–45 and 2020), and is still the largest and longest-running dance festival in the world. A seemingly unlikely place, perhaps, to become the focus of ballroom dancing, or indeed anything of special importance, but Blackpool is unique in Britain. As the influential architectural historian Nikolaus Pevsner noted, referring to the predominance of its built construction, 'English social history of the second half of the 19th century and the first half of the 20th century could not be written without Blackpool.'[2]

In the 1870s, '80 and '90s seaside resort development was taking place all around the British coastline, and entertainment companies set up specifically to cash in on those developments were numerous. According to a historical survey of seaside architecture, *People's Palaces* by Lynn Pearson, more than two hundred substantial new entertainment buildings were constructed between 1870 and 1914 in sixty resorts in England.[3] Those on the south coast, probably with better weather and close to London and other densely populated urban centres, saw the fastest growth. Amid this intense period of development and a new style of seaside architecture even, Blackpool remains unique for its entertainment buildings built at the end of the nineteenth century. The landmark Blackpool Tower stands out, but perhaps less well known are its two vast and spectacular public ballrooms.

Dating from the first phase of resort development, in the last decades of the nineteenth century, Blackpool is considered to be the world's first working-class seaside resort. The wealthier classes had been indulging in sea bathing for some time and resorts around the coastline in the south, such as Brighton, Margate, Southend and Bournemouth, were already undergoing increased development. Unlike other destinations Blackpool had little to recommend it – no historic monuments, no churches, no rock pools with seaweed and shells to tempt amateur naturalists, no trees even, in fact a total lack of any inspiring buildings or natural features of any kind. The beach, which is wide and flat, and the fresh sea air, which supposedly offered health benefits, were sufficient amusement only for a short time for the increasing numbers of working-class visitors seeking novelty and excitement.

Early development had been slow. A church was built in 1825 and a year later the assembly rooms, which included billiards rooms, a library and a hall for dancing that was not considered good enough for concerts. The year 1865 saw the first indication of a plan to cater specifically for the working classes with the construction of the second pier, the South Jetty as it was called, now the Central Pier. Blackpool's North Pier had been built in 1863; it is now famous and listed as the oldest remaining example of a pier by the well-known designer Eugenius Birch, who built fourteen of England's seaside piers. At 2d. (tuppence) to enter, it catered for the 'upturned noses, fashionable clothes and aloofness' of those who preferred more sedate gentle promenading and listening to classical music.[4] The South Jetty had a cheaper entrance fee of just 1*d.* (a penny), a livelier band and a dancing platform specifically intended to attract the more boisterous crowds who were making the North Pier's genteel visitors uncomfortable.

Travelling to the coast had been affordable for only the wealthier classes until the middle decades of the nineteenth century, when the growth of the railways made escape to the seaside much more accessible. For the substantial working-class populations in the mill towns of Lancashire, Blackpool was the closest seaside destination. The first railway line, to Fleetwood, opened in 1840 and a branch line to Blackpool followed in 1846. By the early 1850s the numbers arriving for the weekend had reportedly risen from 100 to 12,000. The railways were quick to offer excursion tickets at low prices which encouraged the new visitors – younger workers, especially young single people, keen on having fun, drinking, dancing and bathing without machines. And as the numbers increased, so did the street traders, hawkers and donkey men who profited by the trippers.

Blackpool continued with its tolerant approach towards the less favourable behaviour of some visitors, where other resorts might have priced them out or found other ways to dissuade them from visiting. The town was welcoming to all, regardless of class, and found innovative ways to manage the potential and actual problems caused by the large and sometimes disorderly crowds. A form of 'zoning', the idea of separating the different sections of society, that had started with the construction of the South Jetty was extended to the town in general. By 1865 the town had taken over the promenade and the seafront, and there was a clear distinction between the north end, where the wealthier visitors stayed, and the south, working-class end. Blackpool Borough Corporation, established in 1876, took charge in order to deal with petty crime and bad behaviour in public places, and set about controlling bathing, licensing traders and generally regulating the various activities in order to keep both the working-class and the middle-class visitors coming. Advertising was also unique to Blackpool, not for individual commercial entities but for the borough council itself.[5] Approval in an 1879 Act of Parliament led to the introduction of a tax on all the town's traders, which was to be used for a band to entertain visitors and to advertise its attractions as a whole. The tax was levied as a percentage of rateable value, thus ensuring it continued to rise along with the rates.

The beach was the last refuge for the huge variety of small-scale traders of all kinds – buskers, conjurors, jewellers, fortune tellers and the like – but by 1893 the corporation, representing the big entertainment companies, had also claimed the beach and foreshore. The corporation aimed to clean up the beach both literally and by replacing the more dubious 'amusements' with more acceptable – indoor – attractions. Leisure time was on the increase for all sections of society in the last decades of the nineteenth century, and why certain activities became popular while others did not must remain a subject for speculation. Ultimately, Blackpool, like seaside resorts everywhere, represented an idea of freedom. The seafront, with its wide open spaces and smoke-free air, offered a physical alternative to overcrowded urban centres, and the idea of a 'day by the sea' was imagined as an escape from the constraints of everyday life. A day 'away' also meant engaging in activities that were outside the norm, encouraging a more laissez-faire attitude; clothes were less formal and social behaviour was more relaxed, which suited the many young and single visitors with no family responsibilities and money to spend.

To contribute to the holiday atmosphere the entertainment companies were all hoping to find something novel and exciting to tempt the more adventurous visitors. Lawn tennis became popular after the introduction of the Wimbledon tournament in 1874, and other recently introduced hobbies such as cycling, which took place in a rink, and golf were all pursued by the wealthier classes keen on sporting activities that were considered beneficial for both body and mind. Ice skating in the winter had been around for a long time in Britain, and indoor skating was soon on the list for developers looking for the next 'new' thing. An initial short-lived 'bout of rinkomania' in the early 1840s reappeared in the 1870s when refrigeration techniques had developed sufficiently to allow rink owners to dispense with the imitation 'smelly' ice made from a mixture of pork lard and salt.[6] Roller skating rinks, an American import, were introduced around the same time in the 1870s. Ballroom dancing, it seemed, had declined in popularity with the wealthier classes in part due to the means and opportunity to try out other, newer physical activities. For the working classes, however, an interest in dancing surged. Dancing needed no specialist equipment and what few 'rules' there were at the time were simple to follow. For the promoters, too, for the potentially high numbers of people it catered for, dancing required relatively little investment other than space. Open-air dancing, such as that catered for on the Central Pier and at the Raikes Hall Gardens, opened in 1872, was the perfect opportunity to let your hair down and socialize, and it drew very big crowds.

Predicting the next craze or popular amusement was not easy, and investing in new building forms to accommodate them was a

Blackpool Tower and its entertainment buildings, including Britain's first public ballroom, opened in 1894 to accommodate the huge numbers of holidaymakers.

high-risk activity. Seaside architecture, as we now refer to the entertainment buildings developed generally in the period 1870 to 1914, had a style of its own: out of the ordinary, often exuberant and flamboyant. Architects with projects to invent buildings for new activities were able to experiment with new styles representing ideas of pleasure and luxury that the visitors and holidaymakers were seeking. They drew on various exotic influences: Indian motifs, Moorish decoration, all kinds of chinoiserie, anything that evoked fantasy or an 'other' place, 'based on everything that is tacky, gaudy and above all imaginative'.[7] Investment in Blackpool was popular, with as many as 22 different entertainment companies registered there between 1870 and 1914.[8] It had its fair share of failures; probably the biggest was the Alhambra, opened in 1899, which housed a circus, a theatre and a huge ballroom that could hold as many as 3,000 dancers. Even though the share launch was oversubscribed and the building was located in a prime position on the Promenade, it was forced to close in 1903 after less than four years in operation. Critics blamed poor design, citing the inadequate circulation space for promenading, which was considered vital to make a visit enjoyable. The Blackpool Tower Company, however – which bought up the Alhambra, remodelled it and reopened it as the Palace in 1904 – must rank as one of the most successful entertainment companies at the time. Its confidence, inventiveness and far-sightedness, combined with the corporation's form of municipal socialism, were unbeatable.

The Blackpool Tower is one of the best known of such early experiments in seaside architecture. It was listed as Grade 1 by English Heritage in 1973, and most would agree with Lynn Pearson's conclusion that of all the entertainment buildings of the period, 'Blackpool Tower Buildings, combining circus, ballroom, tower and other amusements with great decorative splendour, is the best single surviving building.'[9] The idea to create a Blackpool Tower was a simple one: it was a copy of the Eiffel Tower in Paris, built as part of the 1889 Exposition Universelle. Despite much criticism from the intelligentsia for being such a pointless and even ugly structure, it was an instant hit with the public, with 2 million visitors in the first five months. The project to copy it was launched with the establishment of the Blackpool Tower Company in 1891.[10] Starting with a tower that would be a significant landmark like the Eiffel Tower, with an obligatory observation deck at the top, it would also have a building at the base – it became Tower World – which was to be an entirely new type of building encompassing a whole range of entertainment spaces. The project was so popular with the public and such a financial success that similar towers were planned at other seaside resorts. A few were completed and some were popular for a few years, but Blackpool remains the only one still standing. An article in the *New York Times* written in 1994, a hundred years after its opening, pokes fun at the English 'Victorian era fantasy land by the sea' in general, but still recognizes that 'the best part of Tower World is not the circus animals and life-size copies of dinosaurs, but the ballroom, a wonderfully restored bit of Edwardian rococo and gold leaf where scores of graying couples still gather every day.'[11]

The Tower Ballroom, which opened in 1894, was the first in England built specifically as an amenity for the general public to dance. It is located on the first floor of the building that encloses the base of the tower on one side of the circus, which is located in the centre of the building directly under the tower itself. It is reached via a series of oversized grand staircases and promenading spaces. The Grand Pavilion, as the Tower Ballroom was named initially, was so well attended that after only a few years, in 1899, it was closed to be extended and completely refurbished. A report in the *Blackpool Times* praised the architects, Maxwell & Tuke, for their architectural skill in achieving various alterations without 'perceptibly encroaching an inch' and their wisdom in appointing Frank Matcham, 'the pre-eminent theatrical architect-artist'.[12] The alterations were extensive. The width of the already large dance floor was increased by 4.5 metres (15 ft), the roof height was raised and the stage was moved from the long side to one end. An innovative feature, the first in any ballroom, was the huge (15 × 6 metres/50 × 20 ft) sliding panel in the roof that could be opened to the sky in hot weather. Audience capacity was increased by adding curved fronts to the balconies on both sides and adding a gallery at the end, for six hundred seated and two hundred standing. Matcham's explanation for the location for the new gallery demonstrates his understanding of dancers: 'If you have anything like a gallery immediately over the ballroom not a soul will dance under it; and therefore that part of the floor would never be fully utilised. Another thing! The dancers who come here like to be seen and they like to see the people looking on.'[13] The decor was, and still is, unlike anything many visitors to Blackpool would have seen. Matcham's design combines an eclectic mix of late Baroque, Rococo and French Louis xv styles, flamboyant and exuberant, using a range of delicate colours and pastel shades all 'richly relieved with pure English Gold'. The sprung dance floor was relaid exactly as the original.

The redecorations in 1913 were again overseen by Matcham. There were only minor alterations but more extensive adjustments to the colour scheme were carried out, mostly to add yet more gold and imagery, and to replace some of the fake painted marble with the real thing. To add to the impression of height the colours were graded from the palest at upper levels, reaching their deepest tones at the lower ones with the 'luscious claret of the plush curtains and upholstery' and the deep red of the 'rich Turkish pile carpet'. Technical innovations meant that the fake snow could fall more 'naturally' at the end of the evening, as the old boxes that had to be shaken manually were replaced with a remote-controlled concealed mechanism. Most exciting was electrification. The whole ballroom was fitted with electric lighting, which – in combination with the mirrors and the reflective surfaces of the polished marble, gold and other decorations – transformed it into 'a flood of splendour that is wonderful'.[14]

The 1899 refurbishment of the Tower Ballroom had been prompted not only by its ongoing success, but by the opening of the Empress Ballroom – an even bigger and more opulent space – at the Winter Gardens, a near neighbour of the Tower, in 1896. The Winter Gardens as originally constructed comprised a central concert hall space, once again named simply the Pavilion (41 × 22 metres/133 × 72 ft), encircled by a wide ambulatory with a glazed roof extending to halls on either side, giving more than half a kilometre (600 yd) of covered indoor promenading space.[15] Winter gardens in cast iron and glass were a relatively new form of construction which had become fashionable following the creation of the Crystal Palace for London's Great Exhibition in 1851, and had retained their popularity as conservatories for collections of exotic plants and flowers. On a grand scale at the seaside, conservatories had practical benefits, too, as a place to shelter from the bad weather while maintaining a safe way to enjoy a view of the often rough seas. Perhaps due to its limited scale, the 'conservatory' at the Blackpool Winter Gardens did not suffer the fate of the many iron and glass structures built at other seaside resorts. The only other remaining example, which is in considerable disrepair, is the one located on the seafront at Great Yarmouth – so highly valued in 1904 that it was purchased, dismantled, brought there by boat from Torquay and then re-erected.

To create Blackpool's second ballroom, the owners of the Winter Gardens decided to replace the indoor and outdoor skating rinks, the extensive propagation nursery and related spaces and carry out major reconstruction works, demonstrating just how enormous the demand for dancing was. According to Pearson, adding the ballroom was a move downmarket for the Winter Gardens, but one that was necessary for commercial viability. Bigger even than the enlarged Tower Ballroom, the Empress Ballroom claimed to be the finest in the world; with its lofty barrel-vaulted roof and richly decorated plasterwork, it was as impressive as the Tower. The stage is located on the long side, common in dance halls and ballrooms for better acoustics,

The Empress Ballroom in Blackpool, designed by Mangnall & Littlewoods, was added to the Winter Gardens in 1896. It has been the venue for the annual Blackpool Dance Festival since 1920.

Architectural perspective drawing of the new Empress Ballroom at the Blackpool Winter Gardens, from *Building News*, 31 July 1896.

and there are extensive balconies and promenading spaces all round. Whereas the Tower Ballroom was surrounded by such amusements as the circus, menagerie and aquarium, the Empress benefited from the more upmarket rooms in the Winter Gardens. An adjacent themed Indian Lounge provided comfortable and classy sitting-out space, and from there visitors could walk through to the conservatory and Floral Hall to enjoy the exotic plants, palms and ferns.

Vernon and Irene Castle, who became the best-known proponents of the modern style, popularized their eponymous Castle walk.

TWO

Jazz, Ragtime and Tangoitis

*The time-honored cotillion has given way to general dancing and such
unconventional steps as the Turkey Trot and Grizzly Bear, which are the
proper thing now at the most polite functions.*

New York Times, 1911[1]

In the first decade of the new century, the music and dances listed
on the programme at the seaside ballrooms were somewhat different to those at private dances and balls in London. At state balls a
typical programme would consist of fifteen or sixteen waltzes, which
would have been the faster Viennese version, along with two or three
quadrilles and polkas. At other smart dances such as hunt, club or
county balls, again around fifteen waltzes would be typical but accompanied by perhaps the Lancers and two or three two-steps. By contrast,
the usual programme for a popular ball would have included four or
five slow waltzes. The faster Viennese waltz was and remains one of
the most difficult dances to execute well and, in addition to requiring
considerable stamina because of the speed, poses considerable risk
for those who are not expert. The rest of the programme would be
made up of sequence dances along with a whole range of what we
might now call country dances or square dances: Lancers, quadrilles
(two couples), Alberts and the valse cotillion (four couples).

London and other big cities had no equivalent of the new public
ballrooms that were being built at seaside resorts but the newspapers

'London Imitates Blackpool: Everybody's Ball-Room at Earl's Court',
drawn by Frank Reynolds, *Illustrated London News*, 27 June 1908. In the early
twentieth century London had no public ballrooms. The summer theatre in the
Earls Court Exhibition grounds was converted into a ballroom to cater for the
growing demand.

were full of reports of the many private balls. They nearly always
described the interior design and decorations installed for the event
and often, in some detail, the clothes worn by the various dignitaries,
and even the quality of the supper. Only occasionally was there a
description of the kind of music played, the type of band and the
dances that made up the programme. Reports that did focus on the
dancing itself tended to be somewhat negative. There is in general
a hint at a lowering of standards: an increase in the numbers of the
simpler, rowdier 'country' dances previously associated with the
lower classes, which for many was considered the direct result of
young people becoming less interested in attending dancing classes.
Learning to dance had long been part of the education of the upper
classes; it was considered an important social skill for both men and
women. Deportment, etiquette and even suggestions on dress were

included as the responsibility of the dancing teacher, but by the first decade of the new century their influence was waning.

In 1898 the magazine *Hearth and Home*, in a typical lengthy article lamenting the state of dancing, relates a report of an almost unrecognizable version of the Lancers that the writer claims is quite common in London's West End ballrooms. Instead of the good manners one expects in Mayfair and Belgravia, 'the ladies are lifted off their feet . . . and swung round by the gentleman in what is almost a horizontal position.' The young men also link arms and charge up and down the room 'like a troop of cavalry'. The article does not defend the ballroom 'with its artificial excitements and unwholesome gratifications of luxury and vanity' and suggests it is the responsibility of the 'refined women of Society' to 'banish the inrushing tide of boisterous vulgarity from their ballrooms'.[2] We might wonder whether the statement in a 1900 programme for a Wednesday evening's dancing at the Tower Ballroom in Blackpool that declares that 'No Gentleman is allowed to dance without a Lady' was intended to prevent such boisterous behaviour. Contemporary reports blame the trouble in ballrooms on men reluctant to devote their time to dancing lessons, preferring other physical and sporting activities. 'Sandow's symmetrion, tennis, hockey, golf, the chase – yes these things they were interested in, one and all; but of dancing they had no conception. A "rag" Lancers was executed with some brio, and at the end the horn of John Peel caused them all to caper about and around the floor like colts stampeding.'[3] And despite the introduction of the new dances, the lack of discipline continued: 'The ball-room of today is a maze of different styles of dancing . . . the ambition of the dancers seems to be to disregard the music of the band entirely . . . the one-steppers just walk; there is no other word to describe it; it is certainly not dancing.'[4]

Contemporary cartoons in *Punch* magazine had portrayed nineteenth-century ballroom etiquette, and particularly the dance card used by women to 'book' each dance, as outdated – manners

THE

TOWER

BLACKPOOL.

GENERAL MANAGER - - MR. GEORGE HARROP.

WEDNESDAY EVENING
Jan. 3rd, 1900.

Mr. M. MACDERMOTT'S
Premier Orchestra

Master of Ceremonies . Mr. J. BICKERSTAFFE.

*No Gentleman is allowed to dance
without a Lady.*

MAXWELL & CO., BLACKPOOL.

A typical Tower Ballroom programme dated 3 January 1900, including the rule 'No Gentleman is allowed to dance without a Lady.'

were changing. In one cartoon, a man who is refused a dance by a woman because her dance card is full replies, 'Oh, don't worry about that. I'll get you another one.'[5] Clearly, he does not understand the rules. In another a young woman is annoyed at having to leave the man she is enjoying talking to because her card says she is booked by another, less attractive partner. Many cartoons depicted a shortage of male partners; one is entitled 'A Famine in Dancing Men', and plenty more depict men who could not dance properly and some who think it does not matter. When a potential partner suggests the man sit out if, by his own admission, he does not know how to dance the two-step he is not put off, clearly anticipating that he can learn it while dancing with her.[6] In another, when a man comments to his partner on how good the floor is, the response is: 'She (drily). "Then why dance on my feet?"'[7]

The important society events of the upper classes continued with the 'traditional' square dances and polkas which everyone knew. The London correspondent of the *Manchester Guardian*, reporting on one of the first of the season's balls in Covent Garden in 1902 as one of the most successful, described it as being 'decorous' and 'stately' and the dancing as 'good, solid English Dancing, with no frothy foreign nonsense'.[8] The writer, we can assume, was referring to the increasing number of dances imported from Paris and particularly from America – new dances that encouraged much closer physical contact and relied on improvisation to new kinds of music. The perhaps younger and more adventurous of the wealthier classes were less interested in the formal balls of their parents. The rules for debutantes, who were in principle not to be seen anywhere until they had been presented at court, were increasingly less firmly adhered to. Many 'debs' were seen out and about at all the London balls before presentation, and there were reportedly many more applications for the early ones in February among those keen to maximize the season. London's fashionable society was becoming more interested in the opportunities for dancing and socializing, enjoying the different atmosphere of the new cabarets: smaller and more informal relaxed drinking and dining venues which had appeared in European and American cities during the 1890s and 1900s and were beginning to open in London. The atmosphere was more intimate and better suited to the new forms of jazz music; the audience was seated at tables to watch a range of entertainers, musicians, singers, dance demonstrations and sometimes the more risqué burlesque. Cabaret represented the 'alternative' or 'underground' culture, attracting a bohemian and multi-cultural clientele. Some London Clubs such as the Rector's, Grafton Galleries and Murray's had, according to a 1926 article, retained 'very good talk or very good dancing, and occasionally both' but in the many new nightclubs this was often not the case, 'added to which the lighting and decoration of some of them are execrable. Mass production of night clubs seems to have diminished the quality.'[9] The small size of dance floors at such venues, however, and the small bands playing jazz music seemed the natural home for the new kind of 'crush' dancing. Crush, which continued through the 1920s and '30s, is not strictly a dancing style, but overcrowded ballrooms meant that couples danced closer together, could not raise their arms to take up ballroom hold and could take only very small steps, resulting in much more limited movement. The *Dancing Times* tells us that 'The principal Clubs – Ciro's, the Grafton and the Embassy – are crowded each night. Indeed numbers are so great that it is at times impossible to do any serious dancing.'[10]

The physical proximity at dances, exacerbated by overcrowding (particularly at public dances), was seen as a potential risk to morality and did little to improve dancing's reputation. The contemporary American writer Allen Dodworth in *Dancing and Its Relations to Education and Social Life* expressed a common concern that a lack of provision of suitable venues had in part led to dancing's poor reputation. Dancers had become accustomed to overcrowding, colliding with each other on a regular basis and being squeezed into such small spaces that 'positions of indelicacy become no longer offensive.' He defended dancing on the basis of the physical well-being derived from exercise, quoting at length from an article published in the *Lancet* medical journal. He also gave advice on choosing a teacher by making a distinction between the 'teacher' and the 'dancing master', encouraging parents seeking dancing lessons for their children to choose carefully. A teacher can impart the steps for each new dance to their pupil, but it is the master who believes that pupils 'should also be taught what it is that constitutes true gracefulness, and educated to an appreciation of the highest expressions of intelligence and culture that can be given by means of motion'. A true dancing master, he says, relies on the 'study of half a lifetime and in all that relates to gracefulness'.[11] Indeed, this view is still frequently repeated by many teachers and coaches today. People can easily learn steps, but that is of no use if they are not able to execute them with the correct technique and musicality.

For dancing teachers in Britain the ongoing growth in the popularity of dancing – in all its forms – spurred them on to expand and review their role. In common with other trades and professions, dancing teachers in different parts of Britain formed local trade associations, with the common aim to support colleagues, ensure parity, avoid undercutting and generally enhance their status through professionalization. The earliest was the Scottish Association of Teachers of Dancing in 1879. The British Association of Teachers of Dancing (BATD) was formed in 1892, and the Manchester and Salford Association of Teachers of Dancing (MATD) in 1903. These were to be followed by many more regional teachers' associations across the country during the 1920s and '30s. The most influential, which is still in existence today, is the Imperial Society of Teachers of Dancing (ISTD), formed in 1904.[12]

The ISTD – which had an elected chairman, Robert Morris Crompton,[13] and an Executive Committee – had been formed as a result of the first congress of dancing teachers, held in 1904. Its purpose was primarily to establish some rules for dancing and an agreed method of teaching. The following year, in July 1905, around a hundred ballroom dancing teachers met in London to continue their discussions on how they were to 'restore the art of dancing'. Like Dodworth, they were also concerned that some teachers were merely 'dancing room keepers' working on a 'do as I do' principle without technical knowledge of the figures or the correct vocabulary. Teaching dancing by demonstration alone implied a lack of professionalism for which an agreed technique, vocabulary and instruction method would be the best remedy. A uniform teaching system, they believed, would ensure correct technique while still allowing the master to interpret each dance according to temperament. Moreover, an agreed set of properly taught figures would make it so much easier for their pupils to dance with one another, and would put a stop to what were variously described as 'slovenly manners and barbaric antics' in the ballroom.[14]

All had the same aim: to agree on the form of modern dancing and a uniform method of teaching. But there was considerable difficulty in deciding just what the orthodoxy was. The more conservative teachers believed it was important to go back to the origins, to build on what they saw as the true roots of the dances. Those with a less conservative view considered the older traditional dances as primitive, close to folk dancing or country dancing, with no classical or academic credentials, and thought they should remain in the past. They wanted to create a new orthodoxy for modern dancing appropriate for the current age. Until this time all dancing had been based on the same rules used in classical ballet, with the five positions and the feet turned out. Modern dancing would be based on walking steps with parallel feet and a more natural movement. Teaching the vast numbers of keen dancers all over the country was a challenging task, and the plan to teach the teachers first was a laudable aim. Crompton also suggested that the major public schools – Eton, Harrow, Marlborough and Rugby, which educated the wealthy and influential – should teach dancing. This would set an example and avoid the current problem of young men abandoning dancing through lack of ability or treating it as just an excuse for a 'romp'.[15]

Smarter and fashionable dances no longer relied on a programme and all were overcrowded. Everyone eventually agreed that new dances were needed to reinstate some sense of order and reinvigorate the ballrooms. Teachers were encouraged therefore to invent new dances, which would be presented each year to the congress of teachers' associations, with members attending from all over the country keen to compete for prizes. Winning would add prestige, and the dance would then be taught in all the schools. In 1909 the BATD considered dances that we would now categorize as country or folk dances – fifteen round dances, where couples execute set steps in an anticlockwise circle, three square dances, usually with four couples, and three display dances – but one newspaper reported doubts that

The Waltz

Developing ways to impart instructions for dancing was challenging: 'if the pupil will carry the illustration of the ordinary Waltz to a looking glass, and commence by looking at No. 4 and then Nos 5, 6, 1, 2, 3 he will find that the mirror will reflect the correct positions.' From *How and What to Dance* (1906).

anything will 'eclipse . . . the popularity of the two-step, waltz and the Boston' – a slow-moving waltz that was a 'direct descendant of the Kensington Crawl'.[16]

The ISTD meetings to further the debate over what those new dances might be, and how they should be taught, were to continue throughout the first decades of the twentieth century. In 1908, when Crompton and vice president Cecil Taylor attended the first International Congress of Dancing Masters, held in Berlin, they were disappointed at the result of the deliberations and the rather uninspiring keenness of the Germans to 'preserve the Waltz in all its beauty'.[17] The ISTD was of the view that British ballrooms had far too much waltzing and needed more variety. Their conference that year welcomed delegates from France, Germany, the Netherlands and America, who also contributed to the competition for new round dances along with the solo performances of stage dances and novelties in their efforts to introduce something fresh to the ballroom for the coming season. The upper classes, it seemed, no longer took dancing seriously and, when they did dance, it was the waltz. According to the president of the BATD at their meeting in June 1909, reported in *The Observer*, 'The middle classes . . . are not only better dancers than the "upper ten" but favour a greater variety.'[18]

The Boston, a form of waltz that was slower than the Viennese, was the current craze in London. In Paris, too, the dance was so popular that the verb *bostonner* had been coined.[19] Slower waltzing was already becoming the trend, even for the 'smart set', as noted by the past ISTD vice president Charles D'Albert, at the 1910 conference. He thought it was more graceful than the traditional or faster Viennese version and was convinced that the waltz would be back in favour that year, along with the two-step. He said, 'Square dances . . . are absolutely dead. The Lancers and Quadrilles are seldom seen in fashionable ballrooms and when the Lancers were down to be danced at the last Covent Garden Ball only five sets stood up.'[20] The barn dance, cake walk and Washington Post were also dead.

Inventing new dances that could easily be taught to the public was one way to manage the crowds, but a new challenge was going to cause yet more concern for dancing teachers – the arrival of ragtime. The imported American music was brash and vulgar, according to its critics, but it fuelled the already considerable enthusiasm for dancing. Ragtime music, which had started to appear in England from around 1899, with its lively 'honky tonk' piano, banjos and syncopated rhythms coupled with the simplicity of dances like the cake walk, brought an immense sense of fun to dancing. Ragtime music also inspired a whole series of new couple dances in close hold, toe to toe, many with more natural body movements, decried by critics as 'animalistic'. Each new dance seemed to come with a name more outlandish than the last: names we are familiar with now such as the grizzly bear, the bunny hug and the turkey trot. They mostly followed the syncopated rhythm of the music, often stepping on each beat. The turkey trot sometimes turns to promenade position (close hold and facing forwards) and includes steps such as forward and backward points and the pendulum, which were both to become part of the Charleston and were incorporated into today's quickstep. The grizzly bear involved actually mimicking a bear. The partners break away and circle around each other, do-si-do, while holding their hands up as if with claws out ready to pounce on each other. The bunny hug, as the name suggests, had an unusual hold, with a much tighter embrace and the dancers leaning towards each other shoulder to shoulder. Curiosities now, the animal dances, as they are sometimes called, represented a liberation from the constraints of classical dance and the repetitive and sedate square dances, but as novelties each one lasted only a very short time before another one came along to replace it. The maxixe (or mattiche), sometimes referred to as the Brazilian tango, lasted for several seasons in its original form and was referred to as 'purely a thing of the cabaret and low music-hall'.[21] It combined Cuban rhythms with both one-step and two-step figures and the *corta jaca* in shadow hold, now an established samba figure.

After the waltz, the foxtrot – a very different version to the contemporary one – became the most common dance. It could be danced to almost anything in 4/4 time and was based on simple walking steps with any number of variations to suit the dancer or the music. According to some commentators, as the new dances were more fun and more energetic and required knowledge of only a few steps, they encouraged more men back into the ballroom, who were perhaps tempted by the much closer proximity to partners. For many, modern dancing created a much more lively and entertaining picture than the 'days of the all pervasive waltz'. 'If you leant over the balcony in the old days you saw a solid mass of couples all doing more or less the same things and all more or less in the same manner. Now you see a live gathering, couples threading and interlacing, gliding forwards, backwards and sideways like crabs all doing different things in different manners.'[22]

By the beginning of the 1910s in America, where the ragtime dances had originated, the new dances that were all the rage in New York and other cities raised mixed responses. Although the turkey trot was 'not the most dignified of steps', everyone was expected to be 'doing it this season' in Philadelphia; and at a junior dance at Sherry's in New York, favoured by the social elite, the cotillion was waived, based on demand by the young dancers, in favour of the grizzly bear.[23] The *New York Times* reported the increased demand for substantial breakfasts as dances continued very late; in addition, 'the demand on dancing men has been noticeable.' It also mentions that the 'time-honored cotillion has given way to general dancing and such unconventional steps as the Turkey Trot and the Grizzly Bear, which are the proper thing now at the most polite functions'.[24] For early feminists and social reformers, the popularity of dancing and dance halls as public spaces posed a dilemma. On the one hand, the more puritanical thought that dance halls and dancing, with the physical proximity of the new dances, anonymous boisterous crowds, alcohol and syncopated jazz music, which was associated with Black and working-class cultures, could lead to one thing only – promiscuity. On the other hand, dance halls seemed to represent everything that indicated change in the social norms dominated by masculine culture; they could even be seen as a more feminine urban space. At the time women were beginning to have more presence in public, afforded by new kinds of spaces in towns and cities, particularly department stores and railway stations. They shopped, dined out and travelled alone or with female company.

By early 1912 the managers of New York's dance halls held a meeting specifically to decide how best to put a stop to the 'immoral and obnoxious dances': namely, the turkey trot, grizzly bear, shiver dance, Boston dip and bunny hug. They supported the concern at the time for the moral welfare of a new generation of working women who were young and independent without the support of society families. Their express support for dancing – 'girls do not get enough dancing, and indeed there are very few people who do get enough' – led to proposals to start 'model dance halls'.[25] A committee was formed to take their concerns to the chair of the Committee on Amusement and Vacation Resources for Working Girls, the social reformer Mrs Charles Henry Israels, in order to help find a way to put a stop to the inappropriate dances. Various strategies were implemented: new clauses in musicians' contracts, placards posted at dance halls and notices to the musicians' unions requesting them to stop playing the offending dances.

Despite the newspapers' depictions of chaotic overcrowding and boisterous behaviour and the teachers' associations' best efforts to reintroduce some sense of decorum, dancing continued to be extremely popular on both sides of the Atlantic. For the lower classes it was clearly a cheap and easily accessible form of amusement, an escape from everyday life. For a new generation of independent, working women it offered an opportunity to socialize. According to Irene Castle, one half of America's best-known dancing couple of the period, 'By the fall of 1913 America had gone absolutely dance-mad.

The whole nation seemed to be divided into two equal forces, those who were for it and those who were against it.'[26] Despite considerable opposition, the Castles, in a short-lived dancing career, are credited with making the new form of modern couple dancing respectable.

The other half of the couple, Vernon Castle, was born in England and had met Irene during a family visit to New York in 1910. Both worked in the theatre. Vernon had changed his surname from Blythe so as not to be identified with his sister, who was also on the bill, and fell into acting by chance as he gained comic roles mostly based on his physical appearance and athleticism. He was tall, thin and long legged, and was often cast as an affable and stumbling comic drunk. Irene, on the other hand, had been ambitious from a young age, keen on the glamour of a stage career, and had initially befriended Vernon to gain access to his friend the actor and influential impresario Lew Fields.[27]

The Castles' dancing career started soon after their marriage in 1911, and almost by accident, while they were working in Paris. They had been appearing in a revue struggling with the translation of Vernon's comedy sketch and agreed to quit. A disappointed Vernon decided that for their finale they would dance. They performed a version of the grizzly bear he had learnt from newspaper clippings he had been sent from America to Irving Berlin's 'Alexander's Ragtime Band', a tune written that year, which went on to spread the acceptable sound of ragtime everywhere. According to Irene, the dance 'was full of so many acrobatic variations that I was in the air much more often that I was on the ground'.[28] Their performance was a hit with the audience, including an agent, which led to an introduction to Louis Barraya at the Café de Paris. He hired them immediately and the Castles were a veritable overnight success. They appeared every midnight at the Café de Paris after giving demonstrations at private parties. Dancing suited them; as the craze for dancing continued they were able to very quickly establish a reputation, and were soon sought after by every nightclub and party host.

On their return to America in 1912 the Castles took up residence at the Café de l'Opera, New York's version of the Café de Paris, where their regular performances and the public's ongoing passion for dancing reinforced their celebrity status. Their next step was to open their own nightclub, the Sans Souci, in a basement on Times Square. It was decorated by Elsie de Wolfe, the most fashionable interior designer of the period, with bright lights and a vibrant pink and grey colour scheme. A resident jazz band led by Jim Europe, the most prominent figure in Black American music, provided the music. While the avant-garde nightclub put them on the map, their next venture, Castle House, which opened in 1914 with the support of Elisabeth Marbury, established their position in society.

Marbury had established a reputation as a theatrical and literary agent who often represented and supported women. She lived in New York's fashionable Sutton Place, had travelled extensively and was very well connected. She dabbled in various theatrical endeavours, in production and as an agent; her first success had been supporting Frances Hodgson Burnett to stage *Little Lord Fauntleroy*, and she then drifted into personal management, always ready to invest in new ventures. She had seen the Castles perform and laid claim to the idea of setting them up in 'a smart dancing-centre'. Marbury knew that this commercial opportunity would only last as long as the dancing craze lasted and therefore rushed to put her plan into place. She persuaded the Castles to accept her proposal by offering earnings of five times their usual rate, organized redesigning the building, and then held daily teas which included a performance by the Castles. In Marbury's estimation, the Castles were a respectable married couple who would lend dancing the right tone at a time when it was still considered improper and immodest by many. She describes Irene as 'lithe and graceful . . . her features and colouring were beautiful' and Vernon as the dancer; it was he who 'set the pace, it was he who inspired the rhythm, it was he who invented the steps'.[29] Castle House was open for two seasons only but was followed by other similar ventures:

Castles in the Air on the roof at the Forty-Fourth Street Theatre and then Castles on the Sea on the boardwalk in Long Beach.

The popularity of Castle House among the wealthiest in society was ensured by Marbury and her influential circle of friends, who led by example. The twelve 'patronesses' included leaders in high society: Elsie Stillman, who was married to W. G. Rockefeller; their interior designer and author of the hugely influential *The House in Good Taste*, Elsie de Wolfe; and wealthy socialites such as Tessie Oelrichs and Mamie Fish. With endorsements from twelve such influential socialites, the Castles' book, *Modern Dancing*, published in 1914, did much to change opinion about dancing, which, according to the foreword, when 'properly executed is neither vulgar nor immodest, but, on the contrary, the personification of refinement, grace and modesty'. It set out to demonstrate that 'no objection can possibly be urged against it [dancing] on the grounds of impropriety.'[30] In the lengthy introduction written by Marbury, she blames ignorance and lack of proper tuition for the misunderstandings and problems while at the same time eulogizing the Castles. She describes Castle House as a 'model school of dancing' based on 'refinement' and explains that the new modern dances are not like the frowned-upon bunny hug, grizzly bear or one-step if learned correctly. Eliminating improper movements such as 'hoppings', 'contortions of the body' and 'hideous gyrations of the limbs' can result in an 'exquisite expression of joyousness' or 'youthful spontaneity'.[31]

According to Marbury, the Castles were never equalled. Irene Castle claimed that, other than to rehearse a routine for a performance, she did not practise her dancing but merely followed Vernon: 'by keeping my eyes firmly fixed on the stud button of his dress shirt I could anticipate every move he was going to make and we made it together' and 'it was intuitive dancing, to be sure, because I never practiced if I could help it, and if it had been difficult, I'm sure I never would have had the patience to carry on with it.'[32] Gilbert Seldes, an American critic and author, was impressed: 'No one else has ever given exactly that sense of being freely perfect, of moving without effort and without will, in more than accord, in absolute identity with music.'[33] Irene's 'presence' also impressed a young Cecil Beaton: 'Her system of movement, her new flow of line, with protruding stomach, arched back, raised shoulder and lowered chin, swept through Europe like a hurricane,' and 'Her success has been sensational, her influence great, and she is one of the most enchanting souvenirs of an epoch for which she was in so many ways responsible.'[34] The writer Eve Golden suggests that the Castles had sex appeal: 'The couple entwined around each other, wrapped in each other, as they sinuously whirled around,' bringing a level of excitement to the ballroom and sparking admiration in the young, who were eager to emulate them.[35]

The Castles were enthusiastic and inventive, and they developed a distinctive style of their own. They introduced their own Castle walk, a version of a one-step danced on the toes, on every beat of the music, and demonstrated simplified versions of the other popular dances, particularly the maxixe and the tango. Their reputation meant that their endorsement for records and gramophones was sought after by many of the new companies; they gave the Victor Talking Machine Company the exclusive services of the Castle House Orchestra for the making of dance records, and their supervision. Irene's style had many imitators. Trend-setters as she and her husband were in dancing and the music they danced to, Irene moreover had huge influence on changing fashions for women, based in part on the demands of dancing. She altered skirts to include pleats and slits to make it easier to stride out, she cut her hair short and invented the Castle band to keep it in place long before it was to become common-place in the 1920s, and her signature 'Dutch' cap was much copied. She designed hats, modelled for and worked with dress designers, and endorsed corset advertisements. Vernon too was a trailblazer. He wore a wristwatch before they were fashionable and popularized short evening jackets instead of tails – his would cause problems flying around when he danced at crowded parties.

Biographers have focused on their domestic problems and particularly the intense rivalry between them and the Waltons, who were perhaps the best-known of the other popular dancing couples. Introduced by Ziegfeld, Florence Walton, a vaudeville dancer, partnered and married Maurice Mouvet.[36] In 1911 Maurice had been sacked when the Castles refused to share their billing at the Café de Paris with him. The competition between them never abated and the Waltons were fired once again when they returned to New York to dance at the Café de l'Opera and discovered the Castles already installed.[37] The Waltons had a successful career performing and demonstrating ballroom dancing for only a few years – they separated and then divorced shortly after the war ended, in 1920. Florence Walton went back to a successful vaudeville career and Maurice went on to make a significant contribution to the first steps in codifying ballroom dancing in Britain during the 1920s, before his death in 1927.

For a few years the Castles inhabited a fantasy world but one which at the time was considered radical and often less than orthodox. They employed Black musicians, they associated with lesbians, and Irene in particular drew attention to herself by wearing stylish, often daring clothes and keeping unusual exotic animals as pets: she occasionally appeared with a goat on a lead. However, as performers they had the appearance of the ideal celebrity couple – well travelled and extravagant – and as dancers they led a life that was both exciting and glamorous.

At the same time that many different new dances emerged in response to American ragtime and jazz music, the tango also made an appearance. Originally from Argentina, the tango had become hugely popular in Paris before its introduction to London in 1912, where it was immediately welcomed. By 1913 it was already included on the programme at dances. At the Royal Albert Hall in December 1913, of the 25 dances listed there are two tangos along with six two-steps and the rest the 'valse', a version of the waltz. Tango demonstrations had also started to appear as the curtain raiser at West End theatres.

'A Parisian Fashion comes to town: The "Thé dansant." Cousin of the "Tango Tea", in London', drawn by A. C. Michael, from the *Illustrated London News*, 5 July 1913. Restaurant demonstrations by well-known dancers such as the Waltons contributed to the increasing popularity of the Argentine tango among London's smart set.

Belle Harding,[38] who ran a school at the Ralli-Boston Club in the Empress Room in Knightsbridge, is credited with popularizing the dance. She was the first to hold tango teas, which she organized at the Waldorf and the Hotel Cecil. Fashionable society adopted tango as more than just a dance; it was a new, all-embracing style that encompassed music and fashion, as described in socialite Gladys Beattie Crozier's book dedicated to everything tango: 'Everyone is arranging Tango tea parties, Tango dinners and Tango balls . . . and Tangoing both afternoon and night is the popular pastime of the hour.'[39] Her book set out eight basic figures and gave instruction on body position and hold. Further chapters included extensive and detailed advice, including where to go and what to wear and even how to tango on roller skates: 'In order to dance the Tango on roller skates it is wise for a lady to wear a rather short skirt – one which clears the ground by a foot at least – otherwise the bottom edge of it is apt to get under

Photo by Campbell Gray, Ld.

" Scissors " (Les Ciseaux).

Gladys Beattie Crozier's *The Tango: And How to Dance It* (1913) included extensive advice on what to wear. Women's clothing was often too restrictive for modern dancing and new styles were introduced to allow more movement.

the toe, heel outwards, also turns slightly to the left; his shoulders also turning to the left, to correspond. Then he crosses his right foot in

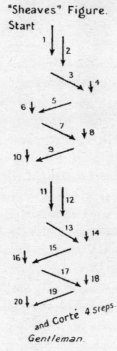

"Sheaves" Figure.

Start

and Corté 4 steps.

Gentleman.

front of his left foot, as before, for 7 and 8, crosses to the right for 9 and 10; he then walks forward with the right foot for 11, and with the left for 12. He then crosses over four times in

Gladys Beattie Crozier's *The Tango: And How to Dance It* (1913) also set out instructions for the steps in each figure using photographs, directional diagrams and textual description.

the wheels during the deep "dips" which are a prominent feature of several of the Tango skating figures.'[40]

A somewhat sensationalist article in *The Observer* in 1913 reported that Berlin, although a season or two behind London, Paris and New York, was suffering from 'Tangoitis in a virulent form', and that it posed a threat to theatre greater even than that caused by the cinema.[41] Dances include other new forms with 'weird steps, trots, wriggles and hugs'; the writer is fearful that teachers are only teaching tango and everywhere will be 'Tangoised'. The tango was criticized for being oversexualized, crude or simply not wholesome enough. Although by now most were accustomed to couples dancing together toe to toe, the tango was thought to have too much body contact. More importantly, it was too stationary: the static nature of the figures meant more body movement rather than actual steps and progression around the room. While many thought it might disappear along with many other novelty dances of the time, it continued to endure. A survey carried out by the Queen's Theatre in January 1914 indicated that at least some sections of the population were not put off by the tango.[42] The answer to the question 'Is the Tango immodest?' was a resounding 'no' with 731 to 21 'yes' votes. It should be noted that by this time the tango was already on the way to being a more decorous version; the many figures had been reduced to eight essentials and it had become more relaxed and much slower. The simplified steps were demonstrated by Belle Harding at the Hotel Cecil in November 1913, danced 'as in Paris, and it is a languid graceful measure in quite slow time.'[43] The demonstration included the scissors, one of the easiest figures, the ruado and media luna, which are still in Argentine tango today but gone from the ballroom version. By June 1914 the tango craze was presumed over – the slit skirts, clutching round the neck and complex movements were too much for the audiences – but a yet more subtle version was to take hold later.

In addition to American dances arriving in Britain, European dances were crossing the Atlantic in the opposite direction, and such was the popularity of dancing that along with their advice columns and reviews, newspapers were regularly printing instructions. One series published each week starting in October 1914 in the *Washington Post* (and its franchised papers) gives us an indication of the kind of dances that were being encouraged. The instructions were written by Evelyn Nesbit with contributions by some of the best-known professional dancers and included illustrations. The first in the series was the roule-roule, which was based on an old French dance.[44] The couple hold their arms out sideways and constantly move in big circles – it was meant to recall the continual movement of a ship at sea. The lulu fado – referred to as the 'latest European Dance' – followed, which was to be introduced in America by Margaret Hawkesworth and her partner Basil Durant, regular cabaret performers, who were featured in the photos demonstrating the steps.[45] Danced to particular Portuguese music, it had been introduced in Paris in 1913. A relatively simple dance based on simple figures, two-step patterns, pivots and slow hesitating walks, it also had what we would now call a 'party' dance element, with dancers changing partners to encourage sociability. After executing a series of the three basic figures, the couples separate and turn while doing various noisy syncopated finger snaps and hand claps before returning to their partner, or indeed moving on to a different partner. The third in the series was the 'Sawyer Maxixe'.[46] Joan Sawyer claimed to have invented the foxtrot as well as the maxixe, claims which are hard to believe. The London correspondent at the *Manchester Guardian* had already written about the maxixe or 'Tango Brésilien' in November 1913, claiming its origins in a cabaret or music hall dance that had been around for five years. It was all the rage in Paris in 1913 and was expected to reach London the following season; it is sometimes credited to Maurice. According to Sawyer, the only relationship between the maxixe and the tango is that they both originate in South America, from Brazil and Argentina respectively. She was insistent also that the maxixe could never be considered improper, as the tango had been, but was a graceful ballroom dance.

However, the illustrations might have made the readers doubt that claim. There are positions outside the normal ballroom hold, steps that resemble lunges more familiar in a gym, underarm turns and kicks from the knee, and most surprisingly both partners hold their arms above their heads in what look like exaggerated contemporary paso doble flamenco-style 'Spanish arms'.

The final article in the series was on the French tango, again by Margaret Hawkesworth.[47] She makes a clear distinction between what she calls the American tango with its many variations and the new streamlined version that had been danced in Paris for several years. Most importantly, the new version is smoother, less jerky and progresses around the floor. According to Hawkesworth, Parisian dancers are not interested in the ragtime dances popularized by the Castles, the syncopated rhythms and dancing as an amusement, but take their dancing seriously as an art form. Less well known than the Castles, Hawkesworth and Durant nevertheless had considerable kudos, having visited Europe and been invited to perform the latest American dances in Paris for the French president, Raymond Poincaré.

As well as the newspapers, record companies were eager to promote sales of their music and new gramophone machines offered dance instruction leaflets free with their records. One such from March 1914 for the Victor Talking Machine Company in the USA is 'Three Modern Dances: Illustrated by motion picture'– the one-step, hesitation (waltz) and tango – alongside a glowing endorsement for their equipment by Vernon Castle. Sawyer's instructions for the foxtrot, published by the Columbia Graphophone Company, were accompanied by a similar endorsement by Vernon Castle, 'Originator of the Castle Walk and other Modern Dances', stating: 'I want to congratulate you on the excellent dance records you have recently issued.' The whole of the dance, comprising four figures, is described in just five photographs with short captions. The rather succinct instructions, such as 'Walk, walk, walk, walk, trot-trot, trot-trot, trot-trot, trot-trot', must have been quite difficult to follow, even for an experienced dancer. Indeed, the caption for 'Picture No. 5' notes that it 'will not help you much, but it illustrates the gentleman's crossing his left foot over in back of the right foot in the "Zag"'.[48]

The teaching associations in Britain struggled with the new dances. With so many of them, it seemed the dancers were more interested in novelty value rather than perfecting the steps, and there was little time to learn one before another took its place. The negative aspects of overcrowding and boisterous behaviour persisted, but on the positive side there are reports that young men had become more adept and the steps were manageable and not boring: 'The Boston and similar developments and varieties of the Waltz are quite unobjectionable and have raised the standard of dancing.'[49] The 'Court and Society' column in *The Observer* in January 1913 lists the

Three Modern Dances: One Step, Hesitation, Tango (1914), published by the Victor Talking Machine Company, USA. The pamphlet includes film stills alongside the written instructions and ends with the Castles' 'Suggestions For Correct Dancing'.

Mr. and Mrs. Vernon Castle's Suggestions

For Correct Dancing

Do not wriggle the shoulders.

Do not shake the hips.

Do not twist the body.

Do not flounce the elbows.

Do not pump the arms.

Do not hop—glide instead.

Avoid low, fantastic and acrobatic dips.

Stand far enough away from each other to allow free movement of the body in order to dance gracefully and comfortably.

The gentleman should rest his hand lightly against lady's back, touching her with the finger tips and wrist only, or, if preferred, with the inside of the wrist and back of the thumb.

The gentleman's left hand and forearm should be held up in the air parallel with his body, with the hand extended, holding the lady's hand lightly on his palm. The arm should never be straightened out.

Page Twenty-eight

THE DIFFERENT FIGURES

Memorize the different figures of the dance in their order, and then I will teach you each figure. The figures are as follows, and I shall use my own terms in defining them:

1. The Walk and "Trot."
2. The Drag-step and "Trot."
3. The Maxixe-glide and "Trot."
4. The Zig-Zag step and "Trot."

Before teaching each figure separately, let me clearly define the "Trot." It is a fast, smooth, gliding run, with heels raised, and with the weight of the body continually on the balls of the feet. There is no taking of the feet from the floor. It is simply an exhilarated, prancing, glide-along, in one direction. Memorize the above.

The dancers face each other and take the same position as for the Waltz.

The gentleman standing with the weight of his body on his right foot, the lady with the weight of her body on her left foot. Now we are ready to begin the

No. 1

First Figure
The Walk and "Trot"

This figure consists of four, long, slow walking steps, followed by eight fast "trot-steps," all in one direction.

The gentleman starts forward with his left foot first (lady starting backward with her right).

All the gentleman has to think is *Walk, Walk, Walk, Walk,* trot-trot, trot-trot, trot-trot, trot-trot, and then he repeats the whole thing again. The lady's feet will move backward in this order, *Right, Left, Right, Left,* right-left, right-left, right-left, right-left.

The walking step is taken with a graceful long stride; see picture of couple taking the very first step No. 1. Note carefully the style of the step.

How to Dance the Foxtrot by Joan Sawyer, November 1914. A Columbia Graphophone Company complimentary booklet that included dance instructions and listings of records. 'Your Columbia Dance Records, with their spritely, clear cut rhythms, are the best records for dancing this season's big dance – the Fox-trot.'

various charity and hunt balls taking place in the counties in the coming month and speculates on 'a very smart function', 'a very full night' and the splendid rooms. The columnist also reports on the decisions to ban some of the new dances by asking that dancers desist or leave. Dances such as the bunny hug and turkey trot, which people might not have dared to perform at London's smarter balls, had caused trouble at country balls.[50]

By 1914 the tenth congress of the ISTD, held in London in late July, was focused on 'smooth dancing' in the continued pursuit of standardization by the 'elimination of exaggerated movements', in order to 'purify ballroom dancing generally'. The conference was attended by some 250 dancing teachers from all over the world, with the largest number of delegates from England and the USA.[51] In general, there was a desire for something more graceful in the ballroom, and in response to the many criticisms of the new dance crazes, some were keen on a revival of the older dances that had all but disappeared from balls. The farandole, an old Provençal country dance, was lively and probably too complicated for a typical ball. But others, the saraband from the period of Louis XIV, the gavotte and minuet, were all more graceful alternatives to the sometimes boisterous and often too energetic American dances.

Delayed by the First World War, the project to standardize modern dancing in Britain was still a few years in the future, but the congress of the Dancing Societies of America, at a meeting held in New York in December 1914, approved the new modern dances; they were published in January 1915 by the American National Association Masters of Dancing.[52] The modern dances listed are the foxtrot, which is the most complex, with several pages devoted to it, the one-step, three kinds of waltz, the maxixe and the Parisian tango. The others with more rudimentary descriptions – la russe, the Brazilian polka, lulu fado and the balancello – have all but disappeared. The descriptions are generally quite brief; they use some existing French and Spanish terminology from classical and folk dancing interspersed

"Fox Trot"

The basis of the "Fox Trot" is two steps, one a slow walking step on two counts, and the other a quick running step on one count.

The gentleman starts with the L. ft. forward, the lady with the R. ft. backward.

The gentleman's part is described; the lady's is the counterpart.

FIGURE I

Gentleman walks forward 4 steps, 2 counts to each L, R, L, R (8 counts).

	2 *measures*
4 running steps, L, R, L, R (4 counts)	1 *measure*
4 running steps, turning to right (4 counts)	1 *measure*
Repeat all	4 *measures*
	8 *measures*

FIGURE II

Gentleman steps L. ft. diag. forward (counts 1, 2), slides R. ft. across behind L. ft (counts 3, 4), and runs forward 4 steps, L, R, L, R (counts 5, 6, 7, 8)

	2 *measures*
Repeat all twice	4 *measures*
Full turn to R., 4 steps, two counts to each step . .	2 *measures*
	8 *measures*

FIGURE III

Gentleman executes a "Maxixe" two-step with L. ft., turn one-half to right (counts 1, 2, 3), hold (count 4), 4 running steps backward, beginning R. ft. (counts 5, 6, 7, 8)

	2 *measures*
Repeat all starting R. ft., complete the turn to R. .	2 *measures*
Repeat all	4 *measures*
	8 *measures*

FIGURE IV
THE ZIG-ZAG RUN

The gentleman moves forward, lady backward; he crosses his foot to the back, and she hers to the front.

Gentleman runs L. ft. to L. side (count 1), R. ft. cross back (count 2), L. ft. to L. side (count 3), R. ft. to R. side (count 4), L. ft. cross back (count 5), R. ft. to R. side (count 6).

The 'Description of Modern Dances', approved by the Congress of the Dancing Societies of America in December 1914 and published in 1915, used a discursive text with simple terminology of steps, counts and measures.

with English. The follower's steps are rarely described in any detail and most simply state, 'The gentleman's part will be described: the lady's is the counterpart.'

In Britain newspaper gossip columns and society pages, and increasingly women's and fashion magazines, were covering dancing from different angles, but the new editor of a professional journal provided a more measured view of the contemporary dancing scene. The *Dancing Times* had been in circulation since 1894, focusing primarily on classical ballet, but in 1910 the new editor, Philip J. S. Richardson, introduced a section dedicated to ballroom dancing.[53]

Richardson was to be a prominent figure in the development and codification of modern dancing, and through him the *Dancing Times* was to become the professional sounding board for ballroom dancing teachers and a key site of the debate around codification.

Josephine Bradley dancing with her husband, Douglas Wellesley Smith. Bradley was chair of the ballroom branch of the ISTD from 1924 until 1947.

THREE

The Democratization of Dancing

Society has tired of society dances! It was impossible to get away from each other. At every private ball they met the same people, the same partners.

Sunday Express, 1921[1]

History associates the 1920s with the Charleston, but many other social dances continued to be popular, and in reality it was just one more American dance craze that came and went. It was attractive to a younger generation, energetic, undoubtedly great fun, and many credit it with encouraging people back to the ballroom. The 1920s saw far more significant events. For professional dancers, it was importantly a decade when the foundations of modern ballroom technique were laid, the 'English style' was established and the Blackpool Dance Festival began. In addition, and with considerable impact on the general public, the music industry was expanding, dance halls were being built and dancing was covered in every newspaper, often with columns contributed by dancers.

Dancing for the working and upper classes in the early 1920s was still very different in terms of both the places at which they were dancing and the kinds of dancing. The working classes were still keen on what might be considered the simpler dances – sequence dances, Lancers and quadrilles – that were easy to learn. They were dancing in town halls and purpose-built public ballrooms, which – following on from the success of seaside developments – were being built all over the country. Hammersmith Palais in London, one of the earliest, had opened in 1919, Birmingham Palais in 1920, Sherry's Dance Hall in Brighton, owned by Bertram Mills, and Dunedin Dance Hall in Edinburgh in 1923. In Glasgow the Piccadilly opened in 1926 for the smart set, followed by the Dennistoun Palais for everyone else. At the end of the decade, the Locarno in Streatham and the Ritz in Manchester both opened in 1929.

The upper classes were also dancing at public venues rather than hosting events in their private ballrooms. Society balls were still taking place, but for the younger generation the rituals were seen as outdated and were increasingly mocked. *Vogue* magazine's amusing story of a young American man going to his first English party tells us a lot about what seemed strange and outmoded behaviour even then. The American visitor is shocked to find everyone wearing gloves and the men still wearing waistcoats and tailcoats, which had long been abandoned in the USA in favour of dinner jackets. He refers to the 'mediaeval custom of the English to have their dances numbered and labelled' and 'the minute bit of pasteboard with an infinitesimal pencil stub attached' handed out at the door for 'booking' partners for each dance. He believes that the English like this system because a woman needs only to dance with those she wants to and a 'duty dancer' will not get stuck for too long with the same partner. 'Cutting in', presumably acceptable in the USA, is absolutely not tolerated. When the American cannot find the seventeenth partner he has booked, he has to rush about looking for her: 'possibly he finds his charmer; possibly she doesn't want to be found; possibly he addresses the wrong girl; probably he has a nervous breakdown; probably his partner has gone home.'[2] The upper classes were dancing in hotels, restaurants and clubs, albeit somewhat exclusive ones. The reason, which must be at least partly due to the more general socio-economic change, is commented on at length by *Sunday Express* journalist Sydney Moseley in March 1921 as a 'sudden love for dancing by the smart set'.[3] Dancing in public places had become popular, especially in the West End, at clubs such as the Embassy and the Criterion. He goes on to tell us the reason: 'Society has tired of society dances! It was impossible to get away from each other. At every private ball they met the same people, the same partners.' Aristocrats and wealthy socialites – the article mentions Phillip Sassoon of the Sassoon Rothschild family and Mrs Dudley Ward, the mistress of the Prince of Wales – could now mix with the new 'elite' on the dance floor: the theatre crowd and stage celebrities, which brought a new kind of glamour.

After the introduction of so many different and often complex dances imported from America or from Paris, Crompton, the ISTD president, had changed his views on the waltz and was keen to promote its apparent revival. He blamed the complexities of the new 'jazz' dances for destroying the sociability of the ballroom. The new dances required combinations of figures that had to be practised with a partner. This often led to the same couple dancing together all evening and not with others. The new dances were also entertaining to watch but often too difficult for the ordinary dancer to carry out.[4] On the other hand, 'With the revival of the Waltz . . . the sociability of former times will be restored to the ballroom, partners will readily be found again, and there will be fewer "wallflowers" than one sees today.'[5] In the 1920s in most European languages the word 'waltz' (or sometimes 'valse') referred to what is now codified as the 'Viennese waltz', which has changed very little for centuries. It comprises a change step and just two rotational, travelling figures, natural (right) and reverse (left) turns, that make a complete 360-degree rotation in six steps, including crossing the feet in the reverse, at a fast pace of 180 beats per minute.[6] Requiring enormous energy and stamina, it was condemned for its fatiguing nature and for its frivolity, similar to other popular country dances such as the polka and galop. The 'English' or 'slow' waltz is still in 3/4 time but at a much slower pace of 84–90 beats per minute. As the first of the standard dances, despite its toe-to-toe, close hold, or perhaps because of its familiarity and simplicity, it survived the opposition by prudish critics.

A newspaper report in 1919 tells the reader that while the waltz is definitely gaining popularity again, the new season's favourite dances are expected to be the paso doble and the tango valse, two new dances that are much calmer than the 'jazz' dances that had been introduced at the Empress Rooms by tango expert Belle Harding.[7] The tango valse was a variation on the Parisian tango without the difficult moves of the pre-war version. The paso doble, also imported from Paris, was promoted as an easy-to-learn dance although reading the description in the *Daily Mail* at the time – 'the double time beat with slightly bent knees. Beginning with a glide, it merges into a fandango movement, finishes with a movement in double time' – we might doubt that.[8]

In his new role as editor of the *Dancing Times*, Philip J. S. Richardson frequently expressed concern about standards. He was worried not that there was a split between the sequence dances at popular assemblies and the non-sequence dances that were danced in clubs, but at the way the dances were 'looked after'.[9] The sequence dances, which had been around for much longer, were being taught by members of the teachers' associations, whereas, apart from a few who had trained at the ISTD, there were not enough properly qualified teachers to support the modern, or non-sequence, dances. In early 1921 Richardson published a list of what he called '15 Dancing Facts'.[10] This is a curious list that reads as not much more than a rant about the lack of understanding and the incorrect use of terminology to describe modern dancing. The sentence 'There is no such dance as the "jazz"' appears three times, and in Fact 2, the description of a sequence dance, his comment that 'certain definite steps have to be done in a certain definite order' demonstrates his pedantic tone. Together with other statements about what is being danced, how and where, and an acknowledgement that the origin of most dances is generally 'wrapt in mystery', a few almost defensive 'facts' are included: '11. dancing in moderation is the finest mental tonic a businessman can take . . . 13. Indecent dancing is practically unknown in this country,' and, somewhat surprisingly, '12. an extraordinary percentage of dancers go to dances for the sake of dancing.' Perhaps Richardson's frustration was understandable. Professional dancers relied on pupils coming to them for instruction, but finding the right balance between dances that were too difficult to learn, which would put people off, and those that were too easy, which would result in lack of interest through boredom, was a considerable challenge.

For those who were keen dancers, the desire to perform and compete in order to demonstrate expertise, fitness and confidence was as strong as for those engaged in other forms of physical activity, and as the popularity of dancing grew, so did the numbers of competitions. There were other benefits too. For dancing teachers, winning at competitions was important to enhance their profile in order to attract pupils. For dance hall managers, competitions offering prizes encouraged attendance and inspired people to improve their standard of dancing, which was in turn also good for the teachers. Early competitions were generally social events organized by dance hall managers but were soon taken up by promoters seeing a sponsorship opportunity. Initially, they were 'one dance' competitions and there was no distinction made between professional or amateur dancers, or indeed 'mixed' couples: at that time more often a professional female teacher dancing with an amateur male leader. The 'mixed' category had been invented for the World's Championships in 1911 when a professional dancer, Louis Bayo, competed with one of his pupils.[11]

The World's Championships, which had started in Paris in 1909, was the first significant competition. It was run by Camille de Rhynal, president of the International Dance Federation (FID) and an influential Parisian choreographer and teacher, in collaboration with several music publishers. It was held at the prestigious Sarah Bernhardt Theatre, now the Théâtre de la Ville, in the centre of Paris. The competition attracted around two hundred dancers for the Boston, grizzly bear, one-step (or rag) and turkey trot. The American dancer Maurice cemented his reputation at the competition, winning in 1911 partnered with Mistinguett, the celebrated dancer at the Folies Bergère. By 1912 the competition lasted for three days, and the even higher numbers each year meant it was necessary to introduce advance registration. Despite a wartime break from 1915 to 1919, the number of participants did not diminish, and for the 1920 competition three hundred couples reached the final heats. They performed eight different dances, the waltz, schottische, shimmy, paso doble, tango, maxixe, one-step and foxtrot (accounts differ on whether the tango was included or not). By 1921 the competition, which had moved to a bigger venue, the Théâtre des Champs-Élysées, lasted for ten days. Rhynal brought the competition to London in 1922 in collaboration with Chappell & Co. music publishers and the *Dancing Times*, where two further competitions were held in 1924 and 1925. The three competitions held in London comprised just four dances, the waltz, foxtrot, tango and one-step. The 'World's', as it was known, returned to Paris in 1926, and for many years afterwards almost every championship was won by a British couple.

The Star newspaper held '*The Star* London and Southern Counties Dancing Championships' from 1925 to 1931, which were considered similarly prestigious. The first was at the now-demolished Palais de Danse in Wimbledon, west London. It comprised just three dances – foxtrot, waltz and tango – and amateur, professional and mixed couples all competed together. It later moved to the Queen's Hall in central London. The *Star* Championships competition was held again from 1938 until 1960 and was resurrected in 1995 by the Ballroom Dancing Federation (BDF).[12] Competitions were staged at local dance halls and ballrooms as they sprang up all over the country, often sponsored by newspapers and supported by local teachers' associations keen to encourage dancers, and frequently also by the *Dancing Times*.

The Blackpool Dance Festival, which has remained the biggest and the most prestigious of any competitive ballroom event worldwide, was launched in 1920 and, apart from a five-year break from

1941 to 1945 and a one-year break in 2020, has continued to take place annually in May.[13] It seems surprising that such a prestigious event, despite the draw of London and its convenience for the many international visitors, has remained at Blackpool – there is still no direct train line from London. The Empress Ballroom at the Winter Gardens must surely play a large role: it is one of the largest ball-rooms in Britain and the most spectacular, and has adjacent spaces for the competitors, audience and congress attendees. The glamorous atmosphere of the Empress Ballroom is perhaps also enhanced by the extreme contrast with the surrounding environment.

The festival was initially supported by local music publishers Sharples, who awarded a Sharples Challenge Shield to the various winners, and until 1923 the chair of the adjudicators was James Finnigan, president of the MATD. For the first few years the festival catered only for novelty dances and sequence dances in different rhythms. The Blackpool Tower Company had taken over the Winter Gardens complex, including the Empress Ballroom, in 1928, and after refurbishing the ballroom revitalized the 1929 festival with the intro-duction of the first major modern dancing competition, the North of England Championships, in both amateur and professional catego-ries. The festival still included the competitions for sequence dances and a veterans' waltz.[14] The first British Championships (amateur and professional) were introduced when the festival was expanded in 1931. The amateur competition saw 31 couples in the final and 22 couples in the professional competition.[15] The North of England amateur had 37 couples and the professional just 13. The field was not as tough as it might have been: that year a clash with the World's in Paris attracted some of the more experienced competitors, including the winning couple, Arthur Milner and Norma Cave, and the *Star* champions, Glasgow's Bobby Philp and Ella Scutts. The *Star* amateur champions, brother and sister John and Elsa Wells, were also absent.

Winning the early championships could lead to immediate offers of employment and was almost certain to guarantee a successful career. The 1920 winners of the World's were immediately booked by both the Hammersmith Palais in London and the Opéra in Paris. The main activity of professional dancers was teaching, and they could also earn money demonstrating; the best-known found work in an advisory capacity to the various associations working to standardize modern dancing. Moreover, the not inconsiderable coverage in newspapers and magazines opened up the opportunity for writing commentaries and dancing instruction. Some individuals' position was assured as the new steps and figures they invented were adopted by the profession, such as the double reverse spin, invented by Maxwell Stuart, five times winner of the World's in the 1920s.

The increased amount of press coverage, particularly of the growing numbers of competitions, meant that the dancing profession was getting more attention and teachers were becoming better known. The early 1920s also saw an increased growth in business activities related to dancing. Music publishers, composers, bands who provided live music, singers and their agents were all in demand and, increasingly, the latest gramophones and records. Competition promoters, particularly newspapers, saw opportunities in a fast-growing entertainment business with little to rival dancing for the public's attention. The middle classes had more leisure time and disposable income, which meant more profits for nightclub and restaurant owners. For dancing professionals, there were more and more opportunities as cabaret and exhibition dancers, teachers, competition adjudicators and commentators. It is difficult to establish how easy it was to make a living as a dance teacher or studio owner in the 1920s – there were no new couples to replace the Castles but there were certainly those who achieved a near celebrity status, albeit within the confines of the profession.

Josephine Bradley had started out playing piano for ballet classes but became so fascinated by dancing that she trained as a ballroom dancer.[16] With her first partner, G. Kenneth Anderson, and while still unknown in dancing circles, she was the surprise winner of a foxtrot competition at London's Embassy Club in November 1920 (both Richardson and Taylor were judges). Bradley and Anderson went on to win several more high-profile foxtrot competitions in 1921 and won the mixed event at the World's Championships in 1924. Bradley is credited with establishing the basics of the foxtrot – the walk, three-step, natural turn and open reverse turn – and with developing the more fluid, flowing style of the slow foxtrot, as it became known. She was the first to introduce the feather step – noting how good it felt when her partner accidentally stepped outside – indicating the earliest contra body movement position (CBMP), where the foot is placed on or across the line of the supporting foot, either in front or behind, to maintain body line.[17] Another important dancer of the 1920s is Santos Casani (1898–1983), who arrived in England from South Africa in 1914 and stayed after the war. He opened Casani's School of Dancing in 1921 in Knightsbridge, and when his business expanded he moved to bigger premises in Regent Street in 1925. He rapidly became prominent in the dancing world. Experimenting with new forms of teaching, he broadcast tango lessons on a fortnightly basis and danced on the stage at the London Coliseum for a week, giving tango lessons to an audience of over a hundred people with his partner, Jose Leonard. An accompanying description of the steps was published in the *Daily Mail*.

The 1920s also saw the establishment of two of ballroom's best-known mainstream figures, Victor Silvester and Arthur Murray,[18] who both became household names. In Britain Victor Silvester attained a celebrity status first as a dancer and teacher and later through his dance orchestra and popular radio and TV broadcasts. On the other side of the Atlantic, Arthur Murray became best known for his worldwide franchise of dancing schools.

Arthur Murray had started out as a dance partner in 1912 at the Grand Central Palace in New York, the first dance hall to offer paid dance partners and instructors.[19] He then worked for a chain of studios part-time while employed in his day job as an architectural draughtsman, before deciding to enrol for lessons at Castle House to learn to teach 'professionally'. The lessons cost him what he earned for four hours' teaching every evening. He left New York to work at various summer resorts, first at Marblehead in Massachusetts and then in the South, often partnering wealthier older women, improving his dancing and his social standing. He says of that time, 'I was tall, single and could dance – in fact I was the best dancer they had seen.'[20] Always image-conscious, he changed his name from Teichman to Murray, continued to dance while studying for a business degree, and tried out various jobs, including working as a journalist, before eventually deciding that, despite it being considered frivolous, self-indulgent and sometimes shocking, he would make dancing his main occupation.

Murray branched out on his own in the early 1920s with a mail-order business based on his belief that 'the written word is more impressive than the spoken word' and that 'Whatever the instructor can TELL you, he can convey to you more forcefully in WRITING.'[21] Murray also believed that learning to dance alone was the most effective way to learn to balance on your own, not lean on others, and know the steps before attempting to dance with a partner. His first substantial book, entitled *How to Become a Good Dancer*, was first published in 1938. It came complete with a set of paper cut-out numbered footprints, inspired perhaps by his training as a draughtsman, which could be laid out on a 60 × 60 centimetre (2 × 2 ft) square grid on the floor for learning the exact foot placements.[22]

His first attempt at a mail-order business was not successful. He bought kinetoscopes – a primitive form of film projector – and made a series of images of himself demonstrating the various figures and positions. Unfortunately, the machines were not robust and regularly broke down, which meant that any profits had to be used to reimburse disappointed customers. Once he switched to the diagrams, however, his success was assured, and by the end of 1925 his mail-order business supported as many as thirty employees to empty the envelopes of cash sent in for the written instructions.[23] Murray also considered that confidence, something he himself was not short of, was as important as technique: 'When you know how to dance and know that you learned direct from America's recognized dancing authority you automatically gain ease and confidence.'[24] Murray may have been a firm believer that the written word is better than instruction in person or even diagrams, but many of the written instructions were so complicated that it seems unlikely that many people were able to interpret them – certainly, reading while doing them balanced on one leg would have been impossible, requiring at least a helper to read out the text as each move was performed.

But Murray was clearly hugely ambitious. His shameless self-promotion, referred to by his wife as 'unique methods of personal publicity', included submitting stories about himself to the society column of the newspaper he had once worked for.[25] He hired press agents – as many as four at one time was not unusual – and rewarded them with bonus payments each time his name was mentioned in the press. His instructions, together with his photographs, were widely published across America. He often invited popular models and actresses to pose with him for photographs, even on one occasion succeeding in persuading Fred Astaire to appear with his then better-known sister, Adele. He did not hesitate to name-drop. To drum up pupils for his first dancing school, his notice to the society editors announced, 'Arthur Murray formerly of Castle House, New York, would be in charge of the dancing at the Georgian Terrace Hotel.'[26] He started classes for children sponsored initially by the society editor of the *Atlanta Journal*, a Mrs Edward Van Winkle, and with her advice pursued the idea of forming a club – the Club de Vingt – which he thought sounded exclusive and would therefore imply membership was a privilege. It quickly grew to twenty pupils and then more, until eventually he was obliged to move to larger premises in early 1920. After teaching children Murray worked hard at advertising to attract adult pupils and especially men, using the

THE CHASSÉ
MAN'S PART

Man's Part

START
HERE

Begin with left foot and go forward, follow the numbers in the foot prints. The right foot is shaded.

This step is one of the standard and most popular steps of the Fox Trot and One Step. It is sometimes referred to as the "Cut Step" because on the fourth step the man draws his right foot up to the left.

Here is how the step is done:

At the "start" stand erect with your heels together, Then—

1. Begin with the left foot and step directly forward taking an ordinary walking step.

2. Walk forward on right foot.

3. Walk forward on left foot.

4. Draw the right foot up to the left, placing weight on right foot. That's all.

Follow the numbers in the foot-steps.

If you want to repeat the step, begin with the left foot.

The Chasse' is one of the most popular steps in the Fox Trot, but it may also be used in the One Step and the Waltz Canter. At first it is advisable to learn to dance the Chasse' to Fox Trot music. After you learn it in the Fox Trot, you will have no difficulty in dancing it to One Step or Waltz music.

The walking steps in the Fox Trot are long and slow. Each walking step takes a full second. The man generally walks forward so that he can see where to go. If the man dances backward he may collide with other couples on the ballroom floor.

The Fox Trot is the easiest and most popular dance. It contains about ten standard variations and many novel steps. Because of its delightful rythm and its syncopated time, the Fox Trot has become the universal dance in every English speaking country. It is interesting because of its many variations,—steps which relieve the monotony of dancing the same thing all the time.

How to Become a Good Dancer by Arthur Murray (1922). Diagrams to show the chassé, 'one of the standard and most popular steps of the Fox Trot and One Step'. The instructions include 'The Lady's part . . . just the opposite of the man's part.'

First Step

FEATHER STEP

Second Step

Feather Step : Third Step

Correct hold

THE FOX-TROT (4)

Casani's Self-Tutor of Ballroom Dancing published in 1927 used photographs and textual description rather than diagrams.

'club' theme again, as it 'attracted many of the manly boys. There is a general impression among them that a dancing school is a place for "sissies". But going to a club in an exclusive club-house is an entirely different matter . . . Everyone wanted to join a club that was particular about its membership.'[27]

In Britain Victor Silvester, like Arthur Murray, had started his dancing career working as a partner for single women. He was whiling away the summer holidays before going to Sandhurst military academy, out at a tea dance with a cousin, when he was approached by Belle Harding, who asked him to dance, telling him, 'Fine young fellow with a figure like that. You'd make a wonderful dancer.'[28] She immediately offered him 'pocket money' to come and join the 35 'girls' training to become teachers and to 'partner unattached ladies' at the dances she ran at the Empress Rooms in Kensington. We might think it hard to believe, but after just two weeks he had learnt the basics and was employed to teach. At the end of the summer holidays Silvester did go to Sandhurst as previously planned, but he lasted just three weeks; he returned to Harding's studio, ignoring his father's disappointment at his son becoming, in his terms, a 'gigolo'. Silvester was less troubled by this insult; indeed, in his autobiography he writes in a chapter entitled 'Teenage Gigolo' that 'one of the perks of the job was partnering rich women who wanted a professional dancer to take them out at night.'[29]

Silvester was obliged to resign from Harding's studio in early 1920 when she discovered that he had been moonlighting at the Ritz Palm Court on his day off. He tried other kinds of employment, working for an entomologist, but that only lasted a few months before he once again went back to dancing, this time to the Empress Rooms, which had been taken over by the Lyons catering company; Lyons offered regular employment and had no objections to his taking on any additional work elsewhere. Silvester won his first competition in Ostend in August 1921 – the judge was Philip J. S. Richardson – and the following summer he won the Cliftonville Trophy with Pat

Victor Silvester and Phyllis Clarke in 1923, winners of the World's Championships held in London at the Queens Hall in December 1922 – the first time they were held in London.

Kendall, which was judged by Pierre.[30] When he heard that the World's Ballroom Dancing Championships, organized by Camille de Rhynal, were to be held in London for the first time in September 1922, Silvester started dancing with a new partner, Phyllis Clarke – he had previously danced with her sister Vera – in preparation. Phyllis and Victor entered and won two local competitions: one at the Frolics Club, the other at Hammersmith Palais. The World's was organized in three categories – professional, amateur and mixed – and once those were decided, the first three couples in each category competed against each other for the overall title. Silvester and Clarke won the overall World's Championships, which, according to dancer and writer Lyndon Wainwright, represented 'the first indications of the British dominance to come'.[31] Silvester continued dancing with Phyllis Clarke, teaching and giving demonstrations not at smart clubs but often at inexpensive venues such as the Lyons Popular Café in Piccadilly.[32] Their partnership came to an end after they came second in the World's Championships in the spring of 1924, soon after he had opened his first dancing school in 1923 at the Rector's Club in central London, before moving to his own premises in Maddox Street.

The practice that both Victor Silvester and Arthur Murray have written about – which they describe as 'escorting' single women at dances – met with disapproval from various camps in the early twentieth century and continues to do so today. However, for anyone setting out to learn to dance, having a partner who is a professional dancer, and more skilled and knowledgeable, is a great advantage; learning is much faster than when learning to dance with a partner who also knows nothing. Many dancers are not prepared to run the risk of dancing with a less adept partner and refuse to dance 'socially' with either friends or strangers; they only dance with their own, paid for, professional partner. It is not clear from either Silvester's or Murray's accounts, but we must assume that they were paid for their services. Whether the practice continued or was common is not clear, but today it is common to see paid partners at social events, almost always older women dancing with much younger professional men, often former competitors or freelance teachers. An advertisement in the *Fulham Chronicle* for the opening night at the Hammersmith Palais, in October 1919, includes '80 lady and gentlemen "instructors"', who were, more accurately, paid partners who waited in 'pens' or 'cages' and could be hired per dance – again a practice that was disapproved of by many. A 'looker-on' writing in the *Daily Express* in 1923 criticizes the somewhat casual attitude of England's freelance professional partners, who are either 'showing people how they ought to dance with their own partners . . . or chatting with them at their tables', comparing it with Parisian dances where 'there are any number of men on the staff who methodically dance with any lady unsupplied with an efficient partner. After the dance the lady is escorted back to their table, formally bowed to and left.'[33]

With his partner Jose Leonard, Santos Casani became well known through his promotion of the Charleston, excessive advertising stunts and innovative teaching techniques.

FOUR

Basic Technique Takes Shape

Because of its delightful rhythm and its syncopated time, the Fox Trot
has become the universal dance in every English-speaking country.
It is interesting because of its many variations, steps which relieve
the monotony of dancing the same thing all the time.

How to Become a Good Dancer (1922)[1]

The most important work to establish the technique for modern ballroom dancing was carried out in the 1920s through what were known as the 'informal conferences' chaired by Philip J. S. Richardson. He had already become a considerable force as editor of the *Dancing Times* and had emerged as the natural leader of the movement to standardize dancing. The first few informal conferences focused on competition dancing, dealing with the basics of technique, and included one that discussed the definitions of professional and amateur status. It was not until the final two, held in 1929, that there was a focus on general or social dancers and the concerns of their teachers.

Richardson organized the first *Dancing Times* informal conference in London in May 1920. Despite the best efforts of leading teachers, in his view 'the bulk of dancers followed their own bent, and freakish movements at times bordering on roughness were very much in evidence' and something should be done.[2] Supported by Maurice, who was then dancing at the Piccadilly Hotel, the conference attracted two hundred attendees and considerable press interest. Chairing the meeting, Richardson made his position clear in his opening remarks: 'Technique is being entirely jettisoned. It is a day of bunny-hug and blatant jazz music.'[3] Maurice, who addressed the conference at length, annoyed some teachers who objected to an American criticizing English dancing, despite the fact that many of the dances had originated in America and that Maurice was, according to Richardson, undoubtedly the greatest American dancer.[4] He proposed a standard hold with both arms at shoulder height and elbows bent, that the basic figures should be agreed for each dance and that all teachers should teach those same basic figures. Demonstrating with Leonora Hughes, Maurice claimed that the biggest problem for English dancers was dancing to the wrong tempo and that the men put their hands too low around their partner's waist, making it much more difficult for her to balance. The problem was partly to do with the growing fashion for backless dresses and men no longer wearing gloves. Cecil Taylor agreed: 'the man ceases to place his hand in the middle of the woman's back. This is primarily in consideration for her and secondarily in consideration for his evening coat . . . he prefers to guard it against powder.'[5]

The conference's first resolution, carried unanimously, was: 'That the teachers present agree to do their very best to stamp out freak steps particularly dips and steps in which the feet are raised high off the ground and also sidesteps and pauses which impede the progress of those who may be following.'[6] Importantly, they agreed to set up a committee that would decide on the figures for each dance and report back to a reconvened conference in the autumn. Richardson was elected to chair the committee, which comprised fifteen eminent dancers such as Maurice and Belle Harding, George Fontana (a leading exhibition dancer), Cecil Taylor (president of the ISDT since 1909) and Edward Scott, the well-known author of several books, including *Dancing as an Art and Pastime* (1892).[7] There was some discussion about the crusade against dancing that seemed to be taking hold in Europe and the need to make it clear that dancing was 'above suspicion', but the main business was to agree on the basic figures. The outline decisions reached in 1920 were revised in more detail at the third conference, held in the spring of 1921, which attracted yet more attendees, up to three hundred, and appointed another committee, this time including Josephine Bradley and Pierre, who were to report back in the autumn. The report of the committee, issued in October 1921, is the first formal description of the English modern or ballroom dances. It made no comment on the one-step and made several recommendations for the other dances; the fox-trot is described in some detail, including what seem oddities now: the 'shimmy step' and 'toddle' movements. The waltz is described very simply as 'step-step-feet together. This movement to be done forward backward and turning.' To encourage the tango, the report suggests that bands should be asked to play a tango immediately after a fox-trot, which they thought would encourage more dancers as they were still on the floor. In addition, under the heading of 'General' were the key recommendations for the basics of modern technique: 'In modern dancing the committee suggest that the knees must be kept together in passing and the feet parallel. They also repeat their suggestion that all eccentric steps be abolished and that dancers should do their best always to progress round the room.'[8]

There was still confusion about the structure of the tango, and a fourth conference was organized in October 1922 specifically to discuss the problems and come to a resolution. Unlike the contro-versial original, which was more suited to exhibition dances and performance than to participation, a much simplified version, more acceptable to the general dancer, had returned to the ballroom. In its now various different forms the tango was steadily gaining in popularity and appeared on many programmes, but there was still considerable disagreement about just how it should be danced. Exhib-ition dancers George Fontana and Marjorie Moss demonstrated at a ball and competition which the *Dancing Times* had organized earlier in the year, and a second event, organized in March 1923, saw Victor Silvester and Phyllis Clarke win the competition. Imported from Paris, where it had been danced regularly for some time, the simplified version of the tango now had just four standard figures. It was to be danced in close hold and, importantly, progress around the ballroom, avoiding close body contact and, even worse, too much undignified body movement, described as 'its apt-to-be-offensive movement of the hips'.[9]

Tango music had presented a stumbling block initially; the particular sound and rhythm of the music was produced by bands playing bandoneons, mandolins and guitars, which were not the kind of instruments found in English dance bands. By 1925 this had changed, in Maxwell Stuart's view; in the same way that it had taken some years for musicians to assimilate 'jazz' music to enable the foxtrot to become established, perhaps for the tango too it was only a matter of time.[10] The introduction of tango bands in dance halls, and new tango music, often by French composers, had also helped to encourage dancers. Rudolph Valentino dancing a passionate tango in the 1921 top-grossing film *Four Horsemen of the Apocalypse* is also credited with contributing to its revival.

By 1924 some teachers and competition dancers still thought it was necessary to develop more detail than had been agreed at the first informal conferences and decided to form yet another 'Society of Ballroom Teachers' in order to focus on developing the modern syllabus. This was averted, however, by the decision taken at the ISTD, which catered for different kinds of dances through a series of specialist branches (known today as faculties), to go ahead with the formation of a dedicated Ballroom Branch.[11] Its president, Cecil Taylor, who had been a member of the first committee of the informal conferences, was supportive and proceeded to appoint a committee including Josephine Bradley, Eve Tynegate-Smith, Muriel Simmons, Lisle Humphreys and Victor Silvester to agree on the syllabus for the entrance examinations.[12] The results were relatively straightforward;

exam candidates could bring a partner of their choice to demonstrate three different elements: knowledge of the basic steps in foxtrot, waltz, one-step and tango, a rudimentary knowledge of the music needed and 'carriage of the arms, head and body'. The syllabus, together with the basic steps, were then published in the ISTD's own publication, *Dance Journal*.[13]

At this time, the early 1920s, the interest in new dances had decreased and nothing seemed to interest the dancing public except the foxtrot, which, although unpopular with teachers, was extremely popular with everyone else. The same was true in America. According to Arthur Murray, as part of his postal course *How to Become a Good Dancer*, 'The Foxtrot is the easiest and most popular dance. It contains about ten standard variations and many novel steps. . . . It is interesting because of its many variations, steps which relieve the monotony of dancing the same thing all the time.'[14] A typical evening's programme comprised mostly foxtrots interspersed with a few waltzes, one-steps or an occasional tango.

Despite the best efforts of the teachers and their teaching associations and the prizes offered by the various teachers' congresses for new dances to replace the foxtrot or even just to gain a space on the evening's programme, nothing new had emerged to capture the public's imagination. The Renil foxtrot, the Kalgoorlie foxtrot, the Ladore waltz, la velda, rosana, rick rock and many others were, according to the press, no more successful than earlier new dances such as the el chucho, which according to contemporary newspaper articles 'two years back was going to be the dance of the year or the camel walk, which last season [1922] was going to oust the foxtrot completely'.[15] There was some hope for the blues (1923), which was sometimes included two or three times in an evening, but few couples, usually only the more expert dancers, would take to the floor. Its slow, languorous movements, which needed a better sense of balance than the faster dances, made it more challenging for the less confident dancers.[16] The *Dancing Times* nevertheless promoted it with a 'Blues

Ball' and competition which did little to popularize the blues; however, it did bring to attention two more individuals who were to become important figures in the history of modern dancing – Alex Moore in first place and Phyllis Haylor in third.[17] Both are credited with inventing new steps that were to be included in the basic syllabus. Haylor, with her partner Alec Millar, are credited with the cross swivel – originally named the Millar cross – and Moore, dancing with Pat Kilpatrick, invented the whisk, another apparently accidental discovery as Moore stepped behind to recover his balance and his 'perfect partner' simply followed.[18]

Other dances, some with the most unlikely names such as the 'dog trot' and 'sixtime', were still being pushed, perhaps over-optimistically, as teachers and commentators alike were frustrated that the foxtrot, which was in effect a walking dance considered by many rather repetitive and simple, had such a hold on the dancing public. Rhynal thought that 'sooner or later dancers will begin to tire of the eternal rhythmic walk.'[19] But the foxtrot continued to be the most popular dance and it was almost by accident that a new dance appeared. For musicians, the syncopated rhythms had become the norm but the original foxtrot speed of 44–6 bars to the minute had been gradually getting faster and faster. Jack Hylton reportedly played foxtrots at 54 bars a minute and the Savoy Orpheans between 52 and 56.[20] This fast version, initially known as the quick-time foxtrot, was to emerge as a new dance with its own name: the quickstep.

Establishing the quickstep (1924) was not only going to help dancers in deciding which steps to do, but was welcomed as a way to help with keeping couples moving, which would in turn reduce problems caused by overcrowding.[21] Overcrowding was an ongoing problem for dance hall owners and for dancers, for its effect on both behaviour and dancing. The inevitable jostling and bumping, especially between the less experienced dancers, often provoked arguments and a loss of good manners. The newspapers continued to be full of advice on what constituted good behaviour in the dance hall.

Gentlemen were encouraged to smile at their partners and enjoy their dancing; they were warned to avoid ostentation and repetitiveness, but crowds caused the biggest problem even for the most skilled dancers. Crowds would make any progress around the floor impossible and would force dancers to stay on the spot, inevitably leading to closer body contact and more body movement, both still considered unacceptable.

British teachers worked hard to eradicate body movements, which were considered undignified, and focused on the approved syllabus. The obsession with new dancing crazes was perhaps over – things had definitely become much calmer by the mid-1920s – but there were always new steps and tricks to learn and teachers could not stop keen dancers picking up new steps and figures wherever they found them. The English upper classes holidaying on the fashionable French Riviera, where the exhibition dancers and professional partners in many of the ballrooms were English, were blamed for the influence of Parisian style and new figures. One example described was spinning – probably pivots – which was frowned upon in social settings, especially when done by inexpert couples, causing bumps and kicks and even falls. Another figure was the drag, now acceptable as part of the waltz's almost stationary figure the drag hesitation. The new steps were credited to the young and fashionable, characterized as 'the young man who goes in for "Oxford" trousers and the type of young woman who has her hair done *à la garçonne*'.[22] Echelon dancing, whereby the couples are side by side instead of toe to toe but facing in opposite directions, was also considered hazardous. The 1925 Riviera season also saw the sidestep introduced in almost all dances – a pragmatic solution to deal with crowded floors.

The teachers' efforts were met with a lack of interest from dance hall owners and promoters keen to attract the public by whatever means. Marathon dances – the subject of the film *They Shoot Horses, Don't They?* (dir. Sydney Pollack, 1969) – did not catch on in Britain, but in America they became very popular. They started in the early

1920s and grew in number until they were eventually banned in 1933. Couples were attracted by the often considerable prize money offered for the couple 'left standing', but watching the humiliation of others on the dance floor provided entertainment for the voyeuristic in even greater numbers.[23] 'Endurance tests', as they were called, were lively events with continuous commentary and crowds cheering on their favourites, but for the contestants it meant non-stop dancing for hours on end, often for several days with no sleep and only minimal breaks for food, showers and rest. According to the historian Peter Buckman, George 'Shorty' Sowden, who was already a champion dancer at the Savoy Ballroom, launched the Lindy hop while competing at the 1928 Manhattan Casino multiracial marathon. When the marathon was becoming monotonous and rather dreary, he threw in some crowd-pleasing, more adventurous steps, while at the same time announcing to the press that this was the Lindy.[24] There was also a trend towards acrobatic elements in exhibition dancing, which the more athletic dancers tried to copy. Such wilder types of dancing were described in *The Observer* as 'a girl being swung round and round, first high, then almost brushing the floor, by a muscular partner who grasps her by one ankle and one wrist and himself twirls with her'; other gymnastics, such as turning cartwheels, were in vogue on the French Riviera in 1925 but for better or worse did not transfer to British ballrooms.[25]

The early dancing competitions had been 'open' events allowing anyone to enter, until the *Daily Sketch* competition in 1921 limited entry to amateurs. Their definition of a professional dancer was as follows: 'For the purpose of this competition a professional is understood to be one who is, or has been, employed as a dancer, a teacher of dancing, or an assistant to a teacher of dancing and who has received payments for this in any form.'[26] We might think that the difference between an amateur and a professional is clear, but for ballroom dancing this was a problem that took much discussion and more than a decade to resolve.

As the number and types of competitions increased, the defini-tions led to confusion over professional status and further clarification was necessary. In place of an established body to take on the task of writing the rules, Richardson and the *Dancing Times* stepped in. Readers were invited to comment and send in suggestions on the pro-posed definitions and their final version, 'The *Dancing Times* Rules', were used for several years. Questions were still raised, particularly about whether winning prize money constituted professional status, and by 1926 the *Dancing Times* hosted another 'informal conference' dedicated to the matter to arrive at a workable and acceptable reso-lution.[27] The revised rules, which were introduced in January 1927, defined amateur rather than professional status: there were to be no fees for demonstrations and no prize money from competitions, and once a dancer had become professional, it would no longer be possi-ble to regain amateur status.

As modern dancing was still evolving and developing beyond the steps and figures laid down by the various associations, instead of learning new dances, finally, it seemed that there was a growing inter-est in focusing on known steps and figures and how to execute them well. Commentators reflected this move – rather than describing yet more new steps, they focused more on 'style'. As the particular tech-nique or characteristics of each of the dances were yet to be fully defined, they tended to rely on nationalistic stereotypes. The English style was regularly described as calm and 'unobtrusive', 'rhythmic' or 'smooth' compared to the 'swooping' style of Paris, which was per-haps more fun and more exhilarating but often resulted in the leader outstepping his partner and not taking sufficient notice of her.[28] A regular column contributed by Rhynal in the *Daily Express* gives an interesting insight into the dancing of the time and particularly his view of the emerging English style. Initially, Rhynal complained that Englishmen did not devote enough time to learning to dance – he was perplexed that they seemed happy to devote time to 'tennis, foot-ball, golf, cricket and other pastimes with such thoroughness', but

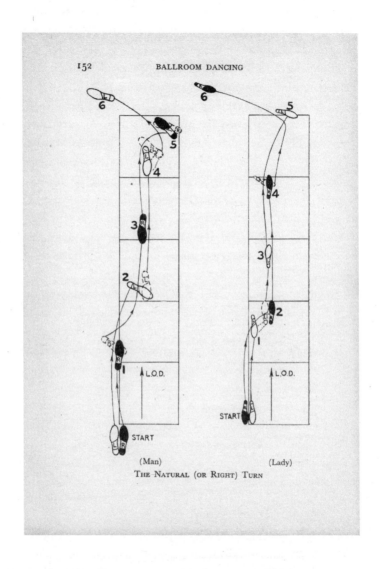

(Man)   (Lady)

THE NATURAL (OR RIGHT) TURN

Ballroom Dancing by Alex Moore (1942). By this time, the follower's steps are included and by the late 1940s Moore is already using charts without diagrams in his book *The Revised Technique*, which was circulated with his letter service.

The Natural Turn

GENTLEMAN

Begin facing L.O.D. and finish facing diag. to centre.

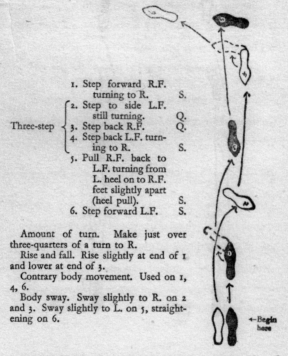

1. Step forward R.F. turning to R.   S.

Three-step
- 2. Step to side L.F. still turning.   Q.
- 3. Step back R.F.   Q.
- 4. Step back L.F. turning to R.   S.

5. Pull R.F. back to L.F. turning from L. heel on to R.F. feet slightly apart (heel pull).   S.
6. Step forward L.F.   S.

Amount of turn. Make just over three-quarters of a turn to R.

Rise and fall. Rise slightly at end of 1 and lower at end of 3.

Contrary body movement. Used on 1, 4, 6.

Body sway. Sway slightly to R. on 2 and 3. Sway slightly to L. on 5, straightening on 6.

←Begin here

Note.—The Natural Turn can be danced along the sides of the room, or round a corner.

Modern Ballroom Dancing by Victor Silvester (undated, *c.* 1945), before the cha-cha-cha and jive were added but including the 'Quick Waltz', rumba and samba. Using a grid with footprints had become the norm for instructions. The follower's steps – going backwards and in the opposite direction to the text – are always more difficult to read.

would not spend time learning to dance properly.[29] In his column in December 1924 he employed what we now recognize as a common stereotype: 'The Englishman dances with his feet and the Latin with his heart' and 'the English stance is ideal for ballroom dancing. Is it because the Englishman is self-conscious and will never have any freak step or any deportment which may lead to the thought that dancing is not really a nice thing?'[30] Rhynal also claimed that the reason the foxtrot had become the 'king of the English ballroom' is because it is a walking dance that can be done with self-control. He complained about the 'robotic' approach to dancing of the typical Englishman and his lack of ability to interpret the 'sentimental' dances such as the waltz. He blamed a hostility to any display of emotion as the reason why the dances he considered more 'temperamental' had so far failed to attain any real popularity in English ballrooms, unlike in Europe, where everyone was regularly dancing the tango and the blues. He also asserted that the preferred English style was one of decorum, unvarying rhythm and repetition.

The idea of style was also becoming apparent in competition dancing, where it was assumed that everyone knew how to execute the steps correctly, which implied that the judges were looking for other qualities, such as dancers who moved gracefully and with ease. Compared to the stage or show dancers with demonstrations of tricks and complicated steps designed to entertain and amaze an audience, competitive ballroom dancing was expected to show competence, which could be demonstrated with a more restrained approach. In addition, the 'English' style – accuracy, poise, a trained physique and musicality – characterized the best dancers, rather than ostentatious displays or temperament. Despite his criticisms, it took only a short time for Rhynal to change his mind and put his weight behind the superiority of the English dancing scene:

Undoubtedly it is in England that the modern style of dancing is purest and most aesthetic. This is achieved by the Englishman's self-control, which allows no careless movement of the body. So even we Frenchmen have to recognise the superiority of the English. Englishmen had displayed a mastership in dancing, and just as English ruling had been accepted internationally in boxing, tennis, golf and other sports and pastimes so English style must prevail in dancing.[31]

By the mid-1920s many new dances had come and gone, dismissed as 'crazes', the waltz had returned, the fast-moving and fun quickstep had emerged, the tango – once considered improper – had been tamed and was gradually gaining ground, and everyone was enjoying the foxtrot. Just as it seemed the professionals had a grip on perfecting the existing dances, another new American dance suddenly arrived to upset the calm: the Charleston.

Before arriving in England from America, the Charleston had met with considerable prejudice. Its objectionable nature was summed up by Henry St John Rumsey, author of *Ballroom Dancing* (1926), as 'an attempt to interpret musical rhythm by eccentric footwork instead of by artistic and rhythmic movement'.[32] Its origins were also considered suspect. A lengthy article in American *Vogue* suggested that we should be amused by the fact that the origin of this new fad was not the New York smart set but was 'shrouded in darkest mystery'. In fact, the new dance had originated in Harlem, the northern edge of Manhattan, already a relatively poor quarter with a largely African American population. The article focused on how much hard work was needed to learn it and the stamina and energy it required; it wondered whether all the effort devoted to it was worthwhile as the 'fad' was unlikely to last long enough for anyone to demonstrate their hard-earned skill. *Vogue* also suggested that talking about the Charleston may have been yet more popular with the smart set than actually doing it.[33]

In England the Charleston was demonstrated for the first time at the 21st Congress of the ISTD in July 1925.[34] While everyone agreed a new dance was needed to bring the ballroom out of the doldrums, there was some doubt that this 'new foxtrot' would be the one. It had potential, but it was perhaps not a surprise that the arrival of yet another 'new-fangled' dance was not greeted with open arms by everyone. Like many of the other 'jazz' dances, the Charleston was criticized for the way it upset good taste and for its complicated musicality and rhythm; moreover, the kicking was a potential nuisance on the dance floor. The signature foot swivel – or 'squiggle' as it was called initially, where the toes and heels are switched in and out – was considered peculiar. The style overall, moving mostly just the legs, with its similarities to African American dances of the southern United States, was not easily accepted, as this damning appraisal written by an *Observer* correspondent in 1926 makes clear: 'It can too easily look like the too-slick, too-deft, too ostentatious dancing of a

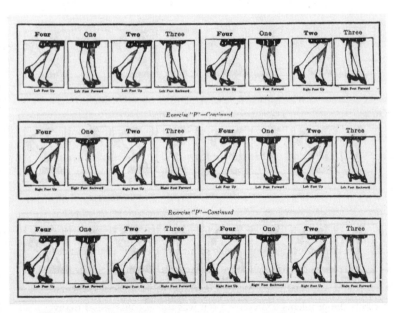

How to Charleston Correctly by Bemis Walker, published in 1926 in the USA, uses drawings based on photographic images with bold type to emphasize the down beat.

This pose is known as the 'Charleston Scarecrow Kick'. From Bemis Walker's *How to Charleston Correctly* (1926).

"jazz boy" with his too-pointed patent shoes, his too-waisted coat and his super-Oxford "bags", in a flashy third rate dance hall.'[35]

Undoubtedly a great form of exercise, the Charleston needed considerable stamina. The ubiquitous and sometimes boring foxtrot had perhaps been a pleasant relief from all the 'crazes' and even a quiet protest against having to learn so many new steps of the dances of the previous decade, but the Charleston's appearance provided excitement, especially for the younger and more athletic dancers. Despite the problems it presented – it was not encouraged at many dance halls and was too ostentatious for smart ballrooms – it very quickly became in vogue at the new small supper clubs. As Victor

Silvester recalled years later in *Dancing Is My Life*: 'Wherever you went people seemed to be practising the Charleston – in bus queues, in Tube stations waiting for a train, at street corners, in shops; even policemen on point duty were seen doing the steps – because in practically every ballroom in London every second dance was the Charleston.'[36]

By 1927 the 'flat' Charleston, a much calmer version without the kicking, devised by the ISTD, had taken over from the original form. It was still lively and had smaller swivels, which according to Silvester did not affect its popularity, which remained undiminished.[37] The dance was so popular that his studio was working thirteen hours every day to keep up with the demand for lessons. It was sometimes called the silent or whispering Charleston; instead of the tap of the feet landing on the floor, minus the kick, there was just the swish of the feet swivelling in and out. The new form was demonstrated by Josephine Bradley and Phyllis Haylor, with their respective partners Wellesley Smith and Alec Millar. Casani and Jose Leonard gave instructions for the new version in a short film released in December 1926, and in 1927 Pathé made another film of them demonstrating on top of a moving taxi in a busy street in central London, which must rank as one of the most extraordinary publicity stunts ever. The Charleston is credited with bringing smiles back to the ballroom; it was clearly a fun dance and it provided a new lease of life to 'jazz' dancing in general.

Despite the swift introduction of the more acceptable, revised, calmer version, the flat Charleston's popularity lasted for only a few years. While the Charleston might have suited the young flat-chested and short-skirted flappers, it was too energetic for many, plus the fashion for shorter skirts was almost over and longer dresses made it difficult if not impossible to do. Furthermore, most dancers were now accustomed to and comfortable with the close hold of modern dancing. The Charleston was best suited to solo dancing, and even with a partner it was necessary to keep your distance. Curiously, for the puritanical who had perhaps given up trying to persuade against the dangers of dancing, the fact that it was more suited to solo dancing was seen by some as a benefit. *How to Charleston Correctly*, published in 1926, makes claims for its physical and also its moral benefits: 'Morally this dance should be considered more favourably than many of the modern dances, which allow the dancing couples to remain in close bodily contact during the dance. The Charleston demands that couples shall not have bodily contact in executing the dance.'[38]

The Charleston, even the flat version, did not last in the ballroom catalogue and a similarly energetic black bottom, which was meant to be the 'next big thing' after the Charleston, did not catch on in Britain. Elements of the Charleston were incorporated into the quickstep, and in America elements of both dances were developed and taken in a different direction and integrated into swing dances, particularly the Lindy hop.[39]

Silvester recounts that other dances such as the heebie jeebies, stomp, rhythm step and Baltimore were little more than 'stunts', but admits that his school in fashionable Bond Street, just like many others, earned a living teaching them.[40] He also recounts how the invention of new dances had become a money-making 'racket', citing a hoax for a new dance called the five-step that had earned its inventor a huge sum of money in just two days. After placing a full-page advert in a magazine – Silvester does not tell us which one – and following it up with a phone call to every local studio asking for a lesson, every teacher signed up for a lesson as quickly as possible, which of course the inventor was happy to deliver for the right fee. Whether or not this is true is uncertain, but several reports in the newspapers in 1924 and 1925, one entitled 'Greatest Gamble on Earth', mentions the new five-step performed at a West End cabaret at the Piccadilly Hotel, and advertisements tell us it was explained in *Woman* magazine, by the dance hostess at the Ritz and in *Home Chat* by its inventor, George Cunningham.

Other short-lived dances include the trebla, which used a mazurka rhythm and was described as the 'new all British dance which experts prophesy will run the Fox-trot and Charleston a close rival'; it was supposedly so simple anyone 'can learn enough steps in three minutes to take the floor in any ballroom', but it failed to engage the public.[41] A dance performed to 'La Java' or 'Valencia', written by Spanish Maestro Padilla in 1926, was popularized in Paris by the burlesque dancer and singer Mistinguett, and criticized for being typically French, 'with its rather cheap effects and persuasion to a jig'.[42] The American band leader Paul Whiteman recorded his version of the song in 1926 and it became one of his biggest hits, at the top of the charts for eleven weeks, helping to establish the popularity of the Spanish one-step or Parisian paso doble, a dance that was to endure, although in a rather different form. Danced in Paris since the First World War, it featured in some London dances initially as more tango music was played, but with its small steps and chassés, it was better suited to the more intimate dance floors in nightclubs and restaurants. It was referred to sometimes as a crush dance because it could be danced in a small space, although the original stamp that lent it a Spanish flavour had gone: 'One doesn't stamp in fashionable ballrooms.'[43] Paso doble refers to the 'double' speed of the music – one step is taken on each beat as in a one-step. The original basic paso doble is still seen regularly at social dances in France, and although the paso doble still exists in Britain it is rarely included at social events; it is usually danced only when choreographed and seen in competition, where it is now one of the international Latin dances.

The early informal conferences were primarily concerned with competition dancing, including one held in 1926, which dealt with the definitions of professional and amateur categories. But after a few years two further conferences were organized to focus on 'general' dancers – those now referred to as social dancers. The sixth and seventh *Dancing Times* informal conferences, the final two, took place in 1929. They were prompted by the National Association of Teachers of Dancing (NATD)[44] and several independent teachers following complaints from the public, who wanted more uniformity so that they could dance more easily with anyone from any studio taught by any recognized teacher. The conference decided that 'the first aim of the profession should be to cater for the general dancer and not the expert, and to attract the man who does not dance today.'[45] Whether this statement was aimed specifically at male rather than female dancers is not clear. They agreed to set out key figures for each of five dances,[46] to be taught by everyone as the basis of simple routines, and to promote the new name 'quickstep': everyone was to insist on using it. 'Freak' steps were to be banned, especially if they were used to show off.

To give some impetus to the project, Cecil Taylor volunteered to share with the other associations the work that had already been done by the recently formed ballroom branch of the ISTD, and again a smaller committee was set up, chaired by Richardson, to prepare proposals for an adjourned conference. Other members of the committee, notably Silvester and Casani, had offered both reputation and considerable experience; both had published quite detailed modern dancing instruction books in 1927, and Casani was now well known through regular contributions to *Eve's Film Review*. *Casani's Self-Tutor of Ballroom Dancing* used a step-by-step list of figures and photographs of each one, and Silvester's *Modern Ballroom Dancing* used diagrams with footprints – the first time these were used in England and one of the reasons the book was so popular. Both were equally keen to promote themselves as teachers of professional dancers.[47] The other members of the committee included, predictably, the well-known competitive dancers and teachers such as Bradley, Tynegate-Smith, Moore, Pierre, Maxwell Stuart and Cecil Taylor. Their report was distributed and agreed to by the 150 dancing teachers who attended the Great Conference, as Richardson named it, in July 1929. The report set out the correct tempo and the basic figures for each of five dances: the valse, foxtrot, quickstep, tango and Yale blues.[48] It listed fifteen 'resolutions' and some 'suggestions for the future'. Although the public was confused by the number of new dances introduced in recent years, the conference agreed that there would still be one new dance each

20. Natural Twist Turn — FOXTROT

Step	Positions of Feet	Footwork	Alignment	Amount of Turn	Rise and Fall	CBM	Sway	Timing	Beat Value
MAN									
1	RF fwd	HT	Facing DW	Start to turn R on 1		1	St	S	2
2	LF to side	TH	Backing DC	1/4 between 1 and 2			R	Q	1/2
3	RF crosses behind LF slightly back	T	Backing LOD	1/8 between 2 and 3			R	&	1/2
4&5	Twist on both feet, ending with RF to side, small step.	T of RF and H of LF with feet flat end on whole of RF, then T of RF and pressure on IE of T LF	Start backing LOD, end facing LOD	1/2 between 4 and 5, body turns slightly more	Rise on 5		St L	Q S	1 2
6	LF to side and slightly fwd	T	Pointing DC	1/8 to L between 5 and 6, body turns less	Up on 6		St	Q	1
7	RF fwd in CBMP OP	TH	Facing DC	No turn on 7	Up on 7 Lower e/o 7		St	Q	1 (2 bars)
LADY									
1	LF back	TH	Backing DW	Start to turn R on 1		1	St	S	2
2	RF closes to LF (H turn)	HT	Facing LOD	3/8 between 1 and 2			L	Q	1/2
3	LF fwd L side leading preparing to step OP	T	Facing almost DW	Continue to turn on 3			L	&	1/2
4	RF fwd in CBMP OP	T	Facing DW	1/8 between 2 and 4		4	St	Q	1
5	LF to side and RF brushes to LF	T and IE of T RF	Backing LOD	3/8 between 4 and 5, body turns slightly more	Rise on 5		R	S	2
6	RF to side	TH	Backing LOD	Slight body turn to L on 6	Up on 6		St	Q	1
7	LF back in CBMP	TH	Backing DC	1/8 between 6 and 7, body turns less	Up on 7 NFR Lower e/o 7		St	Q	1

PRECEDE   Three Step.
At a corner: Change of Direction,   Hover Telemark.
When starting this figure step 1 as Man RF fwd in CBMP OP: Closed Telemark.

FOLLOW   Reverse Turn,   Reverse Wave,   1-4 Reverse Wave followed by Weave,   Closed Telemark,
Open Telemark,   Open Telemark Feather Ending,   Open Telemark Passing Natural Turn Outside Swivel Feather Ending,
Quick Open Reverse Turn,   Open Telemark followed by Weave from PP,   Fallaway Reverse Turn and Slip Pivot,
Lilting Fallaway with Weave Ending,   Extended Reverse Wave,   Curved Three Step.

NOTE   This figure may end DW new LOD.

Man   More turn may be made over steps 4-5 to end LF to side and slightly back backing DC.
Follow with Feather Finish end DW SQ & Q Q Q S Q Q,   or steps 2-7 of Natural Weave SQ&QS Q Q Q Q Q Q.

Figure number 20, the 'Natural Twist Turn', from *The Technique of Ballroom Dancing – Foxtrot* by Guy Howard, published by the IDTA. A typical example of the charts used since the 1970s for both Ballroom and Latin.

year, but that it must have a different rhythm to the 'standard' dances. It was agreed that unless a new one appeared 'of its own accord', as the Charleston and the foxtrot had, the committee would suggest one. No individual teacher was to introduce a new dance independently. The new dance for 1929 was to be the 'six eight'; it was in 6/8 time, as many popular tunes were using that rhythm, and 'all teachers should do their very best not only to push this dance during the coming autumn, but to see that all the standard dances are included in dance programmes.'[49] Teachers were also asked to make use of any press opportunities to stress the simplicity of the modern dances and ensure it was made clear that they were not as complicated as the public thought. Publicity should also be sought to further support the idea of 'Dancing for Health', especially for the middle-aged.

At the conclusion of the 1929 conference, it was agreed that the work of the *Dancing Times* informal conferences was done but that the same committee members would form the first controlling body for ballroom: the Official Board of Ballroom Dancing (OBBD).[50] Any teaching association not already included was invited to send representatives. Importantly, they agreed that the teaching associations would deal with matters relating to syllabus and the OBBD would confine its role to more general administrative matters. During the 1920s the dancing profession had focused on professionalization and establishing a framework for further development of the English style of dancing. But it had also been obliged to deal with ongoing criticism of dancing in general, and sometimes difficult negotiations with dance hall managers and dance promoters keen to see increased audience figures regardless of the standards of dancing and behaviour.

Pierre with Doris Lavelle at Hammersmith Palais, from the official programme
of the procession in celebration of George v's Silver Jubilee in 1935. Pierre was an
accomplished English ballroom and Argentine tango dancer before becoming an
expert in Latin American rhythms.

FIVE

Dancing in Public

Many who visit the Palais de Danse are non dancers. They come alone, or with a party to enjoy the convivial atmosphere, to watch the happy throng of dancers, to catch something of their sheer irresponsible merriment.

'1953 Official Guide to Hammersmith Palais de Danse'[1]

The public ballrooms that offered 'a good floor, reasonable space and a good band' were in part responsible for Britain's success in ballroom dancing. In other countries no such provision existed, meaning that dancers were limited to the studio spaces of their teachers. 'Only Australia appears to have ordinary, everyday, usable dancing halls in the same way as the UK. The rest of the world is just beginning to build them.'[2] During the 1920s and '30s new public ballrooms had continued to appear all across Britain; the seaside resorts had a head start, and the success of the burgeoning leisure industry meant that many more entrepreneurs were ready to invest. Ballrooms were a new kind of large interior space; at a functional level they needed an innovative approach to engineering for wide-span roofs without columns and, most importantly, high-quality solid-wood sprung floors to cushion the impact of dancing.[3] Designers were looking for new ways to appeal to the dancing public, whether with designs clearly associated with the grand houses of the aristocracy or a need to provide detail at eye level to detract from the sometimes overwhelming vast spaces. Like the early examples in Blackpool, many were designed in similar Neoclassical style, decorated with rich materials and highly polished, reflective surfaces.

Ballrooms continued to be a key attraction at seaside resorts. Blackpool drew crowds from northern towns, as did the Isle of Man, which had a long association with dancing. The glass-roofed ballrooms, the Palace and Derby Castle in Douglas, were an important tourist attraction: 'All the roads in Douglas lead in the season to the dancing halls. The vast floor of inlaid woods, polished to glittering point, is crowded with swirling figures dancing light-heartedly in all sorts of styles.'[4] Margate on Kent's north coast had become a popular seaside destination, especially for nearby Londoners, and its two principal dancing venues, Dreamland and the Winter Gardens, have survived various alterations, extensions and adaptations. Dreamland started with a dance hall and restaurant occupying an unused railway building in the late 1860s that was known as the 'Hall by the Sea': 'This mammoth establishment is the largest and most handsomely decorated and fitted place of entertainment out of London,'[5] boasted the advertisements. A new owner acquired the adjacent land and developed it first into pleasure gardens and a menagerie, and then from the late 1880s added amusement rides. It was renamed as Dreamland – which perfectly embodied the fantasy they wished to create – following further development including a ballroom in 1919, when a new owner inspired by New York's Coney Island took over. Another Margate ballroom at the Winter Gardens, built in 1911 (originally the Fort Pavilion and Winter Gardens), is less elaborate than some other seaside ballrooms, but nevertheless according to the English Heritage listing is a 'fine example of a neo-Grecian style'.[6] The building in its original form comprised the main hall on the seafront, with, behind, a semicircular open-air amphitheatre and covered promenade cut into the chalk cliff; it had a stage between the two and large sash windows on either side that opened downwards through the floor. It was extended and altered in the 1930s and again in the 1960s when the amphitheatre was enclosed, but has retained its main features and is still in use as a ballroom and multipurpose hall. Its close relationship with the sea was a common theme, exploiting the contrast between the safe, carefully constructed and ordered space inside and the uncontrolled natural world beyond. Now managed by Your Leisure, the Winter Gardens were originally the responsibility of the fetes committee, made up of local councillors who wanted to provide an entertainment centre for Margate, and later an entertainments committee partially funded through local town council rates.

The new public ballrooms were not for the upper classes, who were catered for with a new breed of 'grand' hotels in London and other urban centres that provided a suitably upmarket venue for their balls. Appearing in the first decades of the twentieth century, 'luxury'

Fancy-dress ballroom dancing at the Winter Gardens, Margate, *c.* 1955.

or 'grand' hotels, as they came to be known, offer a noticeable stylistic comparison as another new kind of 'public' interior space that responded to or marks a reflection of changing society. Some hotels were simply the development of the inns and hostelries of the past that continued to be merely a place to stay temporarily, and of course many of them catered for a growing tourist industry as well as visiting business people. But London's new luxury hotels were to offer much more.

The changing socio-economic situation meant that increasingly the very wealthy were obliged to give up their London residences, which they used perhaps for only a few months of the year during the season; as a result, if they could not borrow a London house from a friend or relative, they were in need of a suitable substitute for entertaining. The listings of private dances published in *The Times*, the 'Dances of the Season', which appeared revised and updated every Monday from January until July, reflect the change from the use of private houses to public venues for entertaining. After being discontinued for the wartime years, the list was reintroduced in May 1919 with a new name, the 'List of Fixtures', which 'during the season in pre-war days was found to be a very practical help to hostesses in enabling them to arrange their entertainments so as not to clash with those given by their friends'.[7] The first post-war list includes the Knightsbridge and Ritz hotels and several untitled hostesses. By 1926 the listing of early balls in March, primarily to advertise the dates, reveals a yet wider range of public venues: the Garden Club, Rembrandt Rooms, Royal Hospital Chelsea, and the Hyde Park, Ritz and Savoy hotels. The change can be seen by making comparison with an earlier listing from 1911, written in very polite discursive style. In this it is clear that almost every dance is given by a titled hostess – duchesses, countesses or ladies – and all are to be held at London's most prestigious addresses; no public venues are used. A sample of the text tells us:

The Countess of Radnor, who gave a successful ball at
Longford a few days ago will be one of the first hostesses
to open the season. On February 15 she is to give a large
dance at 29, Grosvenor Square. The Countess of Altamont
will give a ball at 7, Upper Belgrave Street on February 20
and February 23 is the date fixed for the Hon. Mrs Abel
Smith's dance . . . Other people who are likely to give evening
entertainments are the Duchess of Somerset, the Duchess of
Norfolk, the Countess of Londesborough, Viscountess Iveagh,
Lady Alington, Lady Cheylesmore and Lady Cowdray.[8]

By the 1920s both the upper classes and the working classes were
dancing in public venues. This movement towards the democratiza-
tion of dancing, taking place in the USA too, was seen as a positive
step. In Arthur Murray's pamphlet *The Modern Dances*, a detailed
section on etiquette tells us, 'Time was when a hostess hesitated to
go outside of her own home to give a dance, but fortunately that day
is past. If a home is not large enough or convenient for such a function, a hostess may properly rent a ballroom in a club or hotel.'[9]

The grand metropolitan hotels provided new kinds of space that
in principle were functional, such as foyers, restaurants and sitting
rooms, but they were also eager to meet the ongoing need for ballrooms and associated entertaining spaces. Already keen to socialize
with the new elite – that is, actors and other theatre performers – the
new kind of 'public' spaces were, importantly, places to be seen. By
the 1920s it is probably true to say that appearance could be just as
important as heredity, and increasingly it was money rather than
class that defined society. These new public spaces meant that the
emerging middle classes who had acquired their wealth through trade
or the professions could also visit. The nouveau riche could now
afford the trappings of a glamorous lifestyle previously associated
only with the upper classes; they could buy *objets d'art* and household
furnishings in the new department stores, wear expensive clothes,

pay to educate their children, travel more widely and be seen dining in smart restaurants. Luxury became the new watchword, defined in relation to its association with social standing, both actual wealth and what it represented.

In stylistic terms, there was little difference between the ideas driving the designs for the luxury hotels and public ballrooms. Central to them all was the creation of an 'other' world, an escape from the everyday. The terminology used by the owners of London's new hotels, words such as 'luxury', 'grand' or 'splendid' and embellished with superlatives, contributed to the idea of something 'glamorous', a term that had come into popular use in the late nineteenth and early twentieth centuries. It covered a range of characteristics from enchanting or magical to fascinating or alluring, even theatrical. It is defined in many different ways to describe both people and places. The simple dictionary definition, 'an attractive or exciting quality that makes certain people or things seem appealing', suggests it is an inherent natural quality. Writer Linda Mizejewski further defines the term as 'involving public visibility of a desirable object, its management or control, and its resulting value as a class marker or commodity' through an exploration of the construction of glamorous dancing girls who appeared in the early decades of the twentieth century.[10] Importantly, visual appearance is central to the idea of glamour, but as an illusion or fantasy – an appearance that is knowingly acknowledged to be magnified or glorified – which is accepted nevertheless as being out of the ordinary, attractive and exciting.

The Ritz in 1906 and the Waldorf and Piccadilly in 1908 were the earliest of London's luxury hotels. The Piccadilly, in particular, provided a spectacular ballroom that is still in use today.[11] The Piccadilly had financial problems from the outset, including complex lease arrangements with the Crown Estates who own the land, problems finding tenants for the shop units on the ground floor, and a large overspend on the construction budget. Eventually R. E. Jones, an extremely successful family business with several hotels and catering outlets, one half of the original owners, the P&R Syndicate, took over and was able to turn round the fortunes of the Piccadilly in just a few years. All the usual kinds of economy were made in the staffing, maintenance and service side of the hotel, but R. E. Jones understood that it was necessary to draw in a larger number of visitors, not to the private bedrooms and suites which were of a fixed number, but to the other, 'public' rooms. Dining, music and particularly dancing were to draw in the crowds. Their most important project resulted in the opening of the newly refurbished ballroom at the third basement level. It opened on Friday 6 October 1922 with a gala night and dancing until 2 a.m. Music was provided by the Beneventes Band and the Pic'o Dance Band, and there were demonstrations by well-known Parisian dancers. The *Dancing Times* enthused about 'one of the most beautiful ballrooms of the Metropolis':

> Decorated in the style of Louis XIV, this imposing room will dance four or five hundred people. At one end of the ballroom is a handsome gallery, which can be used either as a sitting out room or for the musicians. The ballroom is lofty and the ventilation is very good. The floor is made of oak . . . A more delightful room for a big dance or for a subscription ball could not be chosen . . . The floor is good, the handsome surroundings are all that could be hoped for. Those who are arranging during the coming months would do well to make an early application, as there is likely to be a big rush for this room when the ball giving hostesses discover it.[12]

As if the opulent decor and spatial design were not enough to attract the dancers, regularly held balls were themed with extravagant decorations, prizes, gifts and souvenirs. On one occasion, the Piccadilly Hotel Ball Room invited 'Dancing in the Caves of the Water Nymphs where the fairy-like seaweed festoons, the Coral rocks and the strange plants of the Ocean rear their heads, swaying to the motion of the

Dancing at the Piccadilly Hotel (now the Dilly), London, 1920; it opened in 1913.

waves.' To create the illusion the room was decorated with tinsel in sea greens and blues, and seaweed, strange fish and marine plants, all suspended and swaying to effect the motion of the waves. The impression was completed with fake corals, soft lighting and real goldfish in bowls on the tables.[13] Any and every event in the social calendar was treated as an opportunity for ever more extravagant ballroom themes. There was a Derby Day Grande Soirée des Fleurs and a Fête d'Oiseaux during Ascot Week when the ballroom became an aviary for the whole week, a Horse Show Ball, an American Independence Day Ball, and a week in Venice complete with striped mooring poles and Italian shawls. The clientele at the Piccadilly clearly included some of the very wealthy, as demonstrated by the high level of effort and cost required to put on the themed balls. Most relied on extensive additional decorations to the space and the provision of prizes and gifts for the 'ladies'. These were generally just novelties, not of any substantial value, although one ball in particular, the Records Gala Ball held on 23 May 1923, stands out with gifts of much higher

The ballroom at the third basement level of the Hotel Dilly is one of the few London ballrooms that retains its original decor and is still in regular use for dancing.

value: a recording of music by the De Groot Band and the Piccadilly Dance Orchestra was presented to every female guest and a lottery draw awarded prizes of two cabinet gramophones.

The ballroom made a considerable contribution to the more stable financial position of the hotel: 'the greatest benefit in increasing our popularity . . . the increase would have been greater still had we not had to bear the heavy expense of improving the ball-room, the excellent results of which are now becoming so apparent.'[14] The second-floor terrace (now built over) overlooking Piccadilly was also used as an al fresco ballroom, and both the Grill Room, where evening dress was optional, and the Louis XIV restaurant had cabaret and dancing too. Free entry to the ballroom was a standard offer to all diners. The Piccadilly's central location and proximity to the West End theatre elite ensured its reputation. It attracted the best musicians and dancers: Bee Jackson, the 'Charleston champion' credited with introducing the black bottom to England, appeared, the London Band and Jack Hylton's Band played there, and it was the first hotel to host a BBC outside broadcast dance band, with the De Groot and the Piccadilly orchestras. De Groot, who was resident at the Piccadilly for twenty years between 1908 and 1928, became a regular feature on BBC radio. The Piccadilly attracted the same high calibre of cabaret dancers as London's best-known venues, such as the Kit Cat Club and Murrays, and was regularly featured in the *Dancing Times* listings.

By the 1930s, when the nightclub scene was growing and patrons were more interested in watching dancing demonstrations by experts and listening to bands, the Piccadilly was employing both male and female dance hosts, 'who all dance perfectly', to encourage more dancers.[15] There was less mention of the ballroom in the press and, as with other venues, it seems that for the stylish upper-class set, cabaret and smaller-scale 'dinner dancing' was becoming much more popular. There were many reports of the closing of the Kit Cat Club in the Haymarket in early 1931, which meant some trade went to other restaurants and nightclubs, including the Piccadilly, but the closure also signalled a change in the 'luxury restaurant trade'; according to the *Evening Standard*, many were experiencing a thin time.[16]

As the interest in dancing among the wealthier classes continued to wane, it seems that interest from the working classes grew even stronger and more purpose-built ballrooms were needed to accommodate the ever-increasing numbers. The first public ballroom to open in London was the Palais de Danse on what is now Shepherds Bush Road, close to Hammersmith Broadway. Various sketchy histories of the building describe its previous use for practical purposes – it was a tram shed at one time – and for different amusements, such as ice skating, roller skating and a cinema, but a reliable source of any detail about the building remains elusive. Some of its history is told in *Earl's Court* (1953), the autobiography of Claude Langdon, the one-time owner of the Palais. Langdon, like the earlier entrepreneurs in Blackpool, had developed his business around the provision of new forms of entertainment spaces, and this tells the story of his various ventures in leisure experiments starting with speedway tracks and 'ice dromes'. Once it opened as a dancing venue in 1919, its popularity was clearly all-important, as witnessed by the many newspaper reports and anecdotal accounts. The Palais was designed by Bertie Crewe,[17] who had trained with Blackpool's designer, Frank Matcham, and the Parisian, Beaux-Arts-trained Victor Laloux, and had worked on many theatre projects in Britain. A report in the *Fulham Chronicle* on the opening in late October 1919 described a magical interior with Chinese-inspired decor – a pagoda roof, Chinese lanterns and a frieze depicting Chinese scenes – and, in the centre of the huge maple dance floor, a model of a village, which included a fountain. The Palais was seen as an important facility for those unable to afford the West End hotels and clubs 'or who risked their reputation in no less expensive but decidedly more dangerous night clubs which had sprung up in recent years'.[18] The Hammersmith Palais very quickly established a reputation for being avant-garde. It was the first venue in London to have a 'jazz' band: the Dixieland Jazz Band, who played there in

Advertisement for the Grand Opening of the Palais de Danse, Hammersmith, in the *Fulham Chronicle*, 24 October 1919. It soon became known simply as the Hammersmith Palais.

The Hammersmith Palais, designed by Bertie Crewe, became one of London's most popular dancing venues, with a floor measuring 41 x 22 metres (132 x 72 ft) surrounded by a colonnaded promenade and seating for spectators.

1921. It remained open for dancing throughout the Second World War, and in 1955 it was the first dance venue whose events were televised. On its opening the Palais did not apply for an alcohol licence; food and drinks were available, but dancing was the focus. The importance of seeing and being seen, essential for success at all dancing venues, is made clear in the 1953 official guide: 'The promenade is one of the most sumptuous in London and is provided for those who do not dance as well as for those who do . . . with an excellent view of the dancing.'

Hammersmith Palais maintained its popular reputation as a ballroom dancing venue up until the 1960s. The best-known band leaders were resident there, including Joe Loss, who took over from Lou Preager in 1959. The Palais also played a significant role in *Dance Hall*, Charles Crichton's film made at Ealing Studios in 1950, which represented the dreams and desires of four ordinary young women and showed the venue as a place where they were able to inhabit an alternative glamorous world.[19] By the early 1960s when music and dancing had once again changed dramatically, it was increasingly used for pop and rock music concerts only and eventually went out of business. Despite efforts to preserve it, the Palais was demolished in 2010.

In addition to the more prestigious and glamorous ballrooms, many 'dance halls' and studios of a less extravagant and more utilitarian style were built all over the country, and often added to working men's clubs and other social clubs. Local councils began to invest in sporting facilities for the public during the 1930s, particularly swimming pools and lidos, which have been studied in detail for their Art Deco designs. Ballrooms were also often a feature of town halls, large spaces that could be used for other functions as assembly rooms and meeting rooms, and hired out for local events.

The innovative Spirella corset factory building in Letchworth, Hertfordshire, has one of the best-preserved ballrooms in England. Even today, it continues to be used regularly for ballroom dancing. The buildings and facilities were unique for its time, befitting the unusual location, designed to promote the health and well-being of the staff. Designed by local architect Cecil Hignett (1879–1946), the building is in Arts and Crafts style. The manufacturing blocks, with full-height windows providing excellent daylighting, are arranged around three sides of a central courtyard with flat roofs intended for sunbathing. The whole of the roof of the central block forms the vast ballroom complete with a sprung maple floor, ornate windows, domed skylights in the vaulted concrete roof, a raised platform at one end and a gallery at the other. Its interiors were listed Grade II* in 1979, and it has been in the ownership of Letchworth Garden City Heritage Foundation since the 1990s. Letchworth, dating from 1907 as the first British Garden City, made considerable efforts to encourage a new population, but by the 1920s its local businesses, in what was a

Decade Club 7th Annual Reunion, 25 May 1927, in the Spirella Ballroom, Letchworth.

rather unusual town, were still struggling to attract workers. Based on Ebenezer Howard's utopian vision, 'New Towns' such as Letchworth were intended to combine the best of town and country. A properly planned and organized environment would provide a sustainable alternative to the overcrowded and insanitary sprawling major cities and would promote a healthy and wholesome lifestyle. Alcohol was banned and Letchworth's first public house, the Skittles – the original pub with no beer – served tea, sasparilla and apple juice. Its quirky reputation drew visitors expecting to see bare-headed, sandal-wearing women, vegetarians and feminists (the alcohol ban was not lifted until 1958). A survey published in 1925 revealed that the main shortcoming, alongside inadequate postal and rail services, was a 'deficiency of popular entertainment opportunities for social life'.[20] Folk dancing, maypoles and Morris dancing were popular, and social dancing was organized on the cricket field mid-week in the summer of 1934; open-air concerts on Saturday and Sunday evenings were eventually followed by sequence dancing.[21] The Spirella Ballroom provided a much-needed facility; it doubled as an assembly room for talks and presentations, and was often reconfigured for regular catwalk shows of new corset designs as well as formal meetings and other social events.

Although many of the commercially operated ballrooms have disappeared, the ballroom at Bridlington, Yorkshire, which – like Blackpool – has its roots in the actions of a benevolent forward-thinking local authority, continues to play a part in the history of dancing. Bridlington town council took control of the existing 1907 Glass Dome concert hall in 1914 and, keen to capitalize on the increasing popularity of dancing in the post-war period, appointed Herman Darewski as musical director in 1924. 'Darewski Dances', as they were called, started after the evening concerts – the chairs were cleared from the floor at 10.30 p.m., and dancing went on until midnight or later. They were initially held on Tuesdays and Fridays on a temporary floor, but after just a few months were such a success, both financially and socially, that they were extended to more nights in the week and the corporation replaced the floor with a permanent version. The corporation then went much further and replaced the Glass Dome with an entire new building that was to have both a concert hall and a ballroom. The opening of the new Royal Hall in 1926 – a veritable people's palace paid for through council rates – drew big crowds. Locals and visitors alike were welcomed and ticket holders could use the balconies at any time. The corporation believed that with their own high-quality dance hall and top-notch band, residents would no longer need to leave town to go to Ilkley or Harrogate for entertainment.

Darewski is credited with ensuring the ongoing popularity of dancing at the Royal Hall by providing for a wide variety of dances and dancers. As the programme from the time claims: 'Not only does he cater for the young people, but he believes in catering for their parents too, who delight in joining in the old-fashioned dances, the

The Spa Ballroom, Bridlington, *c.* 1930. Daylight enters the ballroom through high-level windows and its central glass dome. Glass panels either side of the stage afford views to the sea.

old-fashioned valses, the Barn Dance, the Polka, the Valeta and Military two-step.'[22] He was a successful musician, a graduate of the London College of Music, had spent fifteen years as a composer at Francis Day & Hunter, one of the best-known light music publishers at the time, and had set up his own music publishing company in 1916. He joked about his 'popular' music in an interview published in 1930: 'My father composed only classical music, while I used to compose what he termed trash,'[23] but his music was ideally suited to the new revue format that had gained popularity in theatres during the 1920s and was ideal for dancers. Darewski went on to become musical director at Blackpool's Winter Garden in 1927 and then, after a short stint in London, returned to Bridlington in 1933, where he remained until 1939, still a major attraction. He toured the UK, played at the Opera House in Covent Garden and was regularly heard on the radio. His many songs – he wrote around 3,000 – were simple and often based on current affairs. They connected with a broad audience and earned him royalties at a time when that was extremely rare.[24]

The ballroom to which Darewski returned had been rebuilt following a serious fire in the hall in January 1932. The design work was done 'in house' by borough architect Peter M. Newton. The Italian Renaissance theatre space was retained, largely unharmed by the fire, and the 1926 Royal Hall was reconstructed in a restrained Art Deco style. The new hall was a significant improvement on the earlier version. The dance floor was increased in size by 1,338 square metres (1,600 sq. yd) and an additional storey was added to the height. The

Detail drawings of the construction of a Valtor Spring system, patented by Francis Morton Junior and Co., *Architects' Journal*, 10 March 1926. Spring, or sprung, floors are vital to absorb the impact of dancing and so important they were often mentioned in advertisements for balls and dances.

first-floor balconies that ran round three sides were maintained; above those, additional balconies with glass roofs and furnished with comfortable seating and potted palms provided 'winter gardens' for sitting out. On one side they overlooked the dance floor and on the other was access to roof terraces for sunbathing. The ceiling had papier mâché light fittings with lamps of different colours that could be controlled remotely to give 'atmosphere' to the ballroom. For daytime dancing and summer evenings, the full-height glazing on the promenade side was maintained, giving spectacular views out across the sea and flooding the space with daylight. The dance floor could accommodate 2,000 dancers, and with the addition of the spacious balconies 4,000 people could attend concerts. The holiday guide of 1937 enthused about the Royal Hall, describing it as the 'finest dance and concert hall on the coast' and further on claims that the 'lighting and stage effects are the last word in modern artistry'.

Today the ballroom, renovated in 2016, retains its Art Deco style and character. The windows on the promenade side are gone, so there is no longer a connection to the promenade beyond, and the upper balcony level has been closed off for use as offices. Daylight still enters the space but only via the all-important central glass dome, which, together with the deep circular frieze forming its base, has been fully restored and redecorated. The original dance floor, with a Valtor spring system and locking gear, was replaced, the stage is equipped with up-to-date technical facilities, and decorative coloured lighting can be used to change the mood. Typical Art Deco sunburst gilding decorates the walls and reaches out across the ceiling. After Darewski's departure, the Bridlington Spa ballroom continued to be a major dance destination. Many of the best-known band leaders appeared there in concert – Sydney Kyte, Jack Hylton and Ceres Harper all appeared over the Easter weekend in 1939. Ceres Harper, who had been a big attraction at Filey in the early 1930s, became the musical director from 1946 to 1951 and in 1952 the well-known radio performer Oscar Rubin took over.

Bridlington Spa has continued to host ballroom events, including social dances, parties and competitions. Its magic endured too. Jo Clarke, who works there, remembers the *Yorkshire Evening Post* ballroom dancing competitions she attended as a child in the 1970s:

We would sit cross legged around the edge of the dance floor whilst the competition dances took place. At the end of each section the dancers would leave the dance floor and the children would be allowed to go on to the floor and collect the various adornments that had fallen from the beautiful gowns. By the end of the day's and evening's dancing I would return home with glass jam jars full of feathers, sequins, jewels, and glitter. It was the most exciting treasure to return home with. Later I competed in the very same competition and it was a dream come true to wear my own sequinned gown.[25]

Ann Lawanick holding up her partner Jack Ritof after he has fallen asleep during the marathon dance at the Merry Garden Ballroom in Chicago, 1930.

SIX

Nightlife and Private Clubs

We are entirely opposed to Puritanic interference with amusements, but the policy of the London County Council in permitting dancing and cabaret entertainments in hotels to continue until two in the morning has an ugly appearance of class administration.

Church Times, 1924[1]

As dancing continued to be one of the most popular pastimes, its increased visibility as it moved into the public realm created problems for ballroom managers, dance promoters, restaurant and nightclub owners. Minor worries were expected, such as nearby residents complaining of nuisance and noise and seaside landladies objecting to dancers returning to their lodgings too late at night, but overcrowding was often the most common problem, particularly for the larger public ballrooms. Dealing with big crowds brought its own problems and attracting the right kind of clientele could be difficult. For a dance to be successful, managers needed to create the right balance: on one hand, they wanted to limit the numbers, but still include some expert dancers to ensure there would be enough space for people to dance well and progress around the floor; on the other hand, they needed to attract bigger numbers, at the right prices, to make the event commercially viable but without encouraging the less desirable elements. Alongside the dancing instructions in the press, advice columns on good behaviour suggest that it may have been lacking: 'Ask any manager of a dance rendezvous what has most contributed to his success and he will say that he has consistently banned the "duds" – in other words, the people who don't know how to behave.'[2] The press regularly recorded the efforts of the dancing organizations to discourage what were considered inappropriate moves, 'freak' dancing, or endurance tests and men dancing together in competitions.[3] The bad behaviour frequently referred to includes that related to the dancing itself, such as stopping in the middle of the floor and showing off with ostentatious moves, but there were more serious problems through association with alcohol and prostitution that were damaging to its reputation.

Private clubs, at which most of the criticism was aimed, were not subject to licensing hours; club members could drink at any time of day or night. However, from the numerous newspaper reports of prosecutions for 'keeping a dance hall for public dancing without a licence', many clubs, it seems, were little more than an excuse for drinking and drug taking. The legislation in London at the time for both dancing and drinking was still covered by the Disorderly Houses Act, which had been introduced in 1751 (although it had been amended in most of the rest of the country).[4] Enforcement was the responsibility of the London County Council (LCC), and there were frequent reports of issues surrounding licences for dancing venues of different kinds. Unlike pubs, which required licences and approval of the publican's 'decent' character by a licensing committee, nightclubs could be opened by anyone on payment of a small fee and were not covered by legislation. The situation made it much easier for less scrupulous entrepreneurs to provide the novelty that the fashionable set was looking for; new nightclubs opened frequently and often closed again after a very short time. Lacking the power to enter without a warrant, the police struggled to gather sufficient evidence of law breaking required to prosecute and often resorted to dubious 'undercover' methods.

Objection to the lack of any regulation of private clubs was raised by those on both sides of the alcohol arguments: the temperance reformers and the licensed victuallers.[5] The respectable clubs also suffered. An article in the *Daily Mail* in March 1922 tells us that the 'pussyfoot laws' and 'petty restrictions', as they were known, like prohibition in America, had 'driven pleasure seekers underground into unwholesome places', and added veiled references to prostitution: 'The couples dancing were old men, a few youths, but no elderly women, only girls,' and 'some of the girls looked as though they ought to have been in bed hours before. A number of girls have succumbed to the glamour of the life in these garish surroundings, with very sad results.'[6] Richardson, who considered this was no trivial matter, was prompted to write to the newspaper defending dancing's reputation and the respectable establishments and urging the authorities to 'close all undesirable places which under the disguise of being dance clubs are merely markets for trafficking in drink, drugs, and demi-mondaines'.[7]

Operating without a licence was illegal, but the – perhaps aptly named – Wonderful Units Social and Dance Club on London's Charlotte Street was, according to the mores of the day, guilty of much worse. Two plain-clothes detectives reported that they 'saw black men dancing with white women, overheard grossly indecent conversation, saw very suggestive dancing and on one occasion highly reprehensible conduct by a woman'.[8] Their report was of course intended to either shock or intrigue. Similar police raids on nightclubs, many merely challenging the idea of membership, which was repeatedly overlooked, were reported in the newspapers every week during the 1920s, stirring up tensions and contributing to the poor reputation of London's nightlife. Despite the new 'luxury' hotels, theatres and nightclubs, when compared to Paris or Berlin, London in the 1920s was in general considered a rather dull city. Rain and fog were common, the streets were dreary and more importantly – apart from the rogue clubs – entertainment was limited, especially late in the evenings and on Sundays. American tourists, who were considered an important business source, were often not visiting London but going straight to Europe, to Paris or Brussels, where the nightlife was considered more glamorous. The Brighter London Society, set up in early 1922 with a worthy aim to make the city more attractive by improving the facilities in general, was a formidable lobby against the licensing restrictions – for both drinking and dancing.[9] At that time a licence permitted dancing in hotels and restaurants until midnight. After applying for permission, staying open until 2 a.m. 'to provide entertainment' – but without alcohol – could be allowed on three nights each week but not on Saturday or Sunday. For special occasions or events that brought in more visitors, each establishment could apply for late-night extensions up to a maximum of five nights a week. At the time of the British Empire Exhibition, for example, in 1925, a blanket extension was granted.[10] The committee at the LCC could vary the rules as they saw fit, which led to regular complaints about anomalies, and at whatever time of year extensions for music and dancing licences were routinely opposed on Sundays, even for Christmas and New Year.

The Church in Britain consistently opposed dancing, considering it a frivolous and vain pastime that was merely a distraction from life's more serious issues. It supported a ban on Sunday dancing and did not hold back in offering an opinion on all kinds of dancing activities; there are many press reports of its efforts. A music and dancing licence was refused to a club owner by Folkestone magistrates based on opposition from the nearby church, which claimed: 'It would be an act of vandalism to allow bunny hugging and jazz dancing near the church and graveyard.'[11] It disapproved of the fact that people were 'dancing mad' and that 'work not dancing was wanted.' In Leicester a petition was raised against a Sunday nightclub on the basis of the 'demoralising effects' of dancing.[12] In another example, at the other end of the country in Aberdeen, the granting of a licence for Sunday opening of a dance hall for music and socializing was heavily criticized by the United Free Church Presbytery, which convened a public meeting to discuss how to have the decision reversed; their biggest fear was that the next step would be dancing on Sunday.[13]

The Church was also concerned about the alcohol licensing laws, suggesting that the decision to grant late dancing licences to hotels was based on class bias; the LCC, 'always eager to interfere with the poor, is curiously kindly to the rich'.[14] Dancing until 2 a.m. would only benefit those who could lie in bed until late in the morning and could afford an expensive dinner with drinks at the luxury hotels. There was no benefit to the working classes, who went to the music halls for entertainment, where drinks were not permitted in the auditorium. The Church was also not convinced that the idea of making London more attractive to foreigners through extending licensing hours was of any real benefit, again asking how 'a crowded Savoy Hotel means prosperity for City merchants or East End factories'.[15] At the meeting of the BATD in Aberdeen, the former president J. D. MacNaughton was vociferous in his condemnation of the unsatisfactory state of the ballroom: blaming 'the unrestricted granting of dancing licences to hotels, clubs, dance palaces and adventurous persons', he also considered that the 'dance-palace method of "caging" men and women and hiring them out for gain as dance partners was disgusting'. His answer was that no venue with an alcohol licence should also be able to hold a dancing licence.[16]

From 1928 to 1931 a new police commissioner, Lord Byng, made considerable progress in the plans to clean up London's nightlife. Legislation was sought to differentiate between clubs in 'which there was habitual music or dancing' that would require a licence and consequently inspections, and social clubs or working men's clubs, where dancing might take place from time to time. The changes in legislation – seen as an effective clean-up of rogue club managers and some dubious police practices – resulted in a big reduction in the numbers of nightclubs in London. As a consequence, by the end of the decade, many women working as 'professional dance partners' lost their jobs and others were surviving on very reduced wages. For what had been reliable employment they were paid a minimum wage controlled by the LCC employment regulations, and the rest was made up of 'tips' paid for each dance. Restaurants had mostly given up employing professional dancing partners, and the days when young women could earn a good living and receive presents from satisfied customers were over. According to a *Daily Express* reporter, 'Some of the girls have gone into service and others are training to be waitresses, but it is not much of a life after the carefree gaiety of the ballroom.'[17]

Reports of the young female 'instructresses' or 'dance hostesses' relying only on tips from male partners for their livelihood and the inference of prostitution had, as we have already seen, contributed to damaging the reputation of nightclubs and dancing. Although we hear about respectable male ballroom dancers such as Victor Silvester and Arthur Murray starting out as paid 'partners' for wealthy women in the pre-war days, by the mid-1920s newspaper reports make it clear that many young female dancers were being exploited. There was nothing in the restaurant licences about employment regulations or working conditions for dance hostesses, but holders of licences were expected to make sure that their places were properly run. When asked to comment, Richardson insisted that being employed as a dance hostess was 'perfectly respectable', but added, 'in a well-conducted place'. He suggested that instructresses should not be approached directly; nor should they be paid directly by the customers, but instead be employed properly by the host, who would then introduce them to the customers and oversee conduct. Santos Casani was also asked to comment and agreed that the 'system of dance hostesses without salaries ought to be condemned'.[18]

For most, cleaning up the 'grubby' nightclub scene was a positive move – it contributed to making London's nightlife much more attractive and restored confidence for business. By the end of the 1920s, dancing and cabaret acts were expected to be included at all of the fashionable venues. If there was still any doubt in the best society about the acceptability of dancing, minds might have been changed by three things that happened all in the same week in late September 1929: the exclusive Claridge's Hotel finally succumbed and introduced dancing in the restaurant; Chez Quaglino, described as 'one of that new type of smart, intimate restaurants' opened in St James's; and at the Savoy Hotel a new 'rising floor' – which meant that diners could see the cabaret without having to stand – made its first appearance.[19] Dancing in the smart venues, in public, was clearly becoming accepted as a respectable part of nightlife.

However, the activity of dancing itself – not only the jazz crazes and Charleston – continued to come in for considerable criticism. While some continued with the nineteenth-century idea that dancing was an important social skill and a way to gain poise, grace and good deportment, others were highly critical of both the potential physical damage caused by over-exertion and the risks it posed for morality – particularly for young women. Long before the advent of ragtime and modern dancing, histories of dance relate how the waltz was considered scandalous and the many years it took to be generally accepted sometime in the mid-nineteenth century. Histories of early waltzing are full of descriptions of disreputable behaviour. Eduard Reeser, writing about its beginnings in the late sixteenth century, relates the 'scandalous, shameless swinging, throwing, turning and allurement of the dance devils, so swiftly and at great height, just as the farmer swings his flail, that the skirts of the damsels, lasses and servant girls sometimes fly above their girdles or even over their heads'.[20] A very fast dance, the waltz or valse was criticized as much for its fatiguing nature as for its impropriety, as young women could easily overheat themselves, and the physical exertion was likely to lure young men into bad behaviour. Modern dancing, which required close proximity with a partner, rekindled the fears over impropriety and particularly the risk for young, innocent women.

A somewhat extreme criticism of waltzing, *From the Ballroom to Hell*, had been penned in 1892 by American dancer T. A. Faulkner. Faulkner had been dancing since the age of twelve, was the Pacific Coast champion for several years in 'fancy and round dancing', and was formerly 'proprietor of the Los Angeles Dancing Academy and ex president of Dancing Masters' Association of the Pacific Coast'.[21] The book was supported by a list of churchmen convinced that 'waltzing is the spur of lust' and endorsed by the *Los Angeles Times*, which noted, 'This book has created a greater flutter in social circles than anything published within our remembrance. Its pages should receive careful perusal of parents, and the equally careful attention of the young. We believe every word of it is true.' Faulkner's stated mission was 'the opening of the eyes of the people, particularly parents, who are blind to the awful dangers there are for young girls in the dancing academy and ballroom'. He relates a – supposedly typical – story of a young girl sent to a dancing school who, after initial reluctance, becomes used to the idea of being held in a close embrace and begins to enjoy waltzing with young men. Naturally, lust ensues and a young man takes advantage of her with no intention of making things right by marrying her – all because her 'blood is hot from the exertion . . . every carnal sense is aroused and aflame' and she is carried away by dancing.[22]

The terrible conclusion of the story is that she is shunned by society and ends up in a brothel. Faulkner claimed that two-thirds of girls who are 'ruined' fall through the influence of dancing. He also maintained that no man would choose as a wife someone who has been 'fondled and embraced by every dancing man in town'.[23] The topic of alcohol is taken up in his second book, *The Lure of the Dance*, published in 1916. He compared the dance hall with the saloon, proposing that the evils of drink are the same as the evils of dancing and the rather preposterous idea that the men who seduce the girls are all working for brothel keepers or white slavers.

Today Faulkner's excessive critique of dancing may be laughable, but there were many other, less extreme opponents who were concerned about its effects specifically on young women – including the physical effects. Doctors often warned of dancing indoors because of the stuffy atmosphere of ballrooms and the dangers of too much exercise, particularly waltzing. If the dancers had managed to survive the overheating and perspiring during the dancing, rushing to an open window with their arms and chest exposed to the cold air would mean catching colds – or worse. Some sections of the Baptist Church continue to consider dancing morally dangerous. It was as recently as 1996 that a 151-year-old ban on dancing on campus was lifted at the Baptist Baylor University in Texas. The announcement, which was robustly welcomed by around 7,000 students and reported in the *New York Times*, nevertheless included warnings against 'Dirty Dancing', including 'pelvic gyrations, excessive closeness' and being 'obscene or provocative'.[24]

Others who did not concern themselves with moral questions supported dancing as a good form of exercise – even for women. A 1928 *Daily Express* article informs us that women were regularly doing exercises to maintain their slim figures but that they could be very boring. At the time not all forms of exercise were considered appropriate for women, and articles in the popular press frequently spread worries about how too much sport would make women too muscular and 'masculine'. Dancing, however, was just the right kind of exercise to avoid this, keeping women slim and fit but adding 'easy, graceful movements' and even – curiously – helping to improve footwork in tennis.[25] A few years later the doctor's advice column recommends ballroom dancing as a 'fascinating lesson in muscular co-ordination'. In fact, we are told that it combats almost everything from bad posture to poor circulation as well as indigestion, flat feet and middle-aged spread, and 'it is a mental relief' that will help cure 'nerves'.[26] Ballroom dancing was also often recommended as a way to deal with loneliness and shyness: an inexpensive and easily available hobby to take up in order to meet new friends.

The profession continued to defend its activities and ballroom etiquette was constantly under review. Camille de Rhynal, in one of his *Daily Express* columns in 1924, was keen to defend the dance halls 'from the malignant petty criticisms of killjoys and self-appointed reformers'.[27] Nevertheless, he was keen to remind proprietors and promoters of their responsibility. The New York Metropolitan Dance

The Castles' instructions for the Castle Polka, from the *Ladies Home Journal*, October 1914.

Hall Association had appointed a czar to 'clean up' their dance halls, and if that kind of interference was to be avoided in Britain, it would be necessary to ensure that the highest standards were maintained. Simply encouraging the crowds was not sufficient if there was no discipline and behaviour was allowed to deteriorate.

Vernon and Irene Castle were often credited with representing the more acceptable face of dancing. Polite society accepted that there could not be much wrong with dancing if such an elegant, fashionable and glamorous, happily married couple were doing it, and doing it so well. In her autobiography, *Castles in the Air*, Irene Castle tells of another triumph in changing what she describes as the 'bitter outcry against dancing'. The editor of the *Ladies Home Journal*, Edward W. Bok, considered modern dancing too vulgar for his readership, but after he insisted that 'he would never have any pictures of dancing appear in the *Ladies Home Journal*', Irene was able to persuade him otherwise and he published a feature with the Castles, including instructions and diagrams for learning to dance at home.[28]

The two distinct camps of pro- and anti-dancing continued, and there would be several more new dances that would cause yet more outrage. The modern, codified and organized dances, the new sound of big band music, and the elegance and glamour conveyed by musicals in the 1930s meant the English dances – the slow (or English) waltz, foxtrot, quickstep and ballroom tango – became the acceptable norm and created the enduring image of ballroom that is little changed today. The close proximity of the couples in modern ballroom dances were eventually considered acceptable, but there was to be a new battle, to defend a whole new range of dances that were established in the following thirty-year period, which would be criticized for other reasons. Close body contact would no longer be considered a problem; it was the body movements that characterize the Latin dances, coupled with the high-energy and boisterous jitterbug and rock'n'roll, that were to provoke the critics.

Fred Astaire and Ginger Rogers in *Flying Down to Rio* (1933), their first film together.

SEVEN

Hollywood Glamour

The series of nine films that Astaire and Rogers made for RKO-*Radio Pictures illustrates perhaps better than any cinema house or cocktail lounge or geometrically-patterned dress what Art Deco really meant.*

Velvet Light Trap, 1974[1]

The 1930s was a period of continuing uncertainty: social change with a growing middle class that upset the status quo; a shift in the role of women, as many more opted to work outside the home; the advent of modern technologies affecting everyday lives; and more leisure time for everyone. Trips to the seaside or to explore the countryside, especially for those who lived in the cities, offered a new kind of adventure, and at home the radio, the cinema, popular music and dancing offered another kind of escape. Whether or not a need for escapism was the direct result of the growing economic slump, the 1930s was a time of light-heartedness and frivolity. All histories agree that the most popular leisure activities were going to the cinema and dancing. Both were linked to courtship as dance halls and the cinemas, where there were plenty of other people, were considered safe places for a new generation of unchaperoned young women. Young women went together to the cinema, which regularly ran matinees, and the dance halls' afternoon *thés dansants*. The American cinema industry was booming and within a remarkably short time following the premiere of the first 'talking-picture' in late 1927, a new genre of film musicals was to fuel the continuing popularity of dancing.

Musical theatre, which had grown from the vaudeville shows of the end of the nineteenth century, was well established by the end of the 1920s. In New York, the 1927–8 season is generally considered to be the peak for musicals, when no fewer than 264 shows opened on Broadway.[2] But things were about to change for stage musicals. Remarkably, in the space of just two years, no new venues opened after 1929 and by then 20 per cent of existing theatres had closed down. The introduction of sound in films that started with the premiere of *The Jazz Singer* (dir. Alan Crosland) at Warner Brothers Theatre in New York on 6 October 1927 had changed everything. By the end of 1928, it seems, the whole of the musical theatre industry had moved to Hollywood to make film musicals. The opportunity drew the best-known musicians: George and Ira Gershwin, Jerome Kern, Irving Berlin, Cole Porter and Rodgers and Hart all congregated in Hollywood to write for the big studios. With radio broadcasts, too, popular music spread quickly, and the swing music of big bands was on its way along with more melodic sounds in place of earlier jazz forms.

The first film musicals were based on the traditions of vaudeville or the revue format, with acrobats, juggling acts, ventriloquists, gymnasts and tightrope artists alongside singing and dancing. The emphasis was generally on comedy and more often the physical slapstick kind, or the playful whimsical kind. Many had protagonists spontaneously bursting into song unrelated to the storylines; others had backstage storylines where the musical numbers were closely related to the 'show', which inevitably 'had to go on'. Busby Berkeley, famous for his elaborate geometrical arrangements of female dancers despite being neither a dancer nor a cameraman himself, was prolific, choreographing as many as four films a year, including in 1933 *42nd Street* (dir. Lloyd Bacon) and *Gold Diggers of 1933* (dir. Mervyn Leroy), both made by Warner Brothers. He developed a somewhat mechanistic way of looking at movement and spatial quality in films whereby individual dancers became elements in a much larger moving picture. He favoured shooting with just one camera, rather than the more usual four, to develop his signature overhead shots, which invited audiences to marvel at the synchronized movements and kaleidoscopic pattern making and, perhaps coincidentally, also made it difficult for directors to edit the footage.

Of all the film musicals made in Hollywood in the 1930s, there is one series that stands out – the RKO series of nine films starring Fred Astaire and Ginger Rogers.[3] The films were a financial success, but they also introduced the brand new Art Deco style to cinema audiences and redefined the film musical. Perhaps even more importantly, even if you know nothing of ballroom dancing, you have heard of Fred Astaire and Ginger Rogers. They starred in a series of films made in a short period of time, between 1934 and 1939, that have never been bettered. The films were directed by relative newcomer Mark Sandrich (1900–1945), and included scores written by some of the best names in popular music history: George and Ira Gershwin, Jerome Kern and Irving Berlin. Astaire and Rogers's first film together was *Flying Down to Rio* (1933). They had only small parts but were such a success with the audience and the studio that they were immediately signed up to make several more. As well as being given top billing, the choreography was to change from Busby Berkeley-style excesses to something more like modern dancing when Hermes Pan, one of the assistants on *Flying Down to Rio*, took over from choreographer David Gould. From then on Pan worked closely with Astaire to develop the choreography and perfect the routines before teaching the steps to Rogers. Pan went on to become director of the dance ensembles for the later films.

The new stylistic influence that inspired the films, Art Deco, had come from Paris and was named after the 'Exposition Internationale des Arts Décoratifs et Industriels Modernes', held in 1925. Unlike the modern movement and the already outdated Art Nouveau, which had both focused primarily on architecture, the new style was significant for its focus on design. In an effort to establish the idea of 'total design' and with a focus on interiors, the idea of the 'decorative arts' was intended to establish the importance of all areas of design – graphics, furniture, industrial design, ceramics, textiles and fashion – making distinctions between them redundant. Together with a rejection of historicism, the new style replaced the dark and elaborate designs of the Victorian era, the 'prettiness' of floral patterns left over from the Arts and Crafts movement, and the sinuous loops, pastel colours and fussy spirals of Art Nouveau. Art Deco became fashionable very quickly, in part, it seems likely, due to its extensive use in films. In addition, like other forms of expression such as Cubism, Expressionism, Vorticism and Futurism, it also refused to take a 'static' view of the world, finding ways to express movement and dynamic form. This was perfect for dancing. Native American art – particularly the Maya temples in Mexico – were the inspiration for cubic volumes and ziggurat forms. Ancient Egyptian art, following the discovery of Tutankhamun's tomb in 1922, is cited as a major influence, particularly for the sunburst motif and the stylized angular representations of birds and animals. Geometric patterns, strong vertical and diagonal stripes, chequerboards and Greek key details replaced illustrations of natural forms. An 'assertively modern style', according to historian Bevis Hillier,[4] it nevertheless used vibrant colours, favoured symmetry and rectilinear form, and importantly embraced the demands of industrial production and consumer culture.

The USA had not participated in the Paris exhibition in 1925 but American designers had been quick to adopt the new style, notably in interiors for new kinds of activities – department stores, car showrooms and particularly cinemas. Designers experimented with new materials and industrially produced components such as Bakelite and other early forms of plastic, and there was no limit to the surface effects used: chrome plating, polished and beaten metalwork, silks and satins, animal skins and mirrored glass. Colours were bold and richly contrasting. At the detail level, the more dramatic and geometrically reliable cacti and evergreens replaced softer trailing plants and pretty blooms, and Moorish and Far Eastern furnishings like Chinese paper lanterns and Moroccan-inspired velvet cushions with fringes and tassels completed the picture. The sometimes over-elaborate excesses of early Art Deco had been toned down by Modernist sensibilities by the 1930s, and particularly in America a new element – streamlining – was added to the geometric vertical and ziggurat motifs. The thin parallel lines and shallow curves were inspired by the new science of aerodynamics developed for the trains, cars and planes of the time. The new style, sometimes referred to as American Moderne, was seen as emblematic of a forward-looking successful nation and streamlining became the buzzword in design and market-ing in everything from cars and trains to radios and women's under-wear. Its exponents saw it as the embodiment of the new industrially driven consumer society. Historians have attributed the ease with which the style was adopted to its association with Paris – still con-sidered the leader in taste. Its popularity might also be credited to Hollywood, where the new style pervaded, especially as the visual framework for the new film musicals. The smooth ballroom dancing of Astaire and Rogers perfectly complemented the swooping orches-tral musical and streamlined sets to embody the new American Moderne.

Early film set designers, who were often experienced theatre designers, had continued to work in the traditional theatrical way, using painted flats and various *trompe l'oeil* effects with sloping floors and distorted heights to give an impression of depth. In their new role of 'production designer' or 'art director' they were asked to create atmosphere as well as place. Familiar scenes in early cinema show living rooms crammed with furniture, walls full of pictures, and mirrors and tables covered with crockery, along with costumes: possessions that informed the audience of relative wealth and social position. Scenery had very quickly become subject to an early form of typecasting. A sinister mood for horror films could be created with ruined castles and crooked shadowy spaces, whereas a serious scientist or efficient businessman occupied more reserved and restrained Modernist spaces with rectilinear surfaces, functional furniture and minimal decoration. The style of the scene almost dictated the mood. The advent of sound encouraged more indoor construction for its better control, which also contributed to yet more freedom from reality and functionality in set design. Authenticity became increasingly irrelevant and the designer could invent whatever best conveyed the 'reality' that suited the narrative. According to film historian Juan Antonio Ramirez, the influence of the cinema industry in the 1930s – the over-stylization created by its designers – was even responsible for the invention of what was originally an entirely fictional southern Californian Spanish ranch style, which was loosely based on a southern Mediterranean vernacular mixed with Baroque. He also argues that the popularity of the Mexican Aztec and Maya forms extensively used in early adventure stories influenced the design of the cinema buildings, citing the Aztec Theatre (1926) in San Antonio and the Mayan Theatre (1927) in Los Angeles as early examples of a reciprocity of design which was to continue.[5] We can assume that film musicals were eagerly consumed by dancers following the regular reports in the *Dancing Times* on the latest releases that drew attention to every film that featured dancing.

The introduction of the new style was fully supported by the studios, confident in their influential role as taste makers.[6] Using set designs that both informed audiences about the latest styles and reflected their taste appealed to the aspirational nature of audiences and boosted the popularity of films, following in the footsteps of the French film industry, which had used the talents of contemporary architects and designers for production design since the early 1920s. The first film to use modern architecture was *L'Inhumaine* (1924), directed by Marcel L'Herbier and designed by the architect Robert Mallet-Stevens, author of *Le Décor moderne au cinéma*

(1928), who promoted the cinema as a valid form of artistic expression.[7] The influence of the French avant-garde and Modernist designs arrived in America a decade later, but at a time when there was little work elsewhere, Hollywood's booming film industry attracted a whole new generation of set designers. The more senior production designers supervised unit art directors responsible for teams of illustrators, draftsmen and builders mirroring the hierarchical structures of design and construction work in the real world. Many of them had trained as architects, many in Europe, and they were responsible for bringing with them their experience of European Modernism.[8] The cinema allowed them free rein to employ Art Deco or American Moderne style, perfect to promote an idealistic, even utopian, vision of the modern world to appeal to Depression-era audiences.

At RKO Art Deco style flourished under the art direction of Van Nest Polglase. In collaboration with the unit art director Carroll Clark they created the sets for all nine of the RKO Astaire and Rogers film musicals. Polglase had trained as an architect at the Beaux-Arts school in New York and worked in architectural practice before starting his work in film at Paramount in New York (then Famous Players-Lasky) in 1919.[9] In 1927, as a result of the developments in sound films, he went to Hollywood to work for MGM before moving to RKO in 1932, where he worked until 1943.[10] Together they developed an innovative approach to set design that had not been seen before, with less decor and instead using geometric and abstract composition and exploiting the dramatic use of light. The set was no longer merely a background for the dancers but an integral part of their performance both literally – often physically – and as a part of the narrative, as if another character in the story. Professional dancers were disillusioned with the Busby Berkeley productions that had reduced them to elements of his geometrical pattern-making. They were also bored. The advent of sound had meant that the complexities of cutting and editing, while keeping the dancing and music synchronized, had made anything other than the simplest choreography too challenging for the production team.

Polglase is famed for the introduction of his trademark big white set (which had its own acronym, BWS), which has several key features that reappeared in the various films. The use of white had only become possible at the beginning of the 1930s, when developments in film stock and lighting meant that the pastel colours previously used for sets could be replaced with pure white. This allowed high contrast and greater definition well suited to the sharp geometries of Art Deco. The huge size of the sets was crucial for the dance sequences, to give enough space for movement and to be filmed with as few different shots as possible, although as Astaire was a perfectionist there were often many takes before a scene was completed. Ceilings rarely existed, as any available height was necessary to accommodate the sound booms, lights and camera rigs that allowed focus from wide shots to the characters in the centre, and of course dancing meant the floor was much more important. The floors were usually highly polished surfaces to add to the glamour, to evoke the idea of a frictionless surface so the dancers appeared to glide across it, and to add reflections of the dancing. It is easy to imagine how much work was involved in protecting the surface between takes to prevent damage. The sound for tap dances was often recorded separately after the dances had been filmed without tap shoes to save the polished floors. Balconies or tiered seating in restaurants overlooking the action were a common motif, and stairs, which were everywhere, were usually curving and very often formed a symmetrical pair. The sound was also part of the image-building. Often just a small group of musicians can be seen playing on the stage in the nightclubs and restaurants. The full orchestra that can be heard would have cluttered up the set, yet as film viewers we are happy to believe that the elegantly displayed small group is producing the sound that we hear.

The Brightbourne hotel foyer depicted in *The Gay Divorcee* (1934) shows how the integration of the dancers with the sets was taken to a new level. The set has all the elements we expect: a vast double-height space overlooked by curved balconies; an abstract sunburst pattern on the floor radiating outwards from the centre; and tall, flat, flowerless stems of cacti, hart's tongue ferns and clipped pointed conifers. During the 'Continental' routine – which lasts for an astonishing seventeen minutes, a combination of several versions of the same scene – the dancing couples appear in a variety of different costumes, all in sharply contrasting black and white, alternating black trousers and white tailcoats or short jackets, white tuxedos, and girls in dresses of either black, white or both together. Pattern-making is still in evidence but with couples in formation, something much closer to ballroom dancing, not the high-kicking chorus girls of Busby Berkeley. At the

The foyer of the fictional hotel Brightbourne created for *The Gay Divorcee* (1934). The elements in the film set – the geometric plants, the revolving doors, sunburst floor pattern and dynamic curves of the stairs – play an important part in the choreography.

The elaborate Venice Lido set created for *Top Hat* (1935) is far from an accurate reconstruction. The canal waters are dyed black to enhance reflections and, perhaps inevitably, the bridges include steps to serve the choreography.

back of the set is the entrance to the hotel with a series of revolving doors, and at one point groups of four female dancers position themselves with one in each segment of the door, their feet off the ground, and move only their arms up and down against the glass as the doors continuously revolve. The largest and most extreme BWS was the Venice Lido recreated for *Top Hat*, which required two sound stages knocked together. It was three storeys high and presented a remarkable, though entirely fictitious, version of the Lido. According to Arlene Croce, author of *The Fred Astaire and Ginger Rogers Book*, Italian fascism was the reason given 'to swerve in the opposite direction and construct a Venice so remote from reality that no one would connect it with the Italy of the headlines'.[11] Complete with balconies and cafés, a 'real' canal was constructed – the water was dyed black to enhance reflections – and there were three bridges, two that included steps. Sandrich was even able to use a stock shot left over from *Flying Down to Rio* of a sea plane landing near the hotel to add further glamour. Well fitted to the enchanting surroundings, the romantically linked characters 'spent their lives in evening dress . . . slipping from their satin beds at twilight, dancing the night away and then stumbling, top-hatted and ermine-tangled, out of speakeasies at dawn'.[12] 'Dance Film Notes' in the *Dancing Times*, enthusing about the forthcoming film, says that the dance sequence 'The Piccolino' was so brilliant that on completion 'the whole technical staff broke out into involuntary applause.'[13]

The later films differed only slightly in form and content. *Follow the Fleet* (1936) was set in San Francisco and describes a more work-aday world, with scenes of back streets and drab apartments, and less formal dancing styles to swing music were introduced. Astaire is an ordinary sailor on shore leave and Rogers is a struggling dance hall hostess. In the dance competition scene at the Paradise Ballroom, the standard of dancing was remarkably high, especially given that many of the shag and Lindy hop dancers on screen are non-professional dancers recruited by Pan from local dance halls. Astaire's ship provided the BWS, but the film could not be made without at least one 'trademark' glamorous dance in evening dress. It is an extraordinary scene that depicts an almost suicidal Astaire dancing a sultry standard with Rogers on a flat roof with the obligatory sunburst shape created by dramatic lighting radiating from a domed skylight, to the sound of the distant orchestra playing 'Let's Face the Music and Dance', composed by Berlin for the film.

There are, of course, always scenes in nightclubs or restaurants with dance floors, and in *Swing Time* (1936) the narrative is based around the rivalry between two clubs, Raymond's and the Silver Sandal. The most dramatic design is probably the Silver Sandal, credited to John Harkrider, thought to be based on the Silver Slipper on

Manhattan's West 48th street. Flanked by tiered dining tables, the set has a pair of stairs symmetrically placed either side of the dance floor, which rise to meet in the centre where Astaire and Rogers exit. The design of Raymond's, the rival nightclub, is very much like the Rainbow Room in New York's Rockefeller Center. Whether popular taste and real-life designers were influenced by what they saw of the musical films or whether Polglase was influenced by real nightclubs is difficult to know, but the shared vision and style is evident. The Rainbow Room on the 65th floor of the RCA building at the Rockefeller Center opened in 1934 in grand Art Deco style. It occupied a rectangular space on the west side of the building with floor to ceiling windows on three sides and spectacular views across the Manhattan skyline. Deep reveals of 45 centimetres (18 in.) to the windows were faced with mirrors to reflect both light and the views. The lighting included three crystal chandeliers, wall sconces and a rainbow of coloured lights that changed according to the music being played across the central domed ceiling. The centre of the room had a circular dance floor that could be rotated in either direction overlooked by the dining tables on tiered levels on three sides. The fourth side had a small stage for performers and symmetrical gently curving staircases on either side. Wallace K. Harrison was largely responsible for the design, under the direction of the Rockefeller Center's architect Raymond Hood, and many of the interior furnishings were designed by Elena Bachman Schmidt (1890–1955). The Rainbow Room was immediately known as the most glamorous destination for the elite in Manhattan, European royalty and the best-known actors and performers.

In London's Kensington another Rainbow Room, designed by the American architect C. A. Wheeler, opened at the same time on the top floor of the Derry & Tom's department store.[14] It remains intact, with an oval domed ceiling above the dance floor, and was famous for its roof garden – a 1938 fantasy space complete with pink flamingos in ponds. It was designed by the landscape architect Ralph

Couples dancing on the nightclub set of Astaire and Rogers's *Swing Time* (1936), showing the often-used motif in both film and reality of paired curving staircases and tiered audiences.

Hancock, who was responsible for the gardens at the Rockefeller Center. A description of the gardens – 'couples wandered between flowering shrubs illuminated by concealed lighting' and 'strolled in a Moorish garden', 'Hungarian gypsies strolled about playing Viennese Waltzes' and 'there was the twinkling sound of water from fountains and a tiny stream, while moonlight gave an added touch of romance' – might equally well have been the description of a film musical.[15]

Astaire and Rogers were unique: no other couple then or since has had the same screen presence and no other dancers have ever reached such a wide audience. Astaire and Rogers were dancers who saw dancing as just that – 'not as acrobatics or sexy poses or self-expression'.[16] Aged 34 when he was to make his first film with Rogers, slightly balding and more a comic actor than a conventional male lead, Astaire was an actor about whom producers had expressed some doubts, but they decided that his dancer's posture and elegance gave him sufficient 'presence'. Rogers had had early success as a stage performer in vaudeville and on Broadway, followed by film roles at Paramount, Pathé and Warner Brothers before signing up with RKO. Rogers was primarily an actor and made many more films while working with Astaire and for several years afterwards, and won an Academy Award for Best Actress in 1941.[17] Her acting skills were considerable and once she had learnt to dance like Astaire, they were the perfect couple.

The films depicted the dancers in opulent spaces: hotel lobbies, impossibly large hotel suites, classy restaurants and sophisticated nightclubs. Outside they strolled through gardens incongruously furnished with immaculate parterre, carefully manicured topiary, marble statues dotted here and there, and more often than not a bandstand. The characters they played were beautiful and charming people who sailed the Atlantic aboard the latest ocean liners and decided to take an aeroplane back to New York City at the drop of a hat. The films showed a luxurious lifestyle – not futuristic and not the extremes of magical fairy tales, but a near future, one that might still be beyond most but was believable and potentially within reach. With Astaire and Rogers's impeccable routines, the sleek Art Deco sets, the choruses of couples dancing and the perfect costumes of tail suits and beautiful dresses, the films left the audience in no doubt that dancing was a glamorous activity. The series of films they made together, as Damian Sutton has noted, 'offered more than an escapist fantasy for the passive audience – it engaged audiences physically and discursively to develop an intimate connection between screen aesthetics and financial success.'[18]

It is easy to see much of the design for the movies, unlike the necessarily functional design for the real world, as symbolic or emblematic and to note that different elements might be exaggerated or used to evoke status. But we might also see the design as aspirational. Rather than intending simply to recreate known historical or contemporary spaces, designers naturally looked forward. The new generation had mostly trained as architects and designing for films offered a certain freedom. Unlike working for the theatre, the designer of a film set was no longer just choosing the right backdrop but was responsible for the overall design of the complete scene – the spaces, the props and the lighting. The designers had brought with them their vision of an ideal modern world, their new kind of reality, that existed only in the movies but that many perhaps believed was possible. A new kind of film meant a new design style, one that drew only a very fine line between reality and fantasy.

The Berlin dancing master Walter Carlo dancing a rumba with his wife, 1931.

EIGHT

Everyday Glamour

*Mecca has brought another kind of glamour – an everyday glamour. It
has showed the dignity that could be in ballroom dancing to the whole
country.*

Come Dancing Miss World (1966)[1]

In Britain, perpetuating the glamorous Hollywood ideal that remains
the anachronistic yet enduring image of ballroom everywhere
was in large part down to Mecca, a highly successful entertainment
company whose name was to become synonymous with dancing
and later with other growing forms of popular entertainment. Dance
businesses appeared all over the country in the 1920s and '30s to cater
for increasing demand, but none was to be as successful as Mecca. It
was an offshoot of a much older catering business, Ye Mecca Ltd. Carl
Heimann, originally from Denmark, who worked as a catering manager there during the 1920s, is credited with persuading the company
to invest in dancing, and by 1934 he had become manager of its
subsidiary company, Mecca Dancing. In 1935 Heimann joined with
Alan Fairley, a local Glasgow businessman, to form the Mecca Agency,
which controlled dance halls across Britain and some three hundred
bands. In 1946 they became joint directors of what became Mecca
Ltd, when dancing had become a bigger part of the business than
the original catering activities and the parent company agreed to
surrender financial control to Heimann and Fairley. Their partnership

ran a subsidiary company providing equipment to dance halls and another, DanceLand Publications, which was used to promote their various events and competitions as well as produce books and leaflets.

The biography of Heimann and Fairley, *Come Dancing Miss World*, written by Fairley's wife and published in 1966, tells the almost fairy-tale story of two ambitious businessmen. Heimann's rise to success in the business world started in catering, from his first café, the Black Cat in Coventry, to his year in London working for J. Lyons tea shops for the Wembley exhibition and his first job for Ye Mecca as catering manager at the People's Palace in east London. At Ye Mecca he successfully turned failing cafés into paying concerns, was promoted to catering supervisor and then had the opportunity in 1928 to put into place his first ideas for popular dancing when he was given responsibility for the catering contract for Sherry's dance hall in Brighton, then owned by Bertram Mills.[2] Seeking to emulate the elegance and glamorous atmosphere enjoyed by the wealthy patrons in London's West End dance halls and nightclubs, he made many changes: white linen tablecloths, usherettes and page boys in smart uniforms and new bands. Heimann caused considerable controversy by opening the balcony for spectators, who did not pay to dance but could watch and also buy a drink – according to Roma Fairley, Sherry's was the only licensed dance hall at the time. After Sherry's his next step was the Ritz in Manchester and the Locarno in Streatham and from there on to many more dance halls. Heimann teamed up with Byron Davies, the advertising manager at the Hammersmith Palais, before then taking over his booking agency for bands and cabaret artists.

Alan Fairley, the other half of the successful Mecca partnership, had enjoyed early success with his Dunedin dance hall in Edinburgh, which had opened in 1923 and featured cabaret acts from 1924. Tables and chairs and comfortable sofas lined the walls, food was served in the adjoining hall, and a restaurant and upstairs balcony were available for non-dancers to watch, be seen and socialize. The Dunedin became very well known as the fashionable destination for visiting music hall artists and the smart people of Edinburgh, and included Adele and Fred Astaire among its famous visitors.

The dance hall was modern in style, although the restaurant remained 'Victorian', with red plush and frilly lampshades. Fairley planned non-stop dancing competitions for publicity purposes and introduced paid dancing partners. These had already been introduced at Hammersmith and at Southport Palais, but here they were to enjoy a superior reputation and were known only as 'instructresses'. He also persuaded the BBC to broadcast his 'Romany Revellers', a big band he 'invented' by asking his two dance bands, who performed alternate sets on regular dance nights, to play together to create a more impressive, bigger sound. According to his biography, Fairley was responsible for the first steps to overturn the ban on Sunday dancing. Finding bands capable of bringing in the crowds to make any profit had been an ongoing problem for Fairley, who was in competition with other nearby venues that had residency contracts with popular bands, but Sundays – if he could get permission – offered him an opportunity. He managed to persuade Jack Hylton to agree to his proposition, and Caird Hall in Dundee, which could accommodate 3,000, was to be the venue. His application to Dundee Council was successful but with the condition that they play sacred music only. Jack Hylton, having mislaid his 'sacred music' en route, duly played to a very enthusiastic, capacity audience. The council 'huffed and puffed' over the event, but the result was that Sunday concerts continued on a regular basis.[3]

After his success at the Dunedin, his next big venture when he was all of 22 years old was the Piccadilly, a dance club and cocktail lounge in Glasgow, which opened in 1926. Despite dance halls' common problems often associated with large gatherings, with ruffians and racists and those flouting the strict alcohol licensing laws, it was like no other place in Glasgow and very quickly became the place to be seen. At that time Glasgow already had two big dance halls: the

Plaza for the wealthier classes and the Dennistoun Palais for everyone else. The Waldorf followed and then the Locarno at the other end of Sauchiehall Street, which Fairley was to buy at a knock-down price in 1929. The Locarno was opened in the name of his new business, Scottish Dance Halls Limited, formed in 1934, but it was closed in the summer season as Fairley was doubtful that it would be successful. Rather than closing for a second summer season Heimann was invited to operate it and following the success of his 'Savoy Hotel standards at Palais prices' approach their enduring partnership was formed.[4]

Mecca Dancing very soon became the biggest dance hall owner in Britain. Their target audience was the working classes, which meant affordability was key, but they were nevertheless advertising 'luxury'. Their dance halls offered an image of extravagance associated with the wealthy upper classes of earlier decades and a contemporary version reinvented by Hollywood of elegance and a near-future modern world fuelled by stories of romance and triumph over hard times. Today their approach would be termed 'Experience Design': the sheer size of the spaces, the decor, the facilities on offer, live music, the management style and attentive staff were all to work together to provide a glamorous alternative and an escape from an often drab everyday world.

Dance halls – at the time still novel in many areas – were subject to a strict structure and a careful approach to the selection of staff, including the musicians. Detailed instruction books were issued to all staff with tips on how to behave when delivering what they considered a 'public service'. Like the nineteenth-century classical dance teachers who gave tips on etiquette and general deportment, they set out to educate their clientele in behaviour appropriate to their dance halls. A strict dress code was enforced – no trousers or shorts for women, except at seaside dance halls, and men were not admitted in braces or without collars – and the staff wore easily identifiable smart uniforms. Good organization and adherence to the rules were crucial. There was a reliable programme, with a three-hour session every

Mecca's Stevenage Locarno opened in October 1961. The design was almost
identical to the earlier versions, with a Canadian-maple strip dance floor,
revolving bandstand and 'starlight' ceiling.

afternoon, four hours every evening and only ten seconds between
each dance. All the staff were expected to collude in identifying potential troublemakers and anyone showing signs of drunkenness or
rough behaviour would be asked to leave.

It might be hard now to imagine the effect of visiting the new
luxurious ballrooms. Other venues at the same scale were rare, and
especially for the working classes in big cities like London, this would
have been an entirely novel experience. A newspaper reporter describing going into Mecca's Locarno ballroom in Streatham for the first
time in 1939 is surprised by what he encounters: 'I walked down a
flight of stairs – straight into the Continent. This might have been

Paris or Berlin, this large, octagonal room – with balconies lined with a row of red electric lamps, great Chinese lanterns hanging from the arched roof, the orchestra seated before a backcloth of gold and grey. There was a Continental touch about the assorted costumes too.'[5] Perhaps swayed by the anti-American feeling of the period that encouraged a focus on Europe as the preferred cultural influence, he is nevertheless unwilling to associate it with Streatham – a somewhat nondescript borough in south London – but sees it as somehow verging on the exotic.

The sheer size and grandeur of the main space could be overwhelming in itself, with a vast polished dance floor, high ceiling – often with 'twinkling star' lighting effects – surrounded by tiered balconies, and coloured lighting reflected in the gleaming surfaces. A revolving bandstand, first introduced at the Locarno in Streatham, added to the theatricality of the setting. Without having to interrupt the dancing to change over between two bands, the circular podium would rotate slowly to reveal a second band already in position and ready to play. Boudoirs for the women had seating and make-up

The ladies' powder room at the Stevenage Locarno, 1961.

mirrors; some even provided hair driers. The men's equivalent, the stag rooms, sometimes went so far as to supply razors. No alcohol was served; instead there were various restaurants and cafés or ice cream bars.

The name Mecca became synonymous with ballrooms. The same elaborate decorative design was used in every palais, with variations only to suit the particular building, and sometimes minor differences in pricing and music to suit local demand. They enticed dancers away from the nightclubs and smaller dancing venues, with their association with problems of alcohol, rowdiness and prostitution. They were also keen to encourage women. In the 1930s and up until the 1970s the pub was still a largely male space and ballrooms and dance halls continued to provide an alternative safe and welcoming space for women to meet and socialize as well as for dancing. Mecca's ambition and optimism in business, their strict management style and their constant surveillance reinvigorated the dancing scene in Britain, turning it from a crowded and sometimes chaotic unpredictable social event into the basis for a thriving business. Mecca's success is in part attributed to the almost identical design of their dance halls, offering the comfort of familiarity for their clientele, understood by many successful businesses, avoiding the apprehension and anxiety of the unfamiliar and unpredictable. Some, the more curious and keen to explore new venues, would of course see this uniformity in a negative light, hinted at in a wartime article:

> In the Astoria, you go down two flights of stairs to reach
> the dance floor. In Green's you go up 95 feet in a lift to reach
> the dance floor. But when you get to either you might be
> at the other – you might be at Sherry's for that matter, or at
> Hammersmith or the Tower or any one of the Meccas – the
> general scheme or lack of scheme is the same. The same tunes
> from what looks at first like the same band . . . Look down from
> a balcony, when the main lights are lowered, and the floor is lit

with revolving coloured spotlights and one of those revolving
reflectors that hang from the ceiling and shower bilious light
spots over a smoky ballroom . . . It all seems just the same
everywhere.[6]

While the return of longer dresses and the new Hollywood film
musicals were both credited with having an influence on the desire
to create a more glamorous atmosphere in the ballroom, the dancing
among the public was not considered of a very high standard: 'The
most formless and lazy dancing is to be found in the best hotels and
restaurants, while the best dancing can be seen in the suburban Palais
de danse.'[7] Women wearing longer dresses, which hampered their
movement and in turn hindered the men leading them, was one possible reason for poor performance. Another reason, according to
Santos Casani, was the men, 'who imagine that there is no need for
them to learn steps or rhythm', believing that their partners should
just be able to follow them whatever they chose to do.[8] Whatever the
reason, the Official Board of Ballroom Dancing (OBBD) was doggedly
determined to improve the general standard of dancing. Since its
formation at the conclusion of the *Dancing Times*'s informal conferences in 1929, the OBBD was starting to formulate the set of rules
that were to be recognized by all the various teachers' associations
and seeking to establish itself as the controlling voice in all matters
related to dancing.[9] In July 1931, along with decisions to ban 'freak'
dancing, the OBBD decided to focus on known dances. Not wanting
to risk the introduction of yet more wild dances and crazes of earlier decades, it decided that no new dances would be put forward
for the coming season; instead, it aimed to popularize the waltz and
tango and encourage the Viennese waltz.[10] Marathon or endurance
dances were still popular, especially in America, but the OBBD
doubted that the English would be interested in what it considered
a daft idea. A recent marathon dance contest in Paris at the Medrano
Circus in Montmartre had lasted for 32 days, and only six of the

thirty couples who started were still standing five hundred hours later: 'such a melancholy spectacle', they thought, 'would not attract people looking for "real" entertainment.'[11]

Ragtime and jazz rhythms that had arrived from America in the first decades of the century were still pervasive, but by the early 1930s Latin rhythms were increasing in popularity. They inspired dancers to try out other dances, the rumba or the Brazilian maxixe, which had been around for a while, or the more recent cha-cha-cha and mambo. In 1931, 'El Mansiero', or 'The Peanut Vendor' in English, by the Cuban musician Don Azpiazú and his Havana Casino Orchestra, was an enormous hit, the first of many, and 'was covered almost immediately by, among others, Louis Armstrong and Jack Payne'.[12] Not everyone was confident of the enduring appeal of the Latin rhythms; Eve Tynegate-Smith offered advice to avoid the exaggerated hip movements: 'No attempt has been made to describe the subtle hip movement – natural to Cubans but not to Europeans – as the description on paper would only tend to give a vulgar interpretation, and even without this hip "wriggle" the Rumba is delightful.'[13] According to Bertini, the Tower Ballroom band leader, the fact that the rumba had very quickly increased in popularity was a clear indication the public was ready for something new.[14] He thought that the tempo of a new dance should be somewhere between the slow foxtrot and the quickstep and have a lilting rhythm. He suggested it should be something like the 'Bahama Mamma', which was being played regularly by Henry Hall's BBC dance band in the early 1930s, a tune which sounds more like a bossa nova than any of those that were eventually to become recognized and codified as the International Latin dances. In support, in 1932 the *Daily Mail* launched a 'dance rhythm contest', which generated considerable speculation about what would be most appropriate.[15] Simple easy-to-follow rhythms were the most likely to succeed, although some ambitious proposals for such complex rhythms as 5/4 and 7/4 were put forward. The competition judges were all well known in the popular music or dancing field: Jack

Payne, director of Dance Music at the BBC 1928–32 and leader of the BBC's first official dance band; Lawrence Wright, music publisher and founder of *Melody Maker* in 1926; Santos Casani; and Charles Prentice, the well-known conductor and arranger.[16] Yet despite the enormous number of entries received, close to 2,000, the judges could not pick a winner. They awarded equal prize money to the four best entries, and were unanimous in their decision that none of the entries was good enough to spark interest in a new dance style. They were perhaps hard to please – there were some good melodies, they thought, but nothing that they considered suitable for dancing.

By 1933 introducing new dances seemed to be the only option to improve the situation. The croon, a new variation on the foxtrot, was approved by the ISTD as something that could be easily danced on a crowded floor. Around the same time, the press enthused about a new dance that Victor Silvester had brought back from the USA: the 'Charleston blues', with music specially written by Carroll Gibbons of the Savoy Orpheans.[17] But Silvester tells us again that this was simply a publicity stunt, common at the time, invented at the request of the director at the Savoy Hotel. He made money teaching the dance to other teachers, but like many such inventions it did not catch on.[18] By 1935 the pundits were enthusiastic that another version of the Charleston was making a comeback, although the instruction published in the *Daily Mail* describes something more like today's rhythm foxtrot than a Charleston – albeit with an 'optional foot twist'.[19] The ISTD decided to promote it for the 1935–6 season following a demonstration given by Phyllis Haylor and Charles Scrimshaw at the Empress Rooms in Kensington. They considered it was 'ideally suited to ballrooms either small or crowded' and unlike the original, it was progressive, was to be done without the kicks and swivels, and could be danced in conjunction with foxtrot steps.[20]

Approaching the autumn of 1936 and the coming season, dance teachers were optimistic that there would be announcements about a new dance in preparation for coronation year. Cecil Taylor, then president of the ISTD, was sure that 'somebody is bound to be working out a new idea to mark the occasion. It absolutely cries out for a Coronation Dance.'[21] But no new dance appeared and by the late 1930s the situation had not changed much. The OBBD, the teachers and dancing associations persevered with the modern dances. They feared that the new Latin rhythms would result in the introduction of more freak dances, so continued their struggle to find a way to improve the poor standards of the existing modern dances, with pupils reluctant to learn the complex steps and challenging technique. Dancers and their teachers alike were reportedly enthusiastic about the film musicals, and especially Astaire and Rogers, and their influence on the continuing popularity of ballroom dancing.

Most dancers, it seems, even if they saw themselves as another Astaire or Rogers, were not very interested in learning complex steps, attending classes and practising ambitious routines. They were interested in dances they could learn quickly and easily and in the social aspects of the dance hall – meeting people and having fun. The result was a growth of 'novelty' dances, or 'party' dances as they are called now, with simple steps, simple hold – either side by side or holding hands – and in general a repeated routine easy enough that it can be taught to everybody at a dance in just a few minutes. The simplest of the dances was the 'Boomps-a-Daisy', which involved very little dancing and included the mischievous figure that meant bumping hips with a stranger. In 1938, 'Knees Up Mother Brown', a song that had been around for decades, was finally published and found its way to the ballrooms. The best known of all the party dances of the 1930s is the Lambeth Walk.[22] It was so popular that a whole chapter was devoted to a survey of it in the 1939 publication *Britain* by Mass-Observation. 'This is the song that half the world started singing in 1938. To the song was added a dance that was half a walk, and it caught on as no new dance has done for years.'[23] Everyone danced it everywhere, it seemed, even at some of the smartest private balls and dances. Its phenomenal success was the subject of a 1938 Pathé

INSTRUCTIONS HOW TO DANCE
THE LAMBETH WALK

1. Partners stand side by side, gentlemen on right. Walk forward 8 steps (4 bars), swinging the arms Cockney fashion.

2. Link arms. Go round in circle, 8 steps, to left. On 3rd beat of 4th bar shout "Oi" and give Cockney salute.

3. Side by side again. 2 steps forward 3 quick steps ditto. (1 and 2 and 1.2.3.)

   Repeat. (4 bars in all)

4. Face partner. Back 3 steps, close heels and ...

   slap knees on 3rd beat of second bar.

5. Take 3 steps towards partner and salute on 3rd beat of 2nd bar, shouting "Oi."

THEN REPEAT 1-5, omitting shout and salute as in 2 and 5.

N.B. When the words "Doin' the Lambeth Walk" occur in the chorus, these are sung by the dancers.

CINEPHONIC MUSIC CO., LTD.,
"Dean House," 2, 3 & 4, Dean Street, London, W.1.

Instructions for the dance that accompanies the song 'The Lambeth Walk'. It assumes readers will understand 'swinging the arms Cockney fashion' and 'give a Cockney salute'.

newsreel, along with another popular party dance, the palais glide.[24] The voiceover explains that while the origin of the palais glide – or 'pally' sometimes, because it is friendly – is unknown, the origin of the Lambeth Walk was the stage show *Me and My Gal*. The title song was sung by Lupino Lane, who starred with Adele England. Along with all the comments from 'cockneys', Mass-Observation also interviewed England and Lane about the origins of the dance. Lane was clear that it was he who had invented it based on his own swagger, but Adele had a different story regarding its promotion for commercial purposes:

> There's never been an English dance success like it before. We have so many halls we can push it. I started in the Locarno, then I went to the Ritz Manchester; the Grand Casino, Birmingham; Sherries, Brighton. The Locarno Glasgow and the Piccadilly Club Glasgow; the Palais Edinburgh; and the Royal, Tottenham. I did it all in a month. By the end it had really caught on.[25]

The Lambeth Walk was danced in ballrooms everywhere on both sides of the Atlantic, photographed here *c.* 1940.

Although Mass-Observation was interested to discover the reason for its wide appeal, anti-American feeling is clear when it states that the public 'will take to it with far more spontaneous feeling than they have ever shown for the paradise drug of the American dance-tune'.[26]

Not all novelty dances were so universally adopted. The Lambeth Walk was a surprise success in America, but the American party dances imported to Britain, such as the shag,[27] yam and cherry hop, did not achieve the same popularity. After being introduced by Phyllis Haylor at the Empress Rooms, the write-up in the *Daily Mail* set out instructions and tells us that they were 'typically quick and vigorous in the best American manner'.[28] The British press were correct in their surmise that the Big Apple dance, which required participants to take their turn to contribute a bar or two on their own – with truckin', peckin', high kicks, shimmies or whatever – in the centre of the circle of dancers, was doomed because of the 'natural reserve' of the English. For Arthur Murray, however, the Big Apple – which he claimed to have discovered in 1937 in an old barn in North Carolina – became the craze that enabled him to set up his first set of franchised studios as he sent his staff off to big hotels, department stores and nightclubs armed with the invented call names and records to demonstrate and teach it.[29] The yam, which had been invented together with a comic song for the Astaire and Rogers film *Carefree* (1938), was expected to become a big hit but was not. Alex Moore himself, then president of the NATD, was also responsible for inventing a novelty dance where one man dances with two women simultaneously, for the benefit of wallflowers, but he was wrong in thinking it might be adopted at dances, even when there were twice as many women as men.[30]

To look at dancing as a business – with, on one hand, the consumers or the dancing public and, on the other hand, what might be called the service providers, the dance hall owners and dance promoters – is to oversimplify the relationship. Both rely on the participation of professional dancers to provide demonstrations and instruction.

The dancing profession had long recognized the crucial role played by dance hall managers and promoters and had formally invited the Association of Ballrooms and Dance Halls to send representatives to the OBBD on its formation in 1929. Professional dancers could also be categorized, using business terminology, as a service provider, but with the exception of those who had their own studios or ballrooms, they were obliged to exist in a co-dependency relationship with dance hall owners and promoters. Professional dancers relied on the venue managers to provide the spaces for teaching and the events for them and their pupils to practise what they had learnt. Dance halls equally relied on the professional dancers to teach the public and keep them entertained and interested with demonstrations, new steps and even the invention of new dances.

The often overlapping territories could clearly cause tensions. Professional dancers were keen to educate the public to achieve higher standards and relied on dance halls to support their endeavours by providing musicians to play appropriate, strict tempo music and creating the right atmosphere. However, the dance halls favoured anything, within reason, that would attract customers and had been especially keen on the simple-to-learn novelty dances of the later 1930s, which were popular with dancers. This was not a new problem. In an article published in early 1930, Jack Hylton had offered a robust defence to the suggestion that dance bands were somehow responsible for the growing tensions between dance hall owners and teachers. He argued that dancing relied on dancing teachers, whom he considered to be out of touch with the taste of the public: 'While the dance bands are doing their best to keep dancing as a form of entertainment, the dancing teachers are winning their fight to make it a laborious duty,' Hylton stated. He also suggested that the teachers should make some effort to invite musicians to collaborate with them 'in the invention of a new dance, or even in the putting into practice of an existing one'.[31]

Old time dance experts Sydney and Mary Thompson demonstrate their coronation dance 'A Waltz for the Queen', which was to be shown on television on 22 April 1952.

NINE

Togetherness: Holiday Camps and Sequence Dancing

As for the dances – well, they are an institution. An impeccable floor, top line bands, a gay throng of holiday makers and a grand spirit of companionship – with those ingredients a thoroughly happy time can be guaranteed. There is dancing every evening of course culminating in the Saturday-night Galas that no one could possibly forget.

'Butlin's Clacton Souvenir Brochure', 1946[1]

By the late 1940s an unlikely contribution to the need for more ballrooms and dance halls came about through the development of holiday camps, in particular those owned and run by Billy Butlin. The late 1930s had seen the beginnings of a new kind of organized holiday on offer, aimed primarily at the working classes; the increase in leisure time after the war saw them develop all over the country. The population was increasing, and the recently introduced legislation to give everybody holidays with pay meant, as a Clacton souvenir brochure declared in 1946, 'a vast new class of people . . . for the first time will have the opportunity of getting away with their families for an annual holiday.' Butlin saw the opportunity to provide much-needed capacity; hotels at popular seaside resorts very quickly proved inadequate once more people were able to take holidays. His innovative private 'chalet' accommodation, complemented with a huge range of sporting activities and facilities – pools, vast dining halls, bars and ballrooms with the same 'luxury' branding used by Mecca – formed the basis for what was to become a successful commercial holiday sector. Ballrooms and dancing tuition were an important element in his all-inclusive holidays from the outset. In contrast to the outdoor sporting activities, ballrooms inspired by those designed for film sets presented a glamorous setting and made a key contribution to the idea of luxury, stretching reality to the believable fiction that attracted holidaymakers and dancers in ever increasing numbers.

The success of holiday camps aimed at the working classes coincided with the recently introduced paid holidays and the ongoing growth in hobbies and activities to fill people's increasing leisure time. After many years of debate and campaigning, Britain's Holidays with Pay Act had been passed in 1938, which gave all workers a minimum of one week's paid holiday each year.[2] Although at the time some 70 per cent of the population did not earn enough to afford a holiday, anticipation of the forthcoming Act had prompted interest and investment in camps – to provide those holidays – from the widest sections of society.[3] The Civil Service and National Association of Local Government Officers bought camps, and some local councils thought it might be their responsibility to run camps for the health and welfare of their residents. Municipal camps and the possibility of 'Camps for the Nation' were discussed at some length, and a camps Bill even came to Parliament in March 1939; however, British state camps never materialized. Today's American summer camps and French *colonies de vacances* are the enduring result of similar early efforts, but in Britain children's summer camps never became an established part of childhood. Organized camping for adults, however, became hugely popular, particularly with the younger generation. There was a whole range of different camps that were economically priced to provide a holiday for the lowest paid workers, to attract single people as well as families, and even some specifically for unemployed men. John Fletcher Dodd, a member of the Independent Labour party, pioneered the Caister Socialist Camp, which grew to accommodate 1,000 campers every week during the summer. Tents were eventually replaced by more permanent lodgings, and while there were a certain number of organized dances, socials and lectures, the clientele was largely looking for the sense of freedom offered by camping compared to the constraints of a hotel with dress codes and fixed timetables. A trip away to enjoy the natural environment of either the seaside or the countryside was perhaps another form of diversion or escape from the ordinariness of home life, but by the end of the 1930s the idea that there were health and social benefits to be gained was well established.

Camping was another of the crazes which, along with dancing, 'identified with youth, vigour and the outdoor life' became fashionable for all sections of society during the 1920s.[4] Camping symbolized an idea of freedom: unshackled by family, unfettered by the responsibilities of city life and work, campers were free to go where they wanted as and when they chose, hiking across country, pitching a tent and cooking over a campfire. This extreme did not have enduring appeal for all sections of the population; indeed, most preferred the idea of something that was more organized. T. H. Holding, whose own experiences of camping were of the extreme kind, is considered the founder of organized camping.[5] As a child he had crossed America in a wagon train and later 'cruised' the rivers and lochs in the Highlands of Scotland by canoe. Physical activity, which might be hiking, canoeing, cycling or a combination, was a key element of what we would now call 'adventure holidays', where everyone stayed together in the camp sharing large bell tents. This kind of camping focused on the idea of 'back to nature' rather than independence, with plenty of fresh air and a wholesome, natural way of life. Organized camping enabled an escape from the urban environment into the countryside and for many was the only kind of 'holiday' that was affordable. Sleeping in tents kept the prices low and meant the owners could invest in higher-quality facilities. The notion of holiday as part fantasy or escapism was already evident at the Cunningham Camp site on the Isle of Man, one of the first leisure camps.[6] The washrooms and latrines were housed in a permanent building designed as a miniature castle, complete with fake turrets, battlements and Gothic arched, leaded-light windows. The camp had its own immense dining hall, electric lighting (even before the town was supplied with electricity) and a heated swimming pool. Such facilities would have been an improvement on their other option of staying in Edwardian hotels and probably also on the homes of many of the campers. It became very popular, and by the end of the 1930s other commercial leisure camps were operating alongside the more spartan pioneer camps.

The 'camping holiday' for nature-loving, sporty and adventurous campers, initiated often by socialist and religious groups, settled into something rather different in the 1930s and '40s – the holiday camp. While the pioneer camps continued and developed, they tended to serve the generally well-heeled, educated classes who sought freedom and proximity to nature, and above all independence. Holiday camps were there to serve the working classes. In contrast to the spartan, basic nature of a camping holiday, Butlin's was to offer something quite different – in fact, the exact opposite: luxury or at least the comfort and amenity associated with extravagance. Butlin had already made a name for himself, according to the *Daily Mail*, as 'a pioneer of holiday camps . . . his foresight and genius for thinking in big numbers helped to set this fashion of getting together by the sea like a great happy family.'[7] In addition to the fresh air and sporting activities, not only could the holidaymakers enjoy luxuries of all kinds unavailable to them at home, they 'would do so in a friendly unpretentious and democratic atmosphere in which they need not fear being patronized or intimidated'.[8] For the working classes with no decision-making responsibilities while at work, the camp mirrored this; everything was planned and organized for them; they had only to choose which activities to take part in.

Butlin's name became synonymous with holiday camps and everything they came to stand for, particularly ballroom dancing. The camps continued to enjoy considerable commercial success throughout the 1950s and '60s. They emulated the self-sufficiency of villages or small towns, and were laid out on very simple lines with rows of identical self-contained 'chalets' which, for many, offered more space and a level of privacy, including internal plumbing, that they did not have at home. For families, the children were entertained by day and watched over by night, and for single people, the camps offered an opportunity for socializing with the opposite sex. A whole range of staff were there to cater for all needs: to do all the basic chores, to wait on them in the dining hall. The Redcoats – the genial hosts – were there to attend, amuse and make sure everyone enjoyed themselves. For women, the housewives and mothers, the holiday camp was particularly liberating – the only time they were free from cleaning, cooking and childcare duties. The centrally organized public spaces included dining halls, bars and lounges, and outdoor facilities such as greens for putting and bowls, tennis courts and swimming pools.

Brochure for Butlin's Skegness holiday camp, *c.* 1937. The best-known dance bands played at Butlin's camps, where dancing was a key activity for the holidaymakers.

Above all, there were ballrooms: not just one – each camp usually had three. The design of the ballrooms, bars and lounges, which all followed a set of defined themes, belonged to a make-believe world that 'sought to transport their visitors from a world of everyday drudgery to a make-believe setting. Images were compressed and interwoven to create a world that was everywhere but nowhere. Hawaiian bars and Viennese coffee lounges, Hollywood terraces and South Sea pools.'[9] It was a glamorous world the holidaymakers believed in for a brief time, as George Orwell describes: 'They enjoyed the bright colours, the silly competitions, the make-believe backcloth of a Hollywood film set.'[10] Richard Hoggart, writing in

'Dancing in the Romantic atmosphere reminiscent of those Gay Viennese nights':
Butlin's Luxury Holiday Camp, Clacton-on-Sea. Butlin's camps typically had three ballrooms themed with different decorative designs to create the escapist fantasy that formed the backdrop for the dancing style. From a souvenir brochure, 1939.

1957, tells us that for the holidaymakers the image created was more important than any obvious lack of authenticity; 'if you look closely at the interiors of the great public halls there, you may see the steel girders and bare corrugations of the roofs; but you will have to peer through a welter of artificial trees, imitation half-timbering, great dazzling chandeliers.'[11]

At the new holiday camps physical activity was still an important aspect of the idea of any holiday – no longer the simpler hiking, cycling and canoeing, but the now more skilled sports of tennis, bowling and swimming. Rest and relaxation were of secondary consideration; indeed, the idea that a holiday is for 'rest' did not arrive until the 1970s when foreign holidays, lying on a beach or lounging by a pool in order to achieve the perfect suntan became the epitome of desirability. Ballroom dancing, which could take place indoors, was the perfect holiday activity in Britain's uncertain weather, and Butlin's camps, as Billy Butlin declared in his memoir, 'played an important part in the boom in popularity of all kinds of ballroom dancing'.[12]

Billy Butlin opened his first camp in Skegness at Easter in 1936 and the second in Clacton in 1938. Sure of their popularity, both were supported by the London North Eastern Railway, which met half the cost of advertising. Proposals for his third camp, further along the Yorkshire coast outside Filey, met with considerable resistance, but Butlin was able to convince everyone that as the camp would operate independently, it would not have a detrimental effect on the environment or the good reputation of the resort itself. Butlin's success through the 1940s attracted others. The two competitor names in the British holiday camp business, Pontins and Warners, operated on similar lines and offered similar experiences including dancing, but they operated at a very different scale and lacked the same focus on entertainments. By 1947, with a total combined capacity of 1,300 holidaymakers, Pontins camps were small compared to Butlin's, which by then included five camps that could accommodate a total of 30,000. Deciding they could not compete with Butlin's, Pontins focused on going upmarket, targeting those willing to pay more, and eventually introduced televisions, en-suite bathrooms and buffet-style dining rooms. Later they were quick to take advantage of the new interest in foreign holidays and created Pontinental, a Mediterranean all-in 'package holiday' version of the camps with the most recent must-have: guaranteed sunshine. Warners, the other big name in holiday camps, largely based in the south of England, were also much smaller than Butlin's, catering for between five and six hundred people. They too would have to accommodate changing demand during the 1970s and after several changes in ownership – Warners is now part of Bourne Leisure, the same company that owns the new Butlins[13] – found renewed success as an adults-only holiday company. They all shared the same message: a holiday was not for doing nothing but provided an escape from work into physical leisure activities. Butlin's 1960 brochure invited holidaymakers to 'step out of your work a day world', offering 'tennis courts, putting greens and ballrooms' with 'dancing nightly'.[14]

What distinguished Butlin's camps from his competitors was his – for want of a better word – 'showmanship'. Butlin was by all accounts a charismatic and successful entrepreneur. Through his background in fairgrounds and long experience in show business, he was able to use his connections to arrange for guest appearances by a whole range of celebrities, enticing holidaymakers with the thrill of possible encounters with them. Gracie Fields performed and for several years was a member of competition-judging panels, and other guests included the aviator Amy Johnson and the cricketer Len Hutton. His 'big-name' entertainment policy included all kinds of performers and comedians, and importantly some of the best-known bands. Alan Green, Jack Wallace and Eric Winstone all played at Skegness throughout the summer of 1947, as well as Harry Davidson (1892–1967) and his Old-Time Orchestra, well known through his BBC Radio broadcasts. The idea of the glamour that music and dancing offered complemented Butlin's focus on entertainment. The dancers and musicians employed at the camps were far fewer in number and enjoyed a higher status than the other staff; according to a 1973 survey, the campers' expectations 'of entertainers relate to the quality of performance, clothes, appearance and facial expression. Musicians and dancers tend to keep company with attractive or high-status members of the opposite sex, whether campers or fellow staff.'[15]

With three ballrooms to choose from at Butlin's camps, it was possible to dance all day and all evening. A typical programme from Skegness in 1946 shows the extent of the many instruction sessions in every style and dancing every evening to live bands:

10.00 to 10.30 – Dancing Instruction (Modern)
    in the Viennese Ballroom
10.15 to 11.00 – Dancing Instruction (Old Time)
    in the Old Time Ballroom
10.45 to 11.45 – Coffee Dance in the Viennese Ballroom
11.00 to 11.45 – Dancing Instruction (Formation)
    in the Old Time Ballroom
3.00 to 5.00 – Tea Dance with Leslie Douglas
    in the Viennese Ballroom
3.30 to 5.00 – Old Time Dancing in the Old Time Ballroom
4.00 to 5.00 – Tea Dance to the Sam Ross Trio in the
    Montgomery Ballroom
8.00 to 11.15 – Dancing Time. Leslie Douglas
    and his Orchestra in the Viennese Ballroom
8.00 to 11.15 – Dancing Time with Sam Ross
    in the Montgomery Ballroom
8.15 to 11.15 – Old Time Dancing in the Old Time Ballroom

Dancing at Butlin's was more than just a pastime during the holiday. Reunion balls were organized each year, and according to Butlin as many as 10,000 people attended the first one, which was held on New Year's Eve in 1936.[16] By 1938 the reunion ball had been moved from the National Hall in Olympia to a bigger venue, the Empress Hall at Earls Court, with the best-selling musician Mantovani (1905–1980) and two other orchestras. The number of people trying to attend was so great that the roads were blocked with traffic for miles around, and it was not certain whether future events could be held there. The huge numbers attending the reunion balls indicates just how important dancing was as a part of the holiday camps. Though 1939 was only the second year of full operation, such was the popularity of the holiday camps that by May as many as 50,000 people had already booked for the summer season, only 6,000 fewer than the previous year, making similar crowd problems highly likely: 'every town hall and palais de danse in three or four hundred cities in Great Britain will be crowded on the Butlin Reunion Night which he plans for a certain evening in November.'[17] Butlin rapidly became established as an important figure in the ballroom dancing world; his camps provided the much needed large ballrooms at every camp for every kind of dancing. Moreover, Butlin played an important role in supporting classical sequence or old time dancing.

Before the introduction of ragtime and the early modern dances, apart from the few 'partner' dances such as the polka or Viennese waltz which have only one or two steps, all dances could be called sequence dances. Country dances – or minuets, gavottes and quadrilles – are all scripted; that is, everyone learnt a set routine and could therefore dance with anyone in the ballroom. But even as modern ballroom was growing in popularity during the early years of the twentieth century, old time (sometimes 'old tyme') dancing – or classical sequence, as it is now called – had continued. By the mid-1940s it surged in popularity. The ISTD formed a new division in 1947, the Victorian and Sequence Branch, to reflect this interest, and published its first examination syllabus the following year.[18] The professional syllabus included many dances with a long history that we think of as folk dances, such as the polka, varsouviana and mazurka, and the syllabus for amateurs comprised many dances which are still included

Butlin's Ballroom, created at Earls Court as part of the 'Health and Holidays Exhibition', 1947.

on programmes today, such as the valeta, barn dance and Boston two-step.

The biggest old time dancers' organization was probably the International Sequence Dance Circle (ISDC).[19] It was founded in 1944 by F. J. Mainey and claimed to have a membership in excess of 75,000, including in Australia, South Africa, Denmark and the Netherlands. The ISDC boasted a hundred affiliated clubs, schools and associations and made 'over 500 authentic descriptions of old time dances from the original copies available to all branches'. They also ran a weekend school all year round in Blackpool where 'old time dancing is taught correctly by qualified teachers.'[20] In March 1946 their second old time event, held at the Empress Ballroom in Blackpool, was the biggest that had been seen for more than fifty years. Two thousand members of the ISDC had taken part and, according to the *Dancing Times*, reports had reached the national newspapers and the newsreels.[21] Another key figure in classical sequence is Michael Gwynne, who had taken over an established letter service from a Welsh dancing teacher in 1949. Letter services like those of Alex Moore were a popular way to spread the word in the dancing community.[22] With a determination to make the steps clear for both leader and follower, Gwynne ensured that the dances were correctly scripted, focusing on footwork, tempo, direction, turn and full details of the follower's steps, which were almost always missing in early instruction manuals. His 1950 book (updated in 1971) *Old Time and Sequence Dancing*, with a foreword by Albert Cowan, chair of the OBBD Old Time branch, acknowledged that modern sequence had gained in popularity.[23] However, the foot positions – the five classical dance positions with turnout – and the glossary of largely French terms shows clearly his loyalty to the old time form.

Early radio programmes also played a role in popularizing old time. According to a report on the seventh annual London reunion of the Ball of the Year (hosting 4,500 people at the Empress Hall in Earls Court) in the *Daily Mail* in 1951, another old time specialist, Sydney Thompson, together with his wife Mary, had 'turned a radio diversion into a national pastime and a flourishing industry'.[24] He considered that their radio programme *Take Your Partners*, which had started in 1947, had led to as many as seventy old time dances being reintroduced to the ballroom. As well as the radio programme they sent out leaflets to more than 10,000 people. Thompson had started out learning the dances while working at a factory in Willesden, north London, and teaching them to his co-workers at their socials. Despite his humble beginnings, Thompson was probably as successful as Silvester and Moore through the BBC broadcasts and the annual balls at the Empress Hall at Earls Court – when crowds were often so big 'the police have been turned out to divert coachloads.'[25]

A. J. Latimer, the sometime master of ceremonies for the better-known *Those Were the Days* did much to promote old time through a series of books. The nostalgia promoted is clear in the foreword to his first *Bouquet of Old Time Dances*, published in 1948: 'In glossy pumps and peeping over the top of an absurdly high collar and drawing on very very carefully lest they should split and so shame me, my one and sixpenny pair of white gloves, I took from a tray in the hall a little slip of pink cardboard from which dangled a little pink pencil by a little pink cord.'[26] Despite the nostalgic reminiscences, the end pages and dust jacket reveal a rather more straightforward commercial approach and give more insight into the culture of the old time dancers. Columbia advertised recordings of Harry Davidson and the publisher Danceland advertised their eponymous monthly magazine, which had an 'Old Time corner' and old time records specially recorded by the Danceland Old Time Orchestra (on new unbreakable plastic, no-scratch discs).[27] Mecca Dancing's advertising for '100% Old Time Dancing' in London four nights a week – at the Lyceum, the Locarno, the Palais in Ilford and the Royal in Tottenham – is evidence of its popularity. There are also adverts from the various dance teachers' organizations. The BATD boasts that their prize dances from 1892 to 1920 are the principal 'Old Time Dances of today', and the Midland Association offers 'special attention' to teachers of old time dancing and an invitation to membership of a new association formed specifically for old time teachers. In only a few years the ISDC grew considerably and by 1948 their regular *Dancing Times* advertisements claimed to have '300 branches in 20 countries' and '90,000 members'. More recently, in evidence of its ongoing popularity the Old Time (Classical) Dance Society, with fifty founder members, was formed in 1984 with the aim of 'keeping Old Time dancing alive'.[28]

By the late 1940s sequence dances – the Lancers, quadrilles, the valeta, schottisches and many more – were once again being danced all over Britain, but despite their popularity and the numerous different dances available, the professional organizations still considered it necessary to introduce new dances to refresh the programme. In September 1950 the first competition for new dances was held at Hammersmith town hall, adjudicated by the OBBD. Of the twelve dances presented, the first prize was awarded to the Gainsborough glide, named by the inventors after their school in Edinburgh. The dance was in fact an updated version of a barn dance to a tune composed fifty years earlier.[29] The first modern sequence dance was the waltz Marie, followed by the Catherine waltz and the Georgella blues. Michael Gwynne's letter service was handed on to Holland Brockbank in 1969 and continued with Percy Lane in 1979 as the Brockbank Lane Sequence Script Service, which is exclusively licensed by the BDC. Brockbank and his wife Sylvia hosted the BBC's *Those Were the Days*, which continued to spread news about new dances and keep up interest. The Brockbank Lane service continues today: it organizes annual competitions for new dances in classical (old time), modern (ballroom) and Latin sequence, including in 2020 an online version, and the winning dance is circulated to several thousand subscribers worldwide.[30] Old time societies are still popular. The television journalist and presenter Angela Rippon is the patron of the Old Time (Classical) Dance Society, which has clubs across the UK; the English National Old Time Dance Society, formed as recently as 2015, is another such organization focused on what it refers to as 'traditional' old time, disapproving of the increasing numbers of what they consider to be inauthentic sequence dances.[31]

Why did sequence dancing rather than modern ballroom became so popular? Many of them are straightforward to learn and execute and each set of figures is rarely longer than the customary sixteen bars. Nostalgia might be another reason, both in the 1940s and today, when dancers are looking to find comfort in the idea of a better past. Old time dancers still sometimes perform in period costume and, for modern sequence, men in evening suits and white gloves is not unusual. James Nott records the observation made by women in a 1939 survey stating that they found the old time dancing 'spectacular and graceful' and 'more graceful in deportment and movement'.[32] Perhaps in the late 1930s and 1940s there was also the beginnings of a reaction to the coming of the Latin dances and a much more static approach to dancing in general. Sequence dances introduce variety and an element of sociability into the programme in the same way that party dances do. Similar to the Lambeth Walk and 'Knees Up Mother Brown', which had become hugely popular during the war years and which were more about liveliness and having fun than technique, sequence dances continue to be categorized by some – whether old time, modern or Latin – in the same way.

Modern dancing has always required an ability to improvise, which can be a big stumbling block in a social situation. Improvisation to an unfamiliar piece of music and with an unknown partner is a challenge, sometimes even for the expert dancer. Many leaders will persevere with the execution of a set routine, usually one memorized after a class, taking little notice of the mood of the music or their follower. Others will 'play safe' and resort to the simplest of figures, dancing cautiously without speed or enthusiasm. For followers, similarly, not knowing what will come next and wondering if they will be able to interpret the often imperfect lead can take much of the pleasure out of dancing. Guessing at or anticipating the next figure can cause collisions as well as risking insulting the leader. Sequence dances – once learnt – remove all the uncertainties for followers and particularly for leaders. The dances – and there are hundreds of them – have been choreographed by experts and have been tried and tested over many years by professionals and social dancers alike. We might safely assume, therefore, that those played most often in dance halls everywhere are of high quality. Certainly, once learnt they can be danced anywhere with anyone.

Whatever the reasons for its popularity in the 1940s and beyond, sequence dancing has retained its position alongside modern dancing and is still a feature of many social dance programmes – except perhaps at events where a higher number of competitive dancers or younger people are present, as it now tends to be associated with an older age group. Although some are energetic, we might accept the idea that in general sequence dancing is less strenuous and therefore better suited to those who might be less fit, but this has not always been the case. In the late 1940s the organizers of the Chelsea Week old time dance let over-seventies in free of charge to encourage their participation, stating that 'An old time dance is not really for old people. It is far more tiring than modern dancing.'[33]

Billy Butlin had been a member of the management committee responsible for programming at the Opera House in Covent Garden starting in 1939. The other members were Mecca's Heimann and Fairley, Bernard Mills and Captain J. Russell Pickering.[34] A season was to be reserved for opera and ballet, but their prime aim was to cater for the dancing public and success was expected as 'the boom in dancing is very evident.'[35] Throughout the war years, dancing was scheduled daily from 3 to 6 p.m. and from 7 to 11 p.m., and demonstrations and competitions were part of their plans. The large dance floor was arranged in a circle with tables all round and the band at one end, either William Franklin or Harold Garbutt and His Players. In 1940 they organized the Butlin's Professional Dance Championship, a one-day event approved by the OBBD, whose permission was required for all competitions to take place, but no more were held during wartime, although the social dancing continued.

After the war Butlin continued with his interest as a dance promoter and particularly old time dancing. The camps themselves provided the ideal location for competitions, with large dance floors, stages, top line orchestras, sound equipment and easily accessible, plentiful accommodation for the competitors. After discussion with Richardson a Butlin's National Valeta Competition was launched in 1948 in response to the surge in popularity of old time. According to Butlin, the boom began 'after the lifting of a bizarre ruling barring competitors under 30'.[36] Another reason, Harry Davidson said, was a reaction to the jitterbug and swing, which had arrived with

The valeta, as demonstrated by Michael Gwynne and his wife, one of the many old time and sequence dances once again in vogue by 1950 and popularized by Butlin.

American soldiers. The calmer old time was preferred because 'it gives the ballroom a different atmosphere. The middle-aged mix with the youngsters, and they all enjoy themselves.'[37] The Valeta is one of the first ISTD syllabus dances; partners dance in a variety of different holds, and other than its simplicity it is not clear why it was chosen rather than any of the other sequence dances.[38] The competition was very carefully organized with first heats taking place in dance halls all over the country, including at Butlin's camps. District finals were held in eight different cities across the country with a different dancing teachers' association taking charge of each one. The two winning couples from each district went to the Albert Hall in London for the finals at the two-day-long Butlin's Annual Ball, when six couples were selected on the first night to return to take part in the grand final on the second night. The prizes were generous: a week's holiday at any of the Butlin's holiday camps for all sixteen finalists and for the winners and runners up various cash prizes and trophies, including for the teachers who coached them.

It is not clear whether the standard of modern dancing was particularly high at the camps despite the 'choice of ballrooms . . . some of the best-known dance bands and the many free lessons with professional dancers every morning and afternoon'.[39] A writer in the *Dancing Times* considered that the general standard was very low and put this down to the availability of so many other physical activities. The standard of dancing for the old time session, however, was considered much better: 'If for no other reason than to encourage good ballroom deportment, a session of old-time dancing should be included in every programme; apart from this it is undoubtedly becoming increasingly popular, and will attract many new fans during the winter.'[40] The couples were obviously enjoying themselves too, which, the writer speculated, was due to the presence of Harry Davidson and His Orchestra. Championships in modern dancing covering single dances had ceased to exist once the OBBD took over control of all competitions but it seems there were many dancers enthusiastic about their reintroduction. In old time dancing a selection from three or four dances forms the basis for the competition, but the Butlin's competition – a big single dance competition – was clearly arousing enormous interest as heats were being held all over the country. Butlin continued with competitions with a new Annual

Dance Festival, which was to include a whole range of dance styles. The first one in 1950 was held at the camp in Pwllheli in Wales, and then moved to Filey in 1951. Wilfred Orange, ballroom promoter, studio owner, teacher and one-time chair of the OBBD, who was working for Butlin as entertainment manager at Filey at the time, was the perfect candidate for the job to run the festivals. The competitions were very successful and attracted considerable numbers, especially in the amateur categories. Although Alex Moore wrote that 'unfortunately the dancing seldom reached a high standard,' he had to accept that 'dancing is for the people and Butlin's cater for the people. Can one wonder at its success?'[41]

The atmosphere of the Butlin's holiday camps was perfectly captured by the photographers at the John Hinde Studios.[42] Perhaps considered garish or, worse still, tasteless, the exaggerated colours and extremes of composition reflect the exaggerated reality that was the intentional 'larger than life' ideal of the Butlin's escapist interiors – the perfected reality promoted in advertising campaigns. These were not realistic natural shots but carefully staged images. Exterior shots included strategically placed flowering plants, a bright red van or a girl in a red sweater, swimming pools with carefully draped individuals and dangling fronds and flowers; the interiors showed smiling crowds and themed decorative schemes. These photographs give us an image of the ballrooms, still in use for modern and sequence dancing, but now also for rock'n'roll or disco dancing. In the same way that Hollywood film sets captured a desirable lifestyle, the John Hinde images, commissioned for postcards and advertising, perfectly described the fantasy that Butlin created.

A Teddy boy dances with his girl at the Mecca Dancehall, Tottenham, London. Published in *Picture Post*, 29 May 1954.

TEN

Jitterbug, Rock'n'Roll and Jive

With the advent of Rock'n'Roll in 1956, Teddy boys took to the floor, and
very shortly Rock'n'Roll dancing became a 'sort of art form'.
'Dancing in the Dark: Rationalism and the Neglected Social Dance', 1993[1]

In Britain the post-war boom in the popularity of ballroom dancing continued well into the 1950s. With more leisure time and paid holidays for the working classes, dancing's popularity was ensured. Only the cinema could compete with ballroom dancing's attendance figures; it was to be a while before the widespread ownership of televisions would have a dramatic effect on leisure time. Radio, however, was now in every home and played a key part in its continuing popularity with programmes made specifically for a dancing audience. Harry Davidson's programme, *Those Were the Days*, targeted at older listeners, gave instructions for old time dances such as the barn dance, the valeta and the Lancers. It had started in 1943 and ran until 1976, and also helped to spread the word to a younger audience. As it became increasingly popular, *Those Were the Days* was broadcast on both the BBC's Light Programme and the Home Service. The first programme the BBC dedicated to 'pop music', aimed at a much younger audience, was broadcast for two hours every night at 10 p.m., ostensibly to compete with pirate radio stations active during the late 1950s and '60s but clearly necessary to reflect changing tastes. Radio 1, the first dedicated pop music station, was eventually introduced in

1967 when the BBC's Light Programme, Third Programme and Home Service were rebranded as Radio 2, 3 and 4 to further differentiate between audiences and their differences in musical taste.

The shift in music both in style and from live bands to recorded music during the 1950s was reflected in a similar big shift in the kind of dancing that was eventually to become acceptable. The 'party' dances and line dances, popularized during wartime, as well as the old time and modern sequence dances, were still included at many social dancing events, but the once common ballroom dances were increasingly sidelined as a wave of new dances arrived. First there was jitterbug, which was followed by the Latin dances: the Brazilian samba, the rumba and cha-cha-cha from Cuba and the Spanish-inspired paso doble from France. Latin dances had been introduced to British ballrooms as early as the 1930s, but it took a long time for them to be widely adopted. The body movements continued to be considered rather vulgar, and despite enthusiasm from professionals the rumba was the only Latin dance that had appeared as a single dance contest in the *Star* championships. Dancing professionals were determined to codify the new dances but experienced considerable difficulty reaching agreement.[2] Syllabus examinations for the Latin American dances had been introduced by the IDMA and the NATD in 1946, the Latin Branch of the ISTD had been created in 1947, and the dances had been approved by the OBBD for either three or four dance competitions in 1948. The syllabus was not finally agreed, however, until 1955, and Latin American dances were not accorded championship status until much later.[3] The jive was not added as the fifth dance until 1968.

The jive is very much the odd one out alongside the other Latin dances. It is a very fast dance; competition speed is 176 beats per minute, but it is often danced, especially socially, at a slower tempo of around 160 bpm or less. It has roots in a range of different swing dance forms, which probably contributed to the very long time it took to agree its final international form; but it is probably the best

'Come on you hep-cats and gators – jive!' Programme for Mecca's 1942 jitterbug championship at Sherry's Dance Hall in Brighton.

known of the Latin American dances due to its associations with the rock'n'roll music of the 1950s. The forerunner of the jive or rock'n'roll dances was the jitterbug, which, as most histories agree, was introduced in Britain by American soldiers in the early 1940s. In America dancing to the swing music that developed through the 1930s and '40s after the Charleston had lost its popularity took on various forms – Lindy hop, Balboa and collegiate shag, all very energetic and 'bouncy' – which were danced to various styles of music, such as rhythm and blues, boogie woogie and swing. The jitterbug was banned in many dance halls, because of its wild moves that included people being thrown up into the air and kicking in all directions. Margaret Cox was an enthusiastic dancer in the 1950s: 'I used to go dancing seven nights a week, but I was eventually made to stay in on a Thursday, but I used to love wearing my fluorescent coloured knickers and I had this very full swing skirt which used to fly out with petticoats, but I used to love to show my fluorescent knickers.'[4] Even as late as the early 1970s jive was not welcome in all ballrooms: 'During Saturday night dances with Joe Loss and his Orchestra, jiving was tolerated but only in the corner "stage left".'[5]

In 1940 Alex Moore had described a recent All England Jitterbug Championship in the *Dancing Times* as 'the most disgusting and degrading sight that I have ever seen in a ballroom', but went on to say that he thought there was nevertheless 'room for a mild jitterbug dance in our ballrooms at the present time'. He likened it to the introduction of the Charleston and its similar 'wildness', but suggested that, like the Charleston, 'before the inherent good taste of the average English dancer',[6] the exaggerated movements would soon disappear. Josephine Bradley similarly suggested that there could be a more polite version, and is recorded in a 1943 Pathé newsreel introducing a demonstration of jitterbug that she described as 'hardly a dance that will grace our ballrooms' by comparison with what she considered an acceptable version of the jive.[7] The same year the jitterbug, which was still causing problems, was banned at London's Royal Opera House after it had already been banned at what was still London's biggest dance hall, Hammersmith Palais.[8] Less disruptive versions of jitterbug or swing, of which there were many, grew in popularity and were tolerated at many dance halls until the arrival of rock'n'roll music, which reignited enthusiasm and once again caused an uproar.

The term rock'n'roll, coined in the 1950s, described the style of music with origins in America's long history of rhythm and blues, jazz and swing, and there are many versions of its rich and complex cultural history. The music, so very different from anything which

Jitterbug dancers at the Savoy Ballroom in New York's Harlem, 1954.

had gone before, is so familiar now it is hard to imagine the effect of its arrival in the early 1950s. There are conflicting stories of the 'first' rock'n'roll record. The most often cited contenders are Fats Domino's 'The Fat Man' (1950), The Dominoes' 'Sixty Minute Man' (1950) and Bill Hayley's 'Rocket 88'. Others include 'Gee' by the Crows, 'Rock around the Clock' by Bill Hayley and the Comets and 'That's All Right Mama' by Elvis, but the list is long. Once again, the new American music inspired a rock'n'roll dancing craze very much like those inspired by America's earlier exports of ragtime music in the 1910s and the Charleston in the 1920s.

Films still played a major role in communicating ideas, particularly about the latest tastes and fashions, and were key in spreading both the new rock'n'roll music and dancing. The film *The Blackboard Jungle* (1955) and the follow-up *Rock around the Clock* (1956), both produced by Sam Katzman, were intended to capitalize on the popularity of recent record releases by Bill Hayley and the Comets. *Rock around the Clock* was an enormous financial success, making bigger profits than the recent benchmark multiple Oscar winner *From Here to Eternity* (1953). It broke attendance records and is also often given credit for advancing integration as it included scenes of Black and white musicians playing together, but no one had predicted the astonishing effect it would have on audiences. Audiences, it seemed, were unable to restrain themselves from joining in with the screen action, as recalled by local Teddy boy Tony Lopez:

> I managed to get in with a friend of mine and I had a new Teddy Boy suit made for the occasion. We stood in there with everybody else and waited for the adverts to finish, the advertising films, and then as soon as Bill Haley started up literally the whole cinema got up and started dancing and that's where we, we danced right through the film never saw much of the film at all just danced right through it. That was the type of hysteria which was going around then.[9]

Once dancing in the aisles had become common at screenings, first exuberant and then more excessive behaviour led to disorder and in some instances fighting and riots. As a result the film was banned in several cities across Britain and elsewhere, including Venice for the film festival.[10] Although the bans probably fuelled its popularity, follow-up films *Chachacha Boom* and *Rhythm and Blues*, made to capitalize on the earlier hits, did not reach the same level of success or notoriety. Together with many other movies in similar vein made in the late 1950s, it became clear that young people were less interested in 'traditional' ballroom music and dancing and looking for something very different. They were still dancing in couples, but it was more often than not out of hold and in general much more energetic, signalling perhaps that it was meant to be enjoyed by the young only.

During the 1950s in Britain, a new 'teenage' market, particularly in clothing and music, had swiftly become established, and by 1957, 70 per cent of records were being bought by the much younger consumers. Rock'n'roll music and dancing was initially largely identified with the Teddy boy subculture that had started among London's working-class youth in the early part of the decade and had spread rapidly across Britain. Their distinctive style, which has seen several revivals at much smaller scale, was named after their Edwardian-styled clothing with long jackets and very narrow, ankle-skimming trousers. The Teddy girls or 'Judies' developed an androgynous look, opting for masculine tailoring lines and flat shoes in contrast to the prevalent ultra-feminine 'new look' of Dior with knee-length full skirts and kitten heels. Both Teds and Judies decorated their outfits with sparkly brooches, velvet collars and classy accessories. Rock'n'roll probably did not encourage bad behaviour and juvenile delinquency as some critics thought, but Teddy boys were often responsible for violent behaviour and racist incidents, which gave it a bad name by association.

The unruly behaviour identified particularly with Teddy boys was just one more worry for the dance halls to deal with. The dance hall business continued to expand, but providing venues where people would mix in large numbers meant that managers had to deal with social problems such as sexism and racism as well as drunkenness and rowdy crowds. In the immediate post-war period during central London's rebuilding phase, there were difficulties with building licences which affected key venues such as the Lyceum and the Café de Paris. Later, increasing bureaucracy and the practicalities of revised legislation associated with running dance venues, such as alcohol licensing laws and music copyright, had to be dealt with; the new Copyright Act introduced in 1956 made it clear that the 'copyright in a sound recording is infringed by causing it to be heard in public'; as a result, all teachers were obliged to obtain the necessary licences. One ballroom manager in Birmingham was even fined under the Betting and Lotteries Act for running a 'lucky spot', similar to the lucky programme or ticket number, a random chance to win a prize; in legal terms this constituted a lottery.[11]

As class distinctions were further eroded, the social situation that saw purpose-built ballrooms and dance halls provided for the working classes was now changing. Ballroom dancing was still enjoyed by a wide range of people, but it no longer had a clear social identity. A 1940 article in the *Dancing Times* noted how much dancing had transformed following the First World War: 'The hotel and restaurant dance after dinner or supper became general and the palais came into existence.' It went on to note that between the 'popular palais and the expensive hotel . . . the middle priced dancer was not catered for'.[12] In a different situation, an instance in 1940s Bournemouth reveals class issues in wartime: the strict command structures of the military mirrored hierarchical social structures, forcing the local army command to put the Pavilion Ballroom out of bounds to officers.[13] The reason was that dances tended to be crowded, resulting in officers and men often having to share tables, 'and it was obviously undesirable that these conditions should be allowed to continue' especially if 'after a Paul Jones [when couples change partners], it was said, officers might have to take their partners back to a table where privates were sitting.' Following considerable protest, the matter was eventually resolved by the local Army Command allowing their officers to go dancing during the week and only NCOs and men on the more crowded Fridays and Saturdays. In the mid-1950s the newspapers were still discussing dancing in relation to class. The *Daily Mail* counted dancing as a middle-class activity: 'Dancing as a pleasure to be enjoyed for its own sake, and practised as patiently as snooker or golf, belongs overwhelmingly to one section of society – to the huge, hardworking, decent, mild-mannered, over-taxed, under-paid, expense accountless middle class.'[14] However, an article in *The Times* tells us that 'British ballroom dancing is overwhelmingly a working-class affair attracting support mostly from the under 35s.'[15] We must take into account their respective target audiences – and also the finer distinctions between classes in the 1950s are perhaps not relevant here – to note that both are in agreement that it is definitely not an upper- or upper-middle-class affair. There were still those who condemned dancing, of course, as immoral and dangerous, especially for young women, but they were now in the minority. Dance halls had become an established local social space where the modern dances that had caused such uproar in earlier decades were considered sedate and no longer a matter of concern. The wealthier classes were still dancing but probably in more conservative environments at private events and society balls, where the now acceptable modern and more traditional dances were the norm and their status quo would not be upset.

Racist behaviour was another issue dance halls had to deal with, as well as some clearly racist policies which brought much negative publicity, particularly during the 1950s and early 1960s before the passing of Britain's Race Relations Act in 1965. The closure of the Paramount in London's Tottenham Court Road, where a large Black clientele had danced together with white dancers, as well as Mecca's own door policy, was blamed for incidents at the Lyceum. Black men were admitted only if accompanied by female partners, whether white or Black; managers would not run the risk of potential embarrassment or worse if – as they feared – white women refused to dance with them.[16] A protest against the door policy that refused entry to a group of young Black men resulted in one being arrested for causing an obstruction on the pavement outside. Reports of another incident at the Lyceum suggested Black men were responsible for 3,000 dancers being drenched with fire hoses.[17] A colour bar still in existence in 1958, at the Scala dance hall in Wolverhampton, was defended by the management but led to the musicians' union threatening a boycott along with other local trade union members.[18]

Despite ongoing social problems, one of the main reasons that dance halls enjoyed continued success was not directly related to the dancing itself. The dance hall had very quickly become an established and safe social space, particularly for women. It was a place where boys and girls could meet, where a man could approach a woman and ask her for a dance – something he could not do elsewhere. Mecca promoted the popular assertion that 60 per cent of marriages originated on the dance floor, although no reliable source of the statistic has been found. Schools also exploited the social benefits of dancing in their advertising with slogans such as 'You need never be alone when you can dance' and 'Don't be left out of the Christmas festivities'. Similar advertising material had been used in the 1920s in America by Arthur Murray appealing to those with less self-confidence, suggesting that 'subconsciously, they would like to have more friends and be more popular.'[19] Dancing at the dance halls and taking lessons, they were assured, was a guaranteed way to meet new people, make friends and even meet a mate.

During the 1950s and '60s the problems experienced by dance hall owners, their association with the working classes, and increasingly a clientele more interested in socializing than dancing deterred the more serious dancers. The ballrooms, with their idea of luxury and glamour and their imaginative and opulent decor, which Mecca and Butlin provided, had become familiar. The general dancers were less and less interested in technique and were becoming more interested in different kinds of music and dancing. A broadening range of leisure pursuits, the prevalence of pop music and the influence of TV all contributed to a growing distance between competitive dancers and social dancers. Alex Moore wrote frequently in the *Dancing Times* about the need for better publicity, concerned that TV was having the opposite of the desired effect, deterring potential pupils by showing the inevitably more expert competition dancers: 'We must get people into the studio first and then not make the mistake (so often made in this country) of trying to turn them into medallists before they have acquired and enjoyed the pleasures of simple Social (Rhythm) dancing.'[20]

Earlier in the 1950s, when the divisions between social and competition dancers was already beginning to show, a new competition was launched – one that again reinforced an element of glamour to ballroom dancing. The International was and still is held at a prestigious venue, London's Royal Albert Hall, and was introduced by one of ballroom's most glamorous dancers, Elsa Wells.[21] Wells had enjoyed a successful career as a professional dancer during the 1930s, and with her partner James Barrel (aka James Holland) is credited with originating some of the more athletic figures in the quickstep as well as using flamenco-inspired steps in tango dancing.[22] In the late 1940s, after the early death of her partner, she gave up her competitive career to open a studio in Bayswater. Likened by those who knew her to Marlene Dietrich, 'with a "head turning" air of superiority, elegance and beauty', and frequently referred to as a 'goddess', she became one of the most sought-after coaches.[23] The early International competitions, enabled through contacts of her husband, Lavy Batansky, were held to raise money for Israel's Friends of Jewish Agricultural Training, sponsored by the *Jewish Observer and Middle East Review* and supported by the Israeli ambassador Eliahu Elath, whose wife presented the prizes. The lavish first catalogue, with an embossed cover, large-format photographs of all the patrons, costly advertisements and the principal information interleaved with star-patterned gold pages, perfectly reflected the expectations of Wells and her glamorous reputation. John Kimche wrote: 'As editor . . . it is a great pleasure to follow in the footsteps of my colleague on the "Star" in sponsoring a great Dance Championship. I feel certain that competitors and visitors alike will spend an enjoyable evening and watch some memorable display.'[24] To establish the 'international' nature of the competition three professional couples, from Belgium, France and Holland, and one amateur couple from Denmark, were invited to take part and not obliged to compete in the first round.[25] The only other non-British couples were from Sweden, Ireland and Northern Ireland. The many British couples competing represented schools from across the country: Brighton, Liverpool, Newcastle, Manchester, Birmingham, Glasgow and Leicester. From the beginning and still today, the tickets could be sold many times over. The competition was immediately established in the annual dance calendar and has continued ever since: 'The International rates very highly, very very highly in the world, you get people from all over the world coming to dance at the International . . . it's a very important competition, it's an international competition, basically anybody can dance and it's a great venue.'[26] Today the increase in the numbers of competitors has led to several additional days of preliminary elimination rounds prior to the final heats, which take place on a single day.

In 1959 Mecca's Eric Morley launched the United Kingdom Championships, a professional and amateur competition to include the standard (ballroom) five and three Latin dances. Mecca also lobbied the ICBD for several years for permission to hold the World's Championships, which they were eventually awarded the same year. The World's have never held the same prestige as the other three major championships, but Mecca was keen to align itself with competitive ballroom as well as social dancing. Its proposals to include the Latin dances and add the tango led to much discussion and opposition in the professional press. The UK Championships and the International have both continued and become significant in the competition calendar, together with Blackpool, and have been run by *Dance News* since 1984 and 1977 respectively.[27]

Mecca was always looking at other ways to promote its business and in 1953 introduced the Carl Alan awards for the 'person who has done the most for ballroom dancing'. For Mecca it was, of course, a promotional tool but one that also engaged the professional community keen to see recognition for their discipline. Recipients of the awards include many of the prominent names in dancing: professional dancers as well as promoters, managers and others who make a contribution, such as Billy Butlin for the major dance festivals he sponsored and Peter West for his role as compère on *Come Dancing*. Although a seemingly good idea in the early years that helped sustain interest in dancing and engaged professional dancers and promoters alike, the awards have had a chequered history. Initially they lasted until 1984; after an absence of almost ten years they were reintroduced in 1993 by Butlin's, since when they have changed hands several times. First, the Stage Dance Council took over in 2000 and then *Dance News* from 2001 to 2004. The IDTA took over in 2007, sharing the task with the Theatre Dance Council with a democratic nominations process involving all the recognized dancing associations. The same democratic nominations system has continued since 2011, when the awards were taken over by Lorna Lee-Stylianos and Michael Stylianos.[28]

A *Guardian* article in January 1960 describing the Ritz in Manchester revealed that it was perhaps no longer clear what the dancing public actually wanted and the dancing public could no longer be thought of as one single category. At risk of compromise, the Ritz seemed to offer something for everyone in order to reach as many and as broad a range of customers as possible. It was open every day in the afternoon and every evening except Sunday. The tea dances were still considered important 'for mostly the older ones; night workers and girls who come shopping from out of town in twos and threes and like an hour or two here before they go home'; even for those who did not dance, creating the right atmosphere was still important – to keep the regular dancers – with low lighting, luxury decor and a smart dress code. In order to maintain a sense of decorum, Teddy boys and 'hot' jiving were banned, although ordinary jiving was tolerated in just one corner with only a few people doing it. Perhaps surprisingly, children were welcome – properly supervised, of course – and the manager was insistent that it must not become too 'homely' as this could deter both the businessmen and the teenagers. More significantly, the manager was already dividing the ballroom dancers into two distinct categories: one he described as the 'do-you-come-here-often variety', who were quite distinct from 'couples striding out in the dancing school way'.[29]

Bill and Bobbie Irvine competing in Berlin in May 1966. British dancers Brenda Winslade and Peter Eggleton took first place.

ELEVEN

Latin, the 1960s and Change

For several years my problem has not been to teach Latin and American Dances, but to try to convince the dancing public – and the teachers – that these dances are no more difficult than the English ones.

Latin and American Dances for Students and Teachers (1948)[1]

By the late 1950s the post-war return to ballroom dancing had resulted in around 5,000 schools operating across Britain, run by members of the various teaching associations working to the approved syllabus for the ballroom dances and keeping themselves up to date with the new Latin American dances. By the early 1960s the ISTD listed around 1,000 schools of dancing.[2] At a discussion at the annual conference of the Scottish Conservatives, a 1964 government social survey was used to demonstrate that, contrary to popular opinion, the UK was not a nation of 'TV addicts, football watchers, gamblers and bingo and pop fans'. Instead, the survey revealed that among other active hobbies, no fewer than 5 million people went dancing every week and a further 1 million were attending classes or lessons.[3] The same figures had been reported in the *Ballroom Dancing Times* in 1959 along with other statistics, though the writer made it clear that these were not necessarily accurate figures but the result of 'scanty information and inspired guesses'.[4] Whether or not these figures were accurate, there was considerable optimism that dancing would continue to be popular. Membership of the ISTD in January

1960 was around 6,000, with more than half in the then 'Recreational Dance' branch, the majority, 2,777, in Ballroom and just 459 in Latin American, many of whom would also be in the Ballroom section.[5] The performance-related dances – ballet, stage dance and so on – were then included in the Cultural Dance branch. It was thought that the new music and rhythms that appealed to a younger audience, particularly those new to dancing, would also attract older, more experienced dancers who had enjoyed the standard dances back to classes to learn the Latin dances. In the belief that the Latin dances were to inspire a new generation of dancers, Edmundo Ross, already a well-known bandleader in the nightclub circuit, opened his own school of dancing to concentrate on Latin American rhythms.[6] Interviewed in the *Daily Express*, he predicted that the merengue, a new dance from Dominica, would become far more popular than the cha-cha-cha, owing to its simplicity.[7] While the mambo and the cha-cha-cha had not appealed to British dancers because the steps were too intricate, the merengue offered simple steps that were much easier to learn and provided a foundation for improvisation. However, even this simpler version of Latin did not catch on.

Simplified figures and routines were offered by the 21 Top Rank Victor Silvester studios across Britain. The classes were aimed at people who were primarily keen to socialize and did not necessarily aim to perfect their technique to competition standard but instead wanted to learn enough to have sufficient confidence to be able to dance with anyone and not look foolish. If the simplicity offered by the Top Rank studios was their USP, others took a less modest approach, careful to use the correct terminology – they taught 'sophisticated swing' rather than jitterbug and were keen to promote what they considered 'proper' dances: the cha-cha-cha, paso doble and twist rather than the more casual hokey cokey, pachanga or Big Apple.[8] Some studios had also started offering lunchtime courses aimed at those who could not get to dances in the evenings, 'for the convenience of businessmen and businesswomen, housewives, office staff and shop assistants'.[9] The uncertain period for dancing during the 1960s saw the formation of the International Dance Teachers' Association (IDTA), a combined professional and teaching association to rival the ISTD. The various dance teachers' associations from across the country had been gradually joining forces, amalgamating to form larger groups until eventually the International Dancing Masters' Association (IDMA), formed in 1930, and the Dance Teachers' Association (DTA), following their merger with the Empire Teachers' Association, merged in 1967.

The standard or ballroom dances – the slow and Viennese waltzes, foxtrot, ballroom tango and quickstep, termed 'modern' in the early 1900s to distinguish them from classical dancing – were now deemed old-fashioned and conservative. Despite the hard-fought battle for its acceptability, the 'permissive society' of the 1960s was not bothered by body contact in close hold, 'steps' were largely irrelevant and progression around the ballroom was no longer important. The Latin dances were in general static, danced on the spot, and for the first time all kinds of body movement were considered acceptable, with hips and torso undulating and arms waving in all directions.[10] People were still dancing in couples but as much out of hold as in, or just holding one hand, and often individually executing quite different steps to their partner. By the early 1960s the twist had arrived – the extreme perhaps – a dance without any physical contact at all that would perhaps signal the end of partner dancing.

In the early days of public ballrooms in the late nineteenth century, the entire experience, including the decor and the dancing itself, was designed to reproduce the private ballrooms of the wealthy. That nostalgia continued as ballroom dancing maintained ideas of what was perceived as a more elegant past in the dances of the upper classes and their glamorous ballrooms, with men in tailcoats and women in evening dress. This image was perpetuated, with some Art Deco stylistic modifications, through Hollywood's version of the grand private ballrooms of great houses or the glamorous hotels and exclusive nightclubs of the 1930s. The same style, promoting ideals of luxury and glamour, was emulated by Mecca and other dance hall owners, encouraging their clientele to participate in a believable fantasy. A revival of Art Deco in the late 1960s, during which it was arguably more fashionable than in the original outing, failed to have any real impact on ballroom other than perhaps contributing to the return of longer dresses. Latin dancing, however, was to emulate a different 'other' – a different version of a glamorous lifestyle. It was no longer desirable to emulate the aristocracy – the landed gentry – now associated with a rather conservative, old-fashioned lifestyle. For Britons in the 1960s, when foreign travel to achieve the perfect suntan on a Mediterranean or tropical beach was soon to become available to all, the exotic now replaced the aristocratic as the new fantasy that was almost within reach. Dancer and historian Juliet McMains has written about the desire to emulate what she termed as 'brownness' and 'foreignness', and the necessity to wear dark shades of fake tan when dancing Latin. McMains suggests that fake tanning is not merely the stage make-up required under the harsh lighting but is also related to the changing ideas of glamour. As she writes, 'Both exoticism and glamour merge out of fascination with and fear of difference, a simultaneous desire to understand and to own the Other.'[11]

The Latin dances were not embraced by the British public and never reached the same levels of popularity as the standard or ballroom dances. The jive or rock'n'roll was popular with the public but came in for severe criticism. Leonard Morgan was vehement in his condemnation.[12] He wrote in the *Ballroom Dancing Times* in 1957 that rock'n'roll was merely another version of the jitterbug: 'no better than a violent and spasmodic type of dancing to jazz music' that has 'reached menacing proportions . . . Unless it is curtailed or absorbed it might well do irreparable harm to the English style. In fact it might make nonsense of our efforts over the last thirty years.'[13] The cover picture of the issue containing his tirade against rock'n'roll is of the star of the musical film *Chachacha Boom* – the follow-up flop to *Rock around the Clock* – with a caption that describes the Latin dances as 'bizarre', indicating that they were to come in for yet more criticism from professional dancers. For the Christmas 1957 edition the editor invited two leading exponents, Pierre and d'Erlimont, to contribute their views on the recent International Competition. Neither was very complimentary. Pierre was convinced that 'their knowledge of dancing is practically nil' as the dancers seem to know only one rhythm: 'They Jive to everything! They Jive the Rumba, they Jive the Samba, they Jive the Calypso. Some of them even Jived the Quickstep.' He was also disparaging about the ostentatious performances, pointing out that the competition was intended to find the best dancer, not the most spectacular: 'The old idea that rumba dancing consists of hip-wobbling and partners making goo-goo eyes at each other is unfortunately still very prevalent.' D'Erlimont agreed that 'each dance seemed to me to look like Jive' and had nothing positive to say, admitting to embarrassment at what he had witnessed: 'The exponents of the English Style were elegant in the extreme, but in the Latin American events they were unattractive and inept.'[14]

Despite much negative criticism, for the still growing numbers of competition dancers the Latin dances presented a new opportunity. It took many years for the different controlling bodies and teaching organizations to agree on the structure and regulation covering the new dances, despite the fact that the Latin dances had been enjoyed for several decades and were promoted by some of the best-known professional dancers. Pierre had built his reputation mainly as a tango dancer and went on to become a leading specialist for all the Latin American dances.[15] His 1948 self-published book *Latin and American Dances for Students and Teachers* was one of the first offering Latin American technique. It included a chapter covering instruction for each of four dances, listed as ballroom rumba, Brazilian samba, paso doble and American swing. A final chapter was dedicated to the 'Sistema Cubano o El Son' – the authentic version of the rumba, which places emphasis on the second beat of the bar, and which took many years to be accepted in Britain. Both versions of the rumba are still in use but Cuban is the approved international version. Pierre explored the authentic version of the dances through visits to Cuba and Brazil, and returned with photographs and films which he used to illustrate later editions of his book, including new rumba figures such as the 'Aida' and 'Kiki walks' that he named after his Cuban teachers. Later editions also included two versions of the jive, which he called 'American Swing (Jive)' and 'Slow American Swing (or Blues Jive)' and, of course, the cha-cha-cha.

Dimitri Petrides (1912–1985) too is sometimes credited as publishing the first Latin technique book, *The Latin American Dances*, in 1949.[16] Petrides had trained with and worked for Josephine Bradley, and like Victor Silvester had also spent time as a paid partner at London's ballrooms. Partnered with Gwenethe Walshe, one of Pierre's students, he established a reputation in Latin, winning contests and giving demonstrations.[17] But it was his wife, Nina Hunt, who was to go on to become much better known in the dancing world. Hunt was discovered – so the story goes – by Petrides when (as an out of work actor) she was serving in a shop, he saw her potential and trained her as a dancer.[18] She did not make a name for herself as a competitive dancer but became one of the most successful coaches. She had a reputation for innovative choreography and was reportedly one of the first to take training beyond the dancing itself with advice and instruction on personal appearance, diet and costume. She trained all the champions: Corky and Shirley Ballas, Alan and Hazel Fletcher, Donnie Burns and Gaynor Fairweather, and the Irvines, among many.

Led by Pierre, his partner Doris Lavelle, Doris Nichols, Petrides, Walshe and Hunt were all members of the Latin American branch of the ISTD, which had been set up in 1947. The revised technique was eventually agreed upon in 1955, and the cha-cha-cha was added later after Pierre had visited Cuba again, this time with Lavelle and James Arnell.[19] Walter Laird (1920–2002), another key member of the committee who contributed to the technique and syllabus in 1955, was the only other Latin dancer generally considered a rival of Nina Hunt's. His perfectionism and dedication produced *The Laird Technique of Latin American Dancing*, the first substantial book compared to the slight volumes of Petrides and Pierre. Published in 1961, it is considered the definitive work on the subject and has become the most widely adopted.[20] With his first partner, Ande Lyons, Walter Laird danced ballroom and worked in cabaret shows. Switching to focus on Latin dancing, with his next partner, Lorraine, he went on to win, among others, three World championships. His third partner, Julie Laird, has continued his work updating the technique book and is also credited with the introduction of the batucada in the samba.

In the early 1960s the twist, yet another American dance, was imported to Britain. It became popular quickly – it was very simple to learn, and, perhaps surprisingly, dance halls and schools took it seriously. Rank employed an American to teach it and Mecca's Joe Loss, resident at Hammersmith Palais, had composed a piece of music, 'Twist in the Mood', especially. Mecca, with an eye on profitability, considered that the twist would improve on its already impressive attendance figures, which were up from 300,000 in 1960 to 400,000 in 1961. As it took up so little space, the dance offered an answer to the problems of overcrowding that had dogged the industry for decades.[21]

The growth in the leisure industry in Britain continued, and dancing was still big business in 1961 when Mecca, still hugely successful, planned to merge with the British catering company Forte. Forte owned an impressive list of some of the best-known restaurants in the centre of London – the Café Royale in Regent Street, the Criterion in Piccadilly, the Talk of the Town, chains such as the Quality Inns and Fullers, the Waldorf Hotel, the Festival Pleasure Gardens and, of course, its own chain of around 150 restaurants across the country. Forte also had contracts to provide catering for some of the new kinds

The twist introduced the idea of dancing without any physical contact but still with a partner. Dancing at the Birdland Club, Munich, 1961.

of facilities related to the growing travel industry, such as airports at Gatwick and Edinburgh and motorway service stations, and it saw building motels as another potential investment opportunity beyond the leisure and entertainment sectors. Mecca was still the most successful dance hall business in Britain. It owned forty dance halls all over the country, including the Hammersmith Palais and eleven others in London, as well as dozens of restaurants and pubs. Its continued expansion meant employment opportunities for women in particular. Connie Page was working at the Locarno in Stevenage the first night it opened:

> my friend and I we went down to see what was going on and there were hundreds of young women around about the same age as ourselves. We nearly all had young children and the idea of an evening job was quite appealing and um, so they said yes um you will be divided into two groups Ballroom Staff and Catering, this lot are catering, that lot's Ballroom. It didn't matter what you had done before or hadn't done.[22]

Mecca built new local ballrooms in Bradford (1961), Stevenage (1961) and Hull (1962) and undertook a major project to convert the Empire Cinema in Leicester Square to a new ballroom in the very centre of London, which was completed at the end of 1962. It still owned several subsidiary companies for publishing and a musicians' agency. Mecca had rejected a £30 million takeover bid from another of its rivals, Rank, which owned 29 ballrooms, with a counter-offer to take over its ballroom interests.[23] Mecca also experimented with what it called 'mini-ballrooms'. In a deal with Temperance Billiard Halls it planned fourteen new venues for dancing with full catering facilities, most in the London region and two in Manchester. An innovation by this time was using recorded music in place of live bands.[24]

Mecca (mainly) and Rank (to a lesser extent) still dominated the ballroom and dance hall business but there were other independent operators. The Rivoli Ballroom in Brockley, south London, which was listed in 2007, is one of the few remaining public ballrooms still in regular use for dancing. The design dates from 1957, a conversion of the Crofton Park Picture House designed by Henley Attwater in 1913. From the outside the building is largely insignificant: a modest Art Deco front with a stepped parapet and urns that were added in the 1930s. On regular public dance nights, the hole in the wall outside still operates as the box office and it is cash only. But once inside, the Rivoli brings together all the archetypal elements we expect. The vast sprung maple floor is lined with banquette seating with a stage at one end and, at the other, an upper-level balcony. The high ceiling is a shallow vault with both fringed Chinese lanterns and twinkling French chandeliers side by side. The colour scheme is red and gold. Red velvet covers the banquette seats, red carpet covers the seating areas, and the walls are embellished with framed, padded fabric and gilt-trimmed panels. There is an eclectic mix of Neoclassical motifs, oriental and Art Deco elements, including hardwood marquetry panelled doors to the powder room. A bar stretching the length of one long side completes the late 1950s ambience with booths on either side and original decor. The Rivoli must be one of only a very few buildings that are listed for their contribution to dancing. In addition to the two more usual reasons for the Rivoli's listing – the architectural and historical interest of the interior and as 'a rare surviving example of a once common conversion of an early C20 cinema to a ballroom' – the third is 'as an eloquent and unusual witness to the era of American jive and swing bands, Lindy Hop, Jitterbug and Rock'n'Roll, alongside the continued popularity of traditional strict tempo ballroom'.[25]

Another cinema conversion in Glasgow, where there were no fewer than thirty licensed dance halls – the biggest with a capacity of as many as 1,700 dancers – is another witness to the impact of TV on cinema audiences in the late 1950s. The report in the *Ballroom Dancing Times* tells us that a dance hall, unlike any cinema it might replace, is 'not an impersonal entertainment emporium' but has 'a highly individual character', and that even with so many in and around the main Sauchiehall Street, each has its own loyal clientele.[26]

By the 1960s not all new ballrooms were designed in the Neoclassical style. The Student Union building on the campus at Keele University built in 1963 included a ballroom; it is included here as probably one of the last such spaces to be designed and built in Britain. Together with the ballroom and the Student Union offices, the brief to the architect Stillman & Eastwick-Field included the usual social spaces, bars, offices and games rooms. The three-storey building they designed has a ground floor used for the reception areas, bar, offices and various storerooms and all the main activities on the first floor. The ballroom was already intended to be a multi-purpose space, as with many in town halls and other public places which were often used as assembly halls or meeting spaces for other events. The building is designed in a Modernist style. The double-height ballroom, big enough for three hundred couples, is at one end reached by a long straight flight of stairs in the centre of the building. Unlike the Mecca halls and those of previous decades decorated in Louis XIV style, the Keele ballroom does not conform to the same notions of glamorous decor. It is fully functional, with a perfectly proportioned sprung maple floor, a small dais for a band, and viewing galleries on two sides at the upper level reached by spiral staircases. It is undecorated but the materials are of high quality – there is nothing flimsy or superficial. The timber is all solid hardwood and white marble granules have been added to the concrete to make the surface sparkle. The walls are clad with timber battens with gaps intended specifically to enable the fixing of temporary decorations for individual themed parties and events. The staircase adds to the sense of drama, as it leads directly to the ballroom in one long processional space, recalling the importance of promenading.

The new decade's changes in music style – the advent of Latin dances, the twist and with it more generally an acceptance of solo

The ballroom in the Student Union building at Keele University, designed by Stillman & Eastwick-Field, 1963. One of the very last to be built.

dancing – inevitably had an effect on ballroom, which still represented a significant proportion of the leisure industry. The financial
worth of the dancing business – the dance halls and the individual
dancing teachers and their studios – was the subject of much speculation. Victor Silvester clearly had considerable earning power. Aged
64 when his TV show ended in 1964, he was not considering retire-
ment. With a platinum disc for more than 3 million record sales, a
BBC contract for three sound broadcasts a week, and bookings for
dance halls a year ahead at a minimum of 250 guineas a night, the
rumours suggesting he was worth half a million pounds were probably true.[27] In America the Arthur Murray studios had continued to
grow during the 1950s with an incredible 2,000 new students each
week, but this was a feat they were unable to repeat in Britain.[28] Since
opening his first dance school in 1925, his chain of franchised studios had grown to 72 studios by 1946, and during the 1950s he had
a successful TV programme, *The Arthur Murray Dance Party*. In 1954
the *Ballroom Dancing Times* reported that despite Arthur Murray's
'enormous chain', 'The standard of performance is not, in any way,
as high as the general standard in this country; the technique has not
been developed to such an extent and competitions are compara-
tively few.'[29] He had opened his first studio in England in London's
Leicester Square in 1955, but by 1964 business was slowing down and
the Murrays retired and passed the business to a group of investors.
Although operating as a worldwide franchise, there are just three
Arthur Murray studios in Britain, all in London. They focus primarily
on social dancers and the simplest dances and are not in general associated with the training for competitive Ballroom and Latin.

In the 1950s Alex Moore was still earning a lot of money through
his letter service, which was being sent out to forty different countries,[30] and Sydney Thompson, who had accurately predicted the
rise in the popularity of old time dancing, was holding annual reunion dances that filled the Empress Hall at Earls Court with members
of the 30,000 clubs that now operated across the country. It is

impossible to know what the dance hall business was worth. Some sample comparative statistics reported in the financial pages tell us that, based on entries to dance halls between 1953 and 1956, the numbers of dancers increased from 4 to 5 million. The earnings of the IDMA for medal tests increased from £17,842 to £20,262 in just one year from 1954 to 1955.[31] Peter Millen, chair of the Association of Ballrooms and the manager at the Hammersmith Palais, was keen to establish that ballrooms were no longer the overcrowded, rowdy places they once were. 'Good' managers, the only ones Mecca would employ, could ensure that potential troublemakers were excluded, and 'if a ballroom isn't grossing twice as much money as it did in 1937 there is something wrong with it.'[32] A decade later, despite concerns about changing tastes and their diversification – bingo had already been introduced at many of its venues – Mecca dance halls continued to be successful. The 1964 expansion in both dance halls and 'Bingo casinos' resulted in a 23 per cent rise in pre-tax profits and an almost 50 per cent rise in net income the following year – 'the biggest rise the group has had in one year'.[33]

While it seemed that many of the dancing schools were still experiencing success in terms of the numbers attending, Mecca had already identified changes in its clientele and had been working hard to attract dancers from all sections of society. The professionals were also aware of the growing difference between social and competitive dancers. Keith Jones, president of the NATD, wrote an article entitled 'Social Dancing or Anti-Social Dancing' intending to warn dancing teachers of the coming changes in public taste that threatened the industry as people were becoming less interested in ballroom dancing. While his definition of social dancers is clear, the 'anti-social' dancers, as he described the competitors, were not popular with the ballroom proprietors:

> Their steps are complicated to the extreme and their movement, although beautiful, is developed to cover an enormous amount

of floor. If a reasonable crowd is present we have constant
collisions each followed by either a glassy smile or an indignant
frown. Competitions, I feel sure, do not popularise dancing;
they make the dancers part of another world, with the girls
in exaggerated dresses containing yards of net which makes
them look like tea cosies topped with an extreme hair coiffure
lacquered to the texture of amour plate.

He blamed television to an extent and the cult formed by the competitive dancers who considered themselves better than the rest. The
situation is little changed today; competitive dancers are rarely seen
at social dances, preferring to dance at practice sessions where there
are smaller numbers and the dancers are all expert. His conclusion
was: 'It is obvious that these two paths are moving further and further
apart. The advanced dancers are becoming more stage conscious every
day, becoming almost a ballroom ballet section, and are looked upon
with awe rather than interest by the vast majority of social dancers.'[34]

The increasing division between social dancers and competitors at
a time when there was more interest in much simpler dances and the
Latin dances were not being taken up conspired to make a difficult
time. There were also continuing issues with the various authorities
still working on the definitive versions of the Latin dances, which
were not accorded championship status until 1964. In 1960 a dis-
pute with the BDF led to the British dancers boycotting the World's
Championships held in Berlin because of a decision to include the
Latin dances.[35] The result of the boycott, however, was a dramatic start
for a couple new to the competitive circuit. Bill Irvine from Scotland
and his wife, Bobbie Irvine, a South African champion, despite currently training in England, decided not to withdraw but to enter the
competitions as South Africans. They were well received by the
20,000-strong crowd, were interviewed for the Eurovision screening,
and took second place in the Latin and then first place in both the
ballroom and the Nine Dance competitions held on the second day.

In Irvine's words, 'In a way it was an empty victory because the best couples from Britain were not taking part.'[36] Aware that the situation would not make them very popular with their colleagues in England and despite advice from one of the adjudicators that they should perhaps 'quit while they were ahead' and continue as planned on their way back to South Africa, the Irvines were instead spurred on to prove that they could compete with the best British dancers. They returned to London to train for the *Star* Championship and then Blackpool and made the final in both. They also managed to avert a call to have them thrown out of the BDF for ignoring the boycott. Their competition success continued throughout the 1960s and they went on to win thirteen major titles before retiring.

Describing their visit to the Europa competition in Germany in 1962, Bill Irvine states, 'The English couples were high on the list of probable winners, as they always are at any overseas event. (This isn't conceit – it *is* so.)'[37] In 1966 Peter Eggleton and Brenda Winslade came first in all the modern dances, and Bill and Bobbie Irvine won the Latin American competition, both dancing for Britain. However, Phyllis Haylor noted that German couples were placed second, beating the other British favourites, and suggested that this could signal the end of British supremacy in ballroom dancing.[38] The numbers of competitors from other countries were increasing each year, and eventually in 1975 the Blackpool Dance Festival launched the British Closed, a separate competition that would, of course, allow for easier rankings.[39] For forty years almost all the major championships had been won by British couples. Haylor attributes the change to the impact of an earlier generation of British dancers now teaching worldwide. For years dedicated dancers had visited Britain to attend the annual congresses of the dancing organizations, but the situation was now reversed and as travel became more accessible British dancers were now in demand, visiting other countries, invited to lecture and examine their pupils, and some leading British coaches had also started training couples on a semi-permanent basis abroad.

Sonny Binnick and Sally Brock, British Professional Open champions during the 1950s, who were probably the first British champions to work in America after retiring from competition, had already reported that 'so many teachers are now showing interest in the English Style that it is likely to be adopted on a national basis.'[40] As early as 1953 Victor Silvester had pointed out that 'Ballroom has become one of our most important artistic exports' and 'has been assiduously copied on the continent, in Japan and India as well as in most of the Commonwealth countries'.[41] Sales of technical books and strict tempo records and chains of schools, in North America particularly, employing 'English professionals' to teach, all contributed to establishing English ballroom dancing internationally. A lengthy article in *The Times* in 1956 claims: 'Britain in fact, is pre-eminent in ballroom dancing. No other nation has such style, so many entrants for the annual ballroom events or such support from its public . . . the ballrooms and the Palais de Danse have become an important social influence, an influence, moreover, entirely for good.'[42]

Frank and Peggy Spencer demonstrate a tango hold.

TWELVE

Television, *Come Dancing* and Peggy Spencer

It is difficult to understand the attitude of the British press. Similar successes for British skaters, swimmers or tennis players would be front-page news with interviews and photos. Our dancing champions should be household names. They bring us great prestige abroad. After all we have more competitive dancers than competitive skaters or swimmers or tournament tennis players.

Come Dancing (1968)[1]

The arrival of television during the 1950s was to have a significant impact; it made dancing much more visible and with the well-spoken compères in evening dress it initially gave dancing a new respectability. The first TV programme that showed 'glamorous ballroom dancers' had been broadcast in 1937, according to BBC historian Bob Lockyer, former producer for dance at the BBC and founding chair of Dance UK, although no record remains.[2] The International Championships were broadcast on both radio and TV in 1957, and while the *Ballroom Dancing Times* praised the commentary by Elsa Wells and cricket commentator Brian Johnston, the black-and-white images were considered only a poor second to the real thing.[3] The first BBC programme entirely dedicated to ballroom dancing was the TV *Dancing Club*, launched in 1948 and hosted by Victor Silvester, which ran until 1964. The programme was based on his radio show *Dancing Club*, on air since 1937, which featured his strict tempo

Ballroom Orchestra and included instruction for the various dances. The television version followed a similar format with instruction, competitions judged by popular vote and expert demonstrations 'to bring the glamour and elegance of good ballroom dancing into your homes'.[4]

Silvester had all the right credentials as an experienced and successful dancer, chair of the ISTD from 1945 to 1958, a successful musician and author of several instruction books on ballroom dancing. He had formed a dance band in 1934, the Victor Silvester Ballroom Orchestra, one of the first 'strict tempo' dance bands which ensured that dancers could rely on music played consistently at the correct speed throughout the duration of the dance. By the late 1940s he was already a household name, and his standing in the dancing profession, broadcasting reputation and best-selling records made him the obvious choice to host the transfer of the programme to television. Despite his reputation – or perhaps because of it – he fell out of favour with the dancing profession. Since starting his strict tempo recordings in the 1930s he had sold millions, and his radio and television shows provided the perfect promotion for his record sales. By the late 1950s dancers were tiring of the same tunes and the same arrangements, and Pye Records decided it could compete with something less monotonous and more inspiring. John Warren's 'strictempo' orchestra made the recordings, even utilizing a metronome to ensure that the exact tempo was played throughout.[5] The fact that Silvester effectively held a monopoly on dance music was not the only cause of offence. His approach to teaching was yet more unpopular with professionals.

Silvester had started working with the Rank organization in 1957 with a proposal to run dancing schools in their Odeon and Gaumont cinemas across the country. Cinema buildings, because of their size and layout, often included space for dance floors. Most dance schools were run as very small businesses, and many saw the coming of Victor Silvester and Rank as unfair competition. When the first two schools were announced – at the Gaumont Theatre in Lewisham and the Gaumont State in Kilburn – several London schools and their teachers grouped together to take a complaint to the ISTD, demanding that Silvester be asked to resign his chairmanship in the face of what they considered a blatant conflict of interest. They were unsuccessful and the plans went ahead, with eventually 23 schools which catered for around 22,000 pupils.[6] They taught deportment and good manners as well as dancing, and sold a wide range of Victor Silvester-branded merchandise such as cufflinks, shoes and dance manuals. Silvester was not averse to earning money from advertising; he saw his autobiography, *Dancing Is My Life*, described as 'a story of greater humour and sadness, romance and tragedy than many could ever know', serialized in *Woman's Own* magazine along with his endorsement of a dress pattern.[7]

The complaints did not stop there. Later in 1959 several dancing teachers' associations complained directly to the OBBD, insisting that it take some action in light of what they considered his unethical conduct. Instead of advertising for qualified teachers, Silvester was looking for amateur dancers, whom he called 'personal tuition partners', to dance with the pupils in his classes. They feared this would encourage more unqualified teachers, threaten their own standing as professional teachers and lower standards. In his defence, Silvester argued that dancing with a skilled dancer was of great benefit to pupils who would otherwise be dancing with complete novices, and further argued that in any case paying them was preferable to simply allowing them into classes free, which most other schools did. The OBBD was unable to impose any sanction, as there was no professional code of conduct in place. The OBBD was again asked to intervene concerning the TV *Dancing Club* when Alex Warren brought to its attention the fact that Silvester was not formally qualified to adjudicate Latin American dancing.[8] As with previous complaints, Silvester's position seemed once again unassailable, and he insisted that he knew enough about the dancing through his many

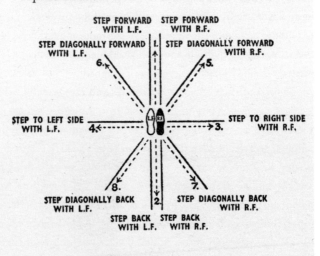

THE DIRECTION OF YOUR STEPS

The diagram below shows you the directions in which steps are taken.

The feet are shown in parallel position in the centre, this being the Starting Position for the Twentieth Century Sequence Dances. For the dances in the traditional style they should be turned out—in 1st Position.

The directions in which steps are taken, as shown below, are exactly the same for both Old Time and Twentieth Century Sequence Dances.

STEP FORWARD WITH L.F.   STEP FORWARD WITH R.F.

STEP DIAGONALLY FORWARD WITH L.F.   STEP DIAGONALLY FORWARD WITH R.F.

STEP TO LEFT SIDE WITH L.F.   STEP TO RIGHT SIDE WITH R.F.

STEP DIAGONALLY BACK WITH L.F.   STEP DIAGONALLY BACK WITH R.F.

STEP BACK WITH L.F.   STEP BACK WITH R.F.

18

As well as instructions for the individual dances, manuals included information on direction and relative position in the ballroom.

years of experience and did not have the time to sit more examinations. Recognition from the establishment for his work came in 1961 when he was awarded an OBE for services to ballroom dancing. But just a few years later, in 1964, his long-running TV *Dancing Club* finally came to an end, unable to compete with its rival, *Come Dancing*.

When *Come Dancing* started in September 1950, it was shown on Mondays alternately with TV *Dancing Club*. Both were live outside broadcasts and were scheduled at 10.15 p.m., a time unpopular with audiences but necessary to allow the amateur dancers enough time to get to the ballroom and into their costumes and make-up, ready for the show after their day jobs. By the time TV *Dancing Club* ended in 1964 after sixteen years, it was the BBC's longest running programme; however, its audience figures had dropped from 9 million at the end of 1962 to 5 million by the end of 1963. It could not compete with *Come Dancing*, which during the same period had seen its audience figures increase from a similar start point of 8.5 million to close to 10 million. TV *Dancing Club* was seen to be more closely aligned with the schools and their efforts to teach the correct way to dance, whereas *Come Dancing* was more closely aligned with the dance halls and embraced the new music and styles and the social aspects of

Peggy Spencer and Victor Silvester demonstrating on TV *Dancing Club*, *c.* 1955.

dancing. *Come Dancing* was also, perhaps, more in tune with a younger audience – Victor Silvester was over sixty – who were now interested in taking up the new kinds of dancing, particularly the Latin rhythms and jive, and it was to become yet more popular with the introduction of formation teams and regional competitions.

Come Dancing, which continued for many more years, had a considerable impact. It was a challenging programme to make but popular with everyone involved. The entertainment format of the show and its high viewing figures attracted a range of commentators and television personalities such as Terry Wogan, Michael Aspel, Noel Edmonds, Pete Murray and Angela Rippon as well as well-known sports journalists Brian Johnston and Peter West. Producers liked the challenge of broadcasting from different locations and the thrill of live shows with an audience. For the professional dancers it offered new opportunities for employment as demonstrators, adjudicators and commentators, and for the competitive dancers it was a chance to appear on TV. For the casual or social dancers, it introduced the best-known names in the competitive world.

For those performing or competing it was often revelatory. Few would have had access to film equipment to assist with their training, so the TV close-ups of particular steps, facial expressions and posture seen in detail could be of great benefit. There were, however, some negative responses. The authorities were concerned that TV might upset the all-important distinctions between professionals and amateurs. Television was also considered to have a rather negative effect on the staging of the World's at the Lyceum in London in 1959. The numbers of contestants per country was limited to two, and although the event was well managed it lacked the atmosphere of a championship, as all focus was on the television presentation.[9] During a programme, the cameras would sometimes focus on just one couple, introducing them by name, which could be construed as a performance or a demonstration – strictly forbidden to those holding amateur status. For some, particularly the less competent social dancers, it had a negative effect too: seeing the high standard of danc-ing and the sophisticated version of familiar dances that they enjoyed in a more casual way was off-putting and even intimidating.

Come Dancing will always be remembered, however, for introduc-ing the grande dame of ballroom, Peggy Spencer. Throughout her life, Spencer was a major influence on the ballroom world through her work as a teacher, choreographer and adjudicator and a wide range of related work in TV and radio that kept her in the public eye.[10] Peggy Spencer had partnered Victor Silvester on his TV show and sometimes provided him with the choreography for his instruction sessions. She was also a member of the ISTD Latin committee working to agree the syllabus and write the technique books. She was ready to embrace all dance styles, collaborating with Edmundo Ross to adapt the new Latin rhythms and one of the first to introduce disco dancing in the late 1970s. Later in her career in the early 1980s she went into busi-ness with Geoff Hearn, initially to sell proper dancing shoes to persuade her pupils out of their street shoes. As Hearn and Spencer Ltd, they took over Alex Moore's letter service and gradually diver-sified into the provision of all things ballroom-related, including a mail-order service. Hearn and Spencer handed over the business to Malcolm Hearn and Keith Hoyle in 1996, and the name was changed to DanceSport International Ltd in 2000.[11]

Peggy had started teaching during the war years. 'With lots of lads at a loose end, she and Frank's then wife, Sylvia, decided to try teaching dancing. They started in crowded air raid shelters then moved on to a local Sydenham café where they would move the tables and chairs back after closing time. In those days she was often just one step ahead of the pupils!'[12] She was taught by Phyllis Haylor and Doris Nichols, but learnt most from her second husband, Frank Spencer, a skilled ballroom dancer, once he returned from overseas postings in 1945.[13] In 1950 Frank and Peggy Spencer established themselves at their own premises, the Royston Ballroom in Penge, south London. They toured with Walter Laird and Ande Lyons as a two-couple performance team in Ballroom and Latin in the late 1950s and became well known for demonstrations and innovative cabaret work.

Among her many achievements, Peggy is probably best known for formation dancing and her famous creation, the 'Penge Formation Teams', which were almost sure to win every competition they entered for nearly forty years. 'Pattern Dancing', as formation was originally known, had been included in competitive dancing events in the 1930s, but there is little information to be found about the content and standard.[14] Frank and Peggy Spencer first entered a formation team competition in 1938, the *Star* ball, with an unsuccessful four-couple quickstep routine. Formation dancing was included in the Blackpool Festival in 1957, and the first European formation team championship was held in 1965. Reporting on their winning the Butlin's formation team trophy, Alex Moore stated that the Spencer 'Penge team proved that clever patterns danced with finish and finesse will always beat the formations which depend on skirt twirling and the static tableau type of formation in which white gloved men stand about looking as lifeless and sometimes as ludicrous as tailors' dummies.'[15]

The appearance of the formation teams on television attracted many to aspire to join, such as Angela Thurgood, who started dancing at Peggy Spencer's school as a teenager in 1962:

> I'd seen the teams on television and they just looked so wonderful . . . and I went to the ballroom. I couldn't dance at the time and just like everybody else took classes. Then I started taking lessons and was eventually invited to join the Latin team as a reserve. In those days, the teams really were very famous, and Peggy could have her pick of people she wanted in the team.[16]

By all accounts Peggy Spencer was a tough teacher, demanding dedication and commitment from everyone involved. For those who did not show the requisite commitment, there were many other

Peggy and Frank together with Walter Laird and Ande Lyons. The 'Dual Dancers' regularly appeared in cabaret performances and gave expert demonstrations.

dancers ready to take their place in the formation teams. Keith Gregory, a member of the ballroom formation team in the 1950s and a successful competition dancer too, recalls how Peggy insisted that, however successful, the dancers should continue to challenge themselves: 'Rita [Withers née Probert] and myself, we were competing almost every weekend and every competition we went into we won. And Peggy says, right, I'm going to change the rules. You can only win a competition four times, then you've got to do something else – go up to a different category.'[17]

Discipline for the formation teams was paramount. As Angela Thurgood noted:

> She was very, very strict, we all called her the sergeant major. We did exactly what we were told . . . we were completely dedicated. All our spare time was dedicated to dancing. We were all having

The Penge Ballroom eight-couple formation team, 1957, photographed at the Royston Ballroom.

private lessons, and the standard was terrifically high. When we were rehearsing, we quite often had to dance on our own, you had to dance your part on your own, without your partner and she would put you with another partner, you had to dance in other positions as well. And we were always told, if anything happens to your partner, if they pass out or whatever, you carry on, you just dance, leave them, don't worry about them, somebody else will pull them off the floor and see to them, but you just carry on – dance on your own.[18]

Regular weekly rehearsals were held on Friday evenings and Sunday afternoons, but they also went on at other times. Frank Fronda, captain of the Latin team during the 1960s, held rehearsal sessions in the school hall where he was a teacher. He also recalls practising until two in the morning at the Royston after it was closed for normal classes and lessons.[19] Angela too remembers the extra effort needed before a competition: 'If there were any big comps coming up – we would get to the ballroom at 10.30 in the evening, when everything finished, for more practice.'[20]

Training teams in the Penge studio started in order to deal with the problem of having too many couples in the studio at the same time. After giving them a short routine to learn, Peggy divided them into two groups to compete against each other – simultaneously helping with the floor space problem and encouraging them to learn faster. Once the competitive spirit took hold, it spread to other studios and continued to grow. By the late 1960s, the Penge studio was still regularly taking in between 3,000 and 4,000 new pupils each year, indicating that dancing had maintained its popularity. And – again – according to Frank Spencer, 'The dance floor is the biggest marriage bureau in the world . . . and with ballads back in the hit parade – especially since Engelbert Humperdinck's "Last Waltz" – teenagers are coming back to learn to dance.'[21] By then the studio's formation

The Penge Latin Formation team competing at Blackpool, *c.* 1960.

teams trained by Frank and Peggy were well known for their regular
TV appearances and for winning almost every formation team
competition.

For the team members, along with the regular rehearsals and
lessons, entering competitions meant additional expense, time off
work and time spent travelling. Angela Thurgood recalled: 'I remem-
ber on one occasion we travelled up to Blackpool, and we did the
competition, and we won. And then after the comp we got the coach
home again, and we drove through the night. I worked near Fleet
Street at the time – I was dropped off there in the early hours, found
a café, had a cup of coffee, waited till it was time to go to work. That's
what it was like, no Razmatazz, no fuss.'[22]

Beyond outings for social dancing and group classes, competitive
ballroom and Latin dancing was, and still is, undoubtedly an expensive hobby. Members of the Penge formation teams contributed
competition subs each week and, as amateurs, were never paid for cabaret or TV appearances. Expenses included dresses and shoes on top
of fees for classes and private lessons. The costumes were a key part of
presentation – even the stripes on a dress played a part as the dancers
moved – and were all-important to Peggy. Her daughter Helena was
a member of a ballroom formation team in the 1950s:

She [Peggy] designed the dresses which were often quite dramatic
contrasting colours, like black and yellow or emerald and white,
and we sat and stuck the sequins on ourselves . . . and we all had
to buy white satin shoes and dye them ourselves with Dylon
dyes in the specific colour. We would stand on a table, with the
scissors ready, to have our dress hems adjusted – to suit the line
rather than the individual – and we all had to have long hair so
that Peggy could have everybody styled in identical French plaits.

In fact, she was very keen that everyone looked the same, so
that individuals could not be identified. She encouraged the TV
cameramen to introduce overhead shots – Busby Berkeley-like

The Tower Ballroom, built by the Blackpool Tower Company in 1894 as part of their ambitious project to provide entertainment spaces for working-class holidaymakers. Designed and extended in 1913 by renowned theatre architect Frank Matcham, it still retains its elaborate decor.

The Rainbow Room on the 65th floor at the Rockefeller Center, 1934, has similar design elements to the nightclubs in Astaire and Rogers's films: a 'luxury ocean liner aesthetic' with symmetrical curved stairs descending to a circular rotating dance floor, a domed ceiling and panoramic views of Manhattan. Refurbished by New York-based Gabellini Sheppard Associates in 2015.

The Rivoli Ballroom, Brockley, south London, 1957. One of the few public ballrooms still in regular use for dancing. Converted from a 1913 cinema, the eclectic interior design combines all the glamorous elements we expect: Art Deco marquetry, chinoiserie, red plush, gold trim and French chandeliers.

BUTLIN'S AYR—*The Old Time Ballroom.*

Photo: E. Nägele, F.R.P.S.

A sequence dance in progress with live music in the Old Time Ballroom at Butlin's Ayr, late 1960s. The decor is minimal but includes the all-important elements: the Art Deco cornicing and chandeliers.

The Mayfair Ballroom in Newcastle, run by Mecca, opened in 1961. The decor is typical of a palais de danse, including an upper-level balcony and a rotating stage. The venue was increasingly used for rock concerts, with the last one held in May 1999 shortly before demolition.

Powder room at the Mayfair Ballroom in Newcastle, 1961. The Mecca Palais de Danse provided cloakrooms and carpeted powder rooms with individual mirrors, seats and shoe bags.

Ballroom dancing champions Caroline Privou and Petra Zimmermann, competing at the German Open Championships in Frankfurt in 2016. Caroline wears a bespoke suit that adapts the lines of a traditional man's tail suit to a female form, made by DSI London.

Brian Dibnah and Georgiana Muja competing in the Rising Star Amateur Latin competition at the Blackpool Dance Festival 2019. They went on to become finalists in 2021.

The Empress Ballroom at the Winter Gardens Blackpool during the Dance Festival,
c. 1980.

– to show the precision of the patterns created by the teams. The intricate patterns were created by Peggy, using a little board, with beans for the gentlemen and peas for the ladies.[23]

The Spencers' book about their achievements, entitled *Come Dancing*, includes descriptions of the events they were involved with as well as some insights into their teaching methods and views on what we might now call 'team spirit'. Some statements seem particularly dated now. Peggy lobbied hard to have dancing included on the school curriculum, particularly for boys, to instil respect for and learn some basic communication skills with the opposite sex. They were keen to avoid there being so many wallflowers – men – at social events and dances and gave a good deal of advice for young men and their parents: 'To be a proficient dancer is a definite social asset.' 'Think of the opportunities you must miss if you can't dance.'[24] Formation teams relied on having equal numbers of male and female dancers, which it seems was much less difficult to achieve in the 1950s and '60s. Corinne Smither, a regular social dancer since 1951, recounts:

When we had our family we encouraged our children to learn ballroom dancing and went to Peggy Spencer's classes at Fairfield Halls in Croydon; at first it was just my son, who was nine, and my husband and I used to take up to eight of his friends in our two cars plus my daughter and her friends. After a while the friends began to drop out but our children kept going. Two of my children plus my two foster boys took their medal tests and were asked to join Peggy's Formation Classes in Penge. The journeys for the dancing practices began for them, sometimes they were at Penge and also at the Rivoli, local competitions, together with the two weekends every year to Blackpool where the children competed against teams from all over the country, usually doing very well indeed and the competition was strong between all the teams as well as in our household! Their clothes for the competitions usually changed each year and were very smart but also expensive so it was not a cheap hobby, but my husband and I were happy for the children to have an activity which they also enjoyed and kept them busy.[25]

In the 1980s *Come Dancing* was still able to inspire. Francesca Canty, then a sixth former at school, says, '*Come Dancing* was still on the TV but I wouldn't say it was the most fashionable thing to watch. It was a bit like Abba – that you probably shouldn't admit you still like, but we did, that's where my love of ballroom took hold.' Taught by Peggy, still living in Penge and now CEO of Bishopsgate Institute, which holds the Peggy Spencer Archive and hosts an annual 'Peggy Party', she tells us: 'What was really interesting about Peggy was it wasn't just about technique, it was also about the social dances and joy. It was about those dances that you could do without a partner, or dances that you could do with a group – a community coming together . . . She'd just got disco on to the ISTD curriculum, I think; she taught us various disco numbers as well as Latin and ballroom.'[26]

Peggy was appointed chair of the ISTD in 2004 and was presented with their Lifetime Achievement award by Lorna Lee-Stylianos, who said, 'No one can be more fitting to collect a lifetime achievement award than this recipient . . . her charm and communication skills, together with her enormous knowledge of the profession have made her one of the most prominent personalities of Dancesport. She has touched the lives of hundreds of students and professionals who have progressed into successful careers as a result of her guidance.'[27] After retiring, Peggy was unable to give up dancing. From her new home in Norfolk she started local classes, trained a senior formation team, and provided support in various ways to local groups and charitable organizations. She always believed that dancing was for everyone, a great form of exercise and a good way to meet people. Most importantly, Peggy was a supporter of social dancing for ordinary people, appreciating from the outset that not everyone wanted to be a competitive

Social dancing at the Royston Ballroom, *c.* 1960, reopened as the Matico Dance Studios in 2021.

dancer: 'If I have anything to give, I also want to share it with as many people as possible, not to make them into champions but just so a husband and wife can go out and have a lovely evening.'[28]

The formation team regional competitions, which represented a kind of middle ground between competition and social dancers, was probably the most important innovation on *Come Dancing*. The programme had an old time section and introduced an off-beat section for which each region could choose its own style of dancing, both to introduce a level of novelty – anything from clog dancing to Morris dancing could be chosen – and to prevent the Home Counties winning every time. Despite the popularity of *Come Dancing*, by the end of the 1960s ballroom dancing still seemed to exist in its own parallel world. The press coverage that had been everywhere since the 1920s had disappeared almost entirely. Even success in major competitions was rarely reported, although couples from competing European countries were rewarded with the same accolades as other returning 'sporting' stars. *Come Dancing* became the butt of many jokes for comedians and commentators, and while it had become the kind of programme that people enjoyed, it nevertheless was also one they liked to laugh at.

By the end of the 1960s ballroom dancing was no longer 'English' but had been renamed 'International Style': 'A way of dancing that used to be peculiar to Britain and a few Western European countries is now very popular in Japan and is known in China.'[29] Although its name had changed – Americans in particular had been uncomfortable with the 'English' branding, especially for dances which had been imported from America and redesigned in England – Britain was still the centre of ballroom dancing, London was considered the world ballroom capital and the British Open at the Blackpool Dance Festival was still the most prestigious competition. Some expressed doubts over whether Britain could maintain its position at the forefront. The Spencers considered competitive dancers to be athletes of the highest calibre, and together with other dancers had been lobbying since the early 1960s for Olympic recognition of ballroom dancing for both couples and formation teams. The art versus sport debate and the development of an increasingly athletic approach to competition dancing amplified the differences and created more distance between competitive dancing and social dancing – a gap that widened when eventually the name of the former was changed to Dancesport.[30]

As social dancers declined in numbers and dance halls began to close, the interdependence of dance hall managers, dance promoters and teaching professionals suffered. While numbers of social ballroom dancers dwindled, solo dances – the twist, the Madison and many others – were to continue and move on to clubs and discotheques. Changes in the idea of a 'holiday' was undoubtedly a factor in the demise of dancing. For the working classes, dancing at holiday camps had been the perfect indoor activity in Britain's uncertain weather, but by the 1970s, for many people active holidays were replaced with more relaxing breaks abroad. Butlin's was still hosting competitions, although Richard Gleave, who became professional ballroom champion in the 1970s, indicated that perhaps their popularity too was fading. Writing in 1964 about the Filey Dance Festival Professional Competition and cabaret night, twenty-year-old Gleave reported that only two 'really good professionals were entered', supposing that the meagre £30 prize money was not enough to attract more. The cabaret, however, comprised some very well-known, successful professional dancers: Peter Eggleton and Brenda Winslade, Laird and Lorraine, and the reigning world champions, Bill and Bobbie Irvine. Gleave noted that he had a 'good week' but hoped that for the next year, 'they will have knocked down the pillars, and the band will play faster quicksteps.'[31]

Michael Stylianos and Lorna Lee-Stylianos giving a demonstration
at the Hammersmith Palais, London, 1973.

THIRTEEN

The End of an Era

It's that it all seems to be ending. You think kids want to come with
their parents and take fox-trot lessons? Trips to Europe, that's what
the kids want.

Dirty Dancing (1987)

By the end of the 1960s there was little interest in ballroom dancing
among the general public. The standard dances, the waltz, foxtrot
and quickstep, once thought risqué because of the close proximity to
a partner, were now considered staid, associated with the older generation and swing music of the big bands or jazz. The music business
was expanding and music itself was changing rapidly with many new
and different styles. In Britain, following the 1967 reorganization of
BBC radio stations to cater for different audiences, the formation of
the Independent Broadcasting Authority in 1972 led to the introduction of commercial radio stations, many of which were dedicated to
pop music. For ballroom dancing, recorded music became the norm
and dance bands were rarely required. After the twist, which was
almost as popular as the crazes of the early 1900s, and other forms of
'beat' music had died down a bit, dancing together in couples again,
this time to Latin rhythms, had been expected to make a comeback.

Many of the competition dancers did not hesitate to learn the Latin
dances, but the continued distinct lack of approval in the dancing
press was less than encouraging. Arlene Croce's 1973 comments in

the *New Yorker* magazine illustrate the widely held opinion, also shared by Jim Cane, editor of the American magazine *Dancer's Digest*. Croce thought they looked uncomfortable – in her words, 'grimly flamboyant'. She then listed such bizarre practices as 'corny flamenco, night club jazz choreography, bits of ballet adagio and a great many figure skating exercises'. There was more: 'flying camel lifts, sit spins, slow circling arabesques, penchees performed by men holding on to girls' waists and stationary penchees performed by girls opposite men in low fondu'. To conclude, 'she accused the World's Latin dancers of being technically limited and aesthetically eccentric.'[1] In contrast to her critique of the Latin dances, she was full of praise for the modern section: 'What a marvellous Programme this Modern Competition was! After Saturday's Latin cum-jazz indigestibles, Sunday was like getting to a first-class English restaurant . . . pure English dancing mastery asserted itself everywhere,' which may be why the editor was prompted to reprint the entire article in the *Ballroom Dancing Times* the following February. Croce concluded that the advantage is because 'England has a huge ballroom-dance public; the strength of the English professional schooling derives in great part from a national passion that never died, as it did in this country [USA].'[2] Despite the criticism and lack of enthusiasm from the social dancing public, Latin dancing continued to grow alongside the more established modern or standard. The first Latin World's was held in 1960, the first British Championship in 1964, and after much deliberation the full syllabus of the five International Latin dances was finally agreed by 1968. Laird and Lorraine were early champions along with the German dancers Rudi and Mechtilde Trautz, and from the mid-1970s the World's was dominated by British couples: Peter Maxwell and Lyn Harman, Alan and Hazel Fletcher and, for more than ten years, Donnie Burns and Gaynor Fairweather.[3]

The Latin dances were probably more popular in America than Britain. An article in American *Vogue* reported that the mambo was the most popular with the big studio chains, Arthur Murray's and

Fred Astaire's, teaching a whole range of Latin dances – the merengue, pachanga, samba, rumba and mambo. It added the unlikely sound-bite: 'We are leaving the hard rock of the sixties for the soft rock of the seventies.'[4] While the dances never achieved widespread approval, a new wave of Latin American singers and bands at the time were immediately popular and created some of the most enduring tunes that are still regularly played. The mid-1960s saw Afro-Cuban Mongo Santamaria's version of Herbie Hancock's 'Watermelon Man', Brazilian Sergio Mendes's 'Mas Que Nada' and South African Miriam Makeba's 'Pata Pata'; in 1970 Mexican Carlos Santana's 'Oye Como Va' was released. Equally, for the standard dances, a high proportion of the tunes played today are the songs associated with the ballroom dancing depicted in film musicals written in the 1930s and '40s by some of the most prolific writers, such as Irving Berlin, Cole Porter, George Gershwin and Richard Rodgers. And though the dancing to their tunes was considered outdated, there was nevertheless the beginning of renewed interest in, or perhaps a reinterpretation of, their work: the 'American standards' or the 'Great American Songbook', as they are known. Examples include Ringo Starr's *Sentimental Journey*, released in 1970, an album of mostly 1940s music, and Harry Nilsson's album released in 1973 mostly from the 1920s.

While the music business was expanding in different directions, ballroom dancing in its social form stagnated, and many ballrooms and dance halls, suffering from lack of business, diversified and either were used for bingo or concerts, or began closing their doors. The lack of interest in ballroom dancing also had a damaging effect on the professional teachers' associations and many studios saw their class numbers dwindle. In 1970 the recently formed IDTA, amalgamating the many teaching associations across the country, launched 'the biggest publicity drive ever undertaken by a dance teachers' organisation in Britain if not in the world' with the slogan 'Start Living Start Dancing'.[5] John Dillworth, the secretary at the time, who was behind the promotion, was inspired by new methods of teaching in Germany, although it is curious that these had not been considered earlier. Rather than teaching everyone in the same way – that is, with a focus on technique with the potential to become competitive dancers – pupils were to be considered 'social dancers'. Dillworth believed the demand was still there and that pupils could be taught the four standard or ballroom dances (the Viennese waltz was, and still is, often considered too difficult and too strenuous), and five Latin American dances but without the pressure of too much technique. *The Guardian* quotes him as stating: 'More people than ever want to dance. Last year 124,000 pupils took our examinations in ballroom dancing, which was 25,000 more than the year before. For the first 6 months of this year entries were 10 percent up on the same period last year.'[6] Despite his enthusiasm there was clearly a decline in interest in ballroom dancing and indeed in any form of partner dancing.

It had further distanced itself from other forms of dance when *Ballroom Dancing Times* was separated from the professional magazine *Dancing Times* by the new editor, A. H. Franks, in 1958.[7] The limited popularity enjoyed by the Latin dances was short-lived, and young people, whether they identified as hippies, rockers, punks or other, seemed content with dancing solo. For most people, dancing, it seemed, was now just moving to music, something that no longer needed lessons of any kind. The new styles of music inevitably brought a whole range of simple-to-learn new dances which appeared in quick succession, in similar fashion to those that had arrived in the early twentieth century, but only one, disco, had a significant impact on the dancing profession. It arrived via a film musical, *Saturday Night Fever* (dir. John Badham, 1977), which inspired huge numbers of people to learn to dance like John Travolta. Such was its impact, including on professional dancers, that many accepted that it might be time for them to embrace some of the new forms of social dancing.

Saturday Night Fever was unlike earlier film musicals, which had continued to be a successful genre throughout the 1940s and '50s but lacked any focus on partner dancing. Individual performers, both singers and dancers, became big stars, but apart from an occasional glimpse, none danced as couples in a familiar ballroom way as Astaire and Rogers had. Dancing in films, too, seemed to have returned to a performing rather than a participatory role, quite separate from the narrative, forming part of the background and much less visible. Inspired by the success of the early rock'n'roll films, 1950s and '60s musicals with stars such as Elvis Presley or Cliff Richard were often merely a vehicle for selling records and therefore focused on music rather than dancing. An exception is the film *Dance Hall*, made at Ealing studios in 1950 and directed by Charles Crichton, which tells

Young dancers at Butlin's Clacton. By the early 1970s, dancing alone had become the norm. It was no longer necessary to have a partner, no longer necessary to move around the floor; there were no longer any 'rules'.

a story from a female perspective of four young women and the importance of the dance hall to their lives. The lead roles are played by actors Diana Dors, Natasha Parry, Jane Hylton and Petula Clark, and along with their 'boyfriends' there was a cast of real-life competitive ballroom dancers, including Len Colyer, Bob Burgess, Margaret Baker, Violet Barnes and Wally Fryer.[8]

By the 1970s the now dwindling cinema audiences were demanding more depth, more realism and a richer variety of films, abandoning musicals as escapist and trivial with little entertainment value. No new couple had taken the place of Astaire and Rogers, although their last film together, *The Story of Irene and Vernon Castle* (dir. H. C. Potter), had been made as long ago as 1939. Astaire and Rogers had been the only dancers to equal or surpass the celebrity of the Castles, albeit confined to the parallel fantasy world of cinema. The biographical film was, of course, intended to be a vehicle for Astaire and Rogers, but according to Irene, Astaire begged her 'not to let her [Rogers] do it'.[9] The film was unlike their others, lacking the comedy element and happy ending, and was not the success that had been expected.

Saturday Night Fever could be considered the first in a series of just a very few films that once again put partner dancing at the centre of the action and seem to have had a disproportionate effect in encouraging the public back to the ballroom. Categorized simply as 'romantic comedies' or 'dance dramas', in these films dancing is not the visual accompaniment or background to the music. Instead, as in the Astaire and Rogers movies, the central characters are dancers and their dancing forms an essential part of the narrative. All enjoyed enormous box-office success, continue to be recognized on a global scale and are frequently cited as inspiration to take up dancing.

In his recent autobiography, *Ballroom Fever: A Strictly Love Affair* (2020), George Lloyd claims that he knew immediately from the way *Saturday Night Fever* depicted 'disco' that it was going to have a major impact on dancing; he goes further to claim responsibility for making disco happen. Lloyd had trained as a dance teacher when very young,

John Travolta as Tony Manero in his famous disco-dancing pose in *Saturday Night Fever* (1977). His dance partner is actor Karen Lynn Gorney.

qualifying in a short space of time, and went on to work for Phyllis Haylor at her Hammersmith studio in the early 1970s. Working at a school in Hendon, which like many dance halls was located above a cinema, he tells us that when taking a break from the studio one Saturday afternoon, he went downstairs to watch the matinee. Lloyd's

enthusiasm is palpable in his description of the intense ambience in
the auditorium: 'the dance and the music were so perfect, so of the
time that watching the film became an almost mystical experience
for everyone there.'[10] He was so impressed that he managed to persuade his doubtful boss to advertise disco lessons. He spent a few days
watching the film four more times to perfect the moves and craft a
series of line dances. After putting just one advert in the local *Hendon
Times*, they taught packed classes every night for weeks. The film itself
was a huge success, and as well as launching a new dancing craze is
often referred to, along with *Star Wars* and *Close Encounters of the
Third Kind*, as one of the three major films of 1977 that marked a
turning point in British cinema attendance.

Lloyd tells us that he learned from the film that it was no longer
sufficient to try to sell just a dance – it was necessary to sell the lifestyle it represented: 'Ballroom had come to represent a faded past, a
world of dinner suits and evening gowns, of shiny wooden floors lit
by glitter balls, a world of middle class aspirations.'[11] The disco, he
believed, was socially inclusive; it was for everyone. Lloyd enjoyed
considerable success with disco; first the local dance schools and
then schools from all over the country wanted the new routines.
Following an invitation to lecture at the annual ISTD congress, he was
invited to write a book on the subject to be used as the ISTD syllabus. Disco competitions followed and the first championship was
held at the Starlight in Streatham with a dancer from *Top of the Pops*
dance troupe Legs & Co. as judge.[12] Michael Stylianos and Lorna
Lee-Stylianos were running their studio in Norbury at the time:
'Full capacity was 250 people; we used to run a *Saturday Night Fever*
class of 250 with another classfull waiting outside for the next one
– it was huge. Not just young people, all ages came.'[13] The disco craze
was so popular – the demand from schools across the country and
in Europe was huge – that Peggy Spencer, who had also been developing the 'new' style, set up a workshop team to travel to venues
around the country to spread the word, demonstrating and teaching

the teachers.[14] The first workshop held at Hammersmith Palais in December 1978 was attended by around five hundred dancers. At the 1979 World Congress during a session devoted to disco – 'Line Dances, Disco Moves and Hustle' – Peggy Spencer proposed a syllabus for a World Disco Dancing Programme to be called 'Together Disco'. Thames Television broadcast the World Disco Dancin' Championships from 1978 until 1984, which included 32 participating countries, televised regional heats and finals at the Empire in Leicester Square. The first Blackpool Disco contest was in 1979 with just seven couples competing. The *Ballroom Dancing Times* reviewer sounded a little bemused by 'entries of a very high entertainment value although one or two went a little wrong'. In response to the view that the reason the American entrants were more adept was because they were some five years ahead of everywhere else, he comments: 'This dance form is so individualistic, I wonder if this can be true.' He then notes that 'a session of disco music for general dancing saw only eight couples on the floor. They all did a form of HUSTLE!'[15] The best-known disco line dance is called bus stop, said to have originated on the U.S. West Coast before moving to the East Coast. There are many different versions, but the one recreated by George Lloyd based on the film is still danced all over the country to the song 'Night Fever' from the original Bee Gees soundtrack.

The *Saturday Night Fever* storyline is a familiar one in romantic dramas, one of social clash that nevertheless does not hamper a developing romantic attachment, but as both leads are dancers their learning to dance together becomes the key element that drives the narrative. Travolta, as the male lead Tony Manero, undergoes the anticipated transformation, leaving his work clothes and humdrum job when he escapes to the disco and the glamour of the dance floor, where his flamboyant appearance and dancing prowess make him the centre of attention, the envy of the other men and attractive to the women. Travolta's follow-up *Grease* (dir. Randal Kleiser, 1978) told another familiar story of teenage ill-fated lovers from opposite sides of the tracks, as had the 1950s' *West Side Story*. *Fame* (dir. Alan Parker, 1980) and *Flashdance* (dir. Adrian Lyne, 1983) followed, both very popular 'dancing' films but of a different type. They both fit to an extent into a 'rags to riches' model of 'if you try hard enough you can succeed', and were popular with a younger generation who were watching the new pop videos fuelled by the advent of MTV in 1981 and the growing popularity of aerobics and other fitness-based interpretations of vernacular 'street dance'.

It was ten more years after *Saturday Night Fever* before another film put partner dancing at the centre of the narrative. *Dirty Dancing* (dir. Emile Ardolino, 1987) was a huge hit, a powerful description of the 'end of an era' state of dancing in the late 1950s and early 1960s. The action takes place in a rural holiday camp somewhere in America, a place away from ordinary life and one – think Butlin's – that has long associations with ballroom dancing, where the emotional final words of the camp's host sums up the situation: 'It's that it all seems to be ending. You think kids want to come with their parents and take fox-trot lessons? Trips to Europe, that's what the kids want. Twenty-two countries in three days.' The dancing in the film tells the story of how Latin music and specifically the mambo, with its exaggerated body movements and sexual overtones, was taking over from the foxtrots and waltzes which belonged to older generations and were now considered outdated and uninspiring. The storyline and central characters have some similarities with those in *Saturday Night Fever*. The camp's dancing teacher is the good-looking male lead, cynical, working class and uneducated, while the female lead is well brought up, well educated, intelligent and naive. She has to negotiate all the dangers, both real and implied, of taking dancing lessons – his corrupting influence, his gigolo behaviour, the proximity and lewd body movements that can only lead to promiscuity – before she inevitably falls in love with him. If the films of Astaire cast the dancer as hero, *Saturday Night Fever* and *Dirty Dancing* both updated the image to cast the dancer as the villain, rebellious and defiant.

The dance dramas continue to be very successful films sharing the idea that dancing represents the fantasy world but one we can reach when we step out of our mundane, day-to-day life. The struggle to master the steps of the dance can be seen to represent a kind of liberation: a way to experience an entirely different world, to overcome difficulties and succeed against the odds. Both tell a story of dancing as both participatory and a performance. They focus on its social aspects, with an element of performance or competition and the importance of the couple's relationships away from the dance floor.

As the number of ballrooms and dance halls aimed at social dancers disappeared or were put to other uses, smaller venues – the ballrooms and practice studios dedicated to professional training – continued to thrive but were mostly invisible, known in general only to competitive dancers and their coaches. Some who taught social dancers also took disco on board, notably Peggy Spencer's Royston Ballroom in Penge, but many did not. They rarely hosted social events and many of them discouraged all except those ready to train for competition. Dancing continued in the more established, dark and smoke-filled jazz clubs, like the 100 Club on London's Oxford Street, which remained unchanged for decades, but the newer 'discotheques' were different. The music was recorded and the French name made it clear, as for the Palais previously, that a French name still represented something stylish. Very soon it was abbreviated to 'disco' for both the place and the dancing. Disco was important because it encouraged people back into dance studios to learn new dances; also in common with classical dance and ballroom, it was a style of dancing that appeared – at first glance at least – to transcend any obvious connection with a nationality or a particular subculture. Disco dancing had universal appeal and was perhaps bland; it attracted the more conventional youth and initially appealed to a wide demographic. As a different kind of venue to the one patronized by their parents, the disco was brighter and louder, the music was continuous, the decor was vivid and colourful with flashing lights, and there were bars serving alcohol. It represented a new version of the sophistication and glamour that the Castles in 1910 might have represented. A flamboyant display of luxury was once again acceptable, even fashionable; foreign travel, ready-to-wear clothes and dining out were the new desires. More expensive than the palais, which had specifically sought to attract the working classes, discotheques were aimed at all sections of society. Disco dancing itself appeared to be egalitarian; everybody dances solo and nobody is leading or following: there is no host and often the DJ was not important as long as the music was continuous. Disco dancing expressed an idea of freedom in dancing that had not been enjoyed previously. Gwenethe Walshe had been bold enough to suggest as early as 1958 that 'girls can express themselves more in Latin-American, and are not so restricted by a partner,' not a widely held view at the time.[16] The upbeat mood of the music and the constant and regular beat meant it was easy to anticipate, and everyone could invent their own moves and be as ostentatious as they chose.

There were, of course, discotheques that became the fashionable place to be and be seen mingling with a more glamorous crowd. The Bains Douches in central Paris, which opened in 1978, was designed by a then relatively unknown Philippe Starck, and hosted acts like Joy Division, Prince and Depeche Mode. 'It was very very glamorous but it was not slick,' noted the *New York Times*.[17] From 1977 to 1980, Studio 54 in New York was intended to attract creative people from all walks of life and very quickly became the place to be seen rubbing shoulders with musicians and other media stars. In London the Embassy Club opened in 1978 in imitation of Studio 54, and was followed in 1979 by the legendary Heaven. The sociologist David Walsh suggested that disco dancing, with its upbeat mood, freedom from any partnership and 'anything goes' attitude, 'led to the remasculinisation of dancing by helping to give the male a place of eminence in which he can engage in display just as easily as women and without embarrassment as a result'.[18] If we consider that the conventional male role for a long time had been one of the leader, to support and allow a female partner to 'show off' with more elaborate steps, this may be true. The opportunity for display and for individual expression without any responsibility for a partner would almost certainly have encouraged men to dance, especially with John Travolta leading the way.

While many were keen to join the crowds at Studio 54 in New York or at the Embassy in London, and disco dancing was everywhere, *Come Dancing* was still on the TV every week, compered by Terry Wogan from 1973 to 1979 after his move from Radio 1 to Radio 2 in 1972. As Bill Irvine, then one of the judges, is quoted as saying in the *Daily Mail*: 'Of course John Travolta and the disco craze has brought more people into the studios wanting to learn the Hustle and the Bus Stop. But there are many many people who want to learn the Waltz that mother used to do and *Come Dancing* just carries on regardless.'[19] However, if ballroom dancing was ever mentioned on TV or ever appeared in the newspaper columns, it was almost certain to be satirized. A review in the *Listener* in 1976 suggested that the programme took dancing too seriously: '*Come Dancing* is a curious business in that it has nothing to do with dancing at all: I mean the ordinary toe stubbing variety, where one used to hold a girl pretty firmly and smooch around a bit when the lights were low.'[20] The advent of colour television in the mid-1970s, which fans of *Come Dancing* thought would make it so much more enjoyable, led only to more criticism: 'A woman can knowingly go into the public eye wearing 80 yards of chiffon in five different colours . . . so many northern ladies can wear such brilliant and short skirts over such awful white legs.'[21] A report on a visit to the Latin Championships in Blackpool in 1984 similarly poked fun at the costumes, with dresses that look 'as though they started life as ballgowns and are in the process of being converted to swimsuits . . . The men are in figure-hugging catsuits with sequined flashes across the torso.'[22] Ballroom dancing retreated further. Association with the Miss World beauty contest,[23] which was also sponsored by Mecca, didn't help dancing's reputation. Miss World was considered mainstream TV viewing in the 1960s and '70s despite ongoing protests particularly from feminist organizations, and was considered in extreme bad taste even by those who did not identify as feminists. Satirical write-ups became the norm and were to be expected, it seemed. As late as 1993 when the Penge Latin formation team was preparing for the final of the *Come Dancing* competition, Peggy Spencer's knowing first question to the reporter – 'You're not going to send us up, are you?' – was ignored, and the article was published with descriptions such as 'the women, their faces painted like Barbie dolls', 'regulation cleavage', the 'ladies' colour coordinated partners resembling waiters at a chichi Italian wedding'.[24] There is little comment about the dancing itself, only that it resembled 'synchronised swimming on land'.

Disco, although huge, was not the only story in the 1970s. Considered conventional rather than edgy, disco had a wide mainstream appeal – unlike punk, which existed alongside it on the margins. The rock music scene of earlier decades had largely excluded women, but the punk scene, like disco, appeared to have a more inclusive attitude and also identified with an anti-fashion stance. For women an androgynous look, wearing men's clothing, dungarees and baggy trousers, heavy boots, ripped T-shirts, plastic and safety pins, all conspired against the delicate and soft 'feminine' look. Punk rejected all conventional conceptions of female beauty. Clothes were not expected to enhance the female form but aimed at covering it up in a way that had not happened in the past. At the same time, the continuing growth in the feminist movement supported the ongoing questioning of the pervasive and stereotypical idea of womanhood as 'delicate', 'feminine' and 'pretty'. By the 1980s wearing trousers had become the new normal for women, and it was only a short step, in the shadow of punk fashions that had developed in opposition to the material and flamboyant excesses of disco and rock music, to wearing flat shoes and cutting their hair short. The much more 'sober' look

Richard Gleave and Janet Gleave performing a show dance at the Royal Albert Hall, *c.* 1980. Competitive ballroom dancing continued regardless of the changing times.

presented was in extreme contrast to that depicted on *Come Dancing*, which was guaranteed to be off-putting. Jacky Logan, who was awarded a British Empire Medal for services to same-sex dancing in the 2020 New Year honours list, recalled her impressions of ballroom dancing at that time:

> We were all wearing trousers, flat shoes and no make up . . .
> the idea of dressing up like the women on *Come Dancing* was
> anathema . . . it seemed to be the image we were all fighting
> against . . . The women seemed so subservient – following their
> male leaders – and dressed in such a way that seemed to hamper
> every move, decorated to within an inch of their lives . . .
> The posture and posing seemed so abnormal.[25]

According to David Walsh, writing in 1993, the dance hall had 'acted as a centre of and focus for all the leisure time activities of adolescents and young unmarried adults, providing them with, through dancing, the opportunity to mix together and date one another'.[26] We would probably agree that dance halls at any time during the twentieth century did just that, from the earliest dance halls and ballrooms to the palais of the 1930s onwards. But by the 1990s the social scene had changed, women were more independent, bars and cafés had replaced the male-dominated atmosphere of pubs and were growing in number, and there were other places to meet. Ballroom, including the codified Latin dances, was increasingly seen as old-fashioned, conservative and sexist – a long way from the disco culture in the late 1970s, which had probably provided the first highly visible, openly gay space in Britain's cities. Many of the mainstream dance schools and studios, while struggling with dwindling numbers of pupils, were still uncomfortable with men dancing together. Allowing women to dance together was considered less threatening; the teaching profession had long accepted that dancing was popular with young girls especially, and held dedicated competitions for them, but otherwise it was assumed that a couple would be a man and a woman. But by the mid-1990s, in London at least, change was coming.

The various music genres had, it seemed, finally 'liberated' both men and women from the cultural associations of ballroom and Latin – that is, strong men leading their more fragile female partners – and freed them too from the need to dress up in costumes that belonged either in the Neoclassical ballrooms somewhere in the nineteenth century or the sultry bars of Rio or Havana. They were also free from the need for detailed knowledge of a technique often seen as overly restrictive, apt to stifle enjoyment and musicality and thwart individual expression. As early as 1948 Pierre's book said that 'too much technique kills dancing.'[27] By the 1980s, via the twist and disco and many other versions, dancing solo had become the norm and for many has remained the norm. For keen dancers, however, the 1990s saw renewed interest in partner dancing, not in the codified ten Ballroom and Latin dances, but instead those that were considered the original or authentic versions of national social dances, before they had been imported and modified to suit English tastes. The salsa, Lindy hop, ceroc and Argentine tango had all been around for decades but saw a marked increase in popularity. These were social partner dances that encompassed perhaps just one or two related styles; they could allow individual expression but without the demands of complex technique and knowledge.

Salsa dancing, a term which initially referred to a range of related dance styles such as cha-cha-cha, mambo and guaracha, originated in New York and had grown in popularity, as had all the Latin-inspired dances, during the 1960s. Its name is credited to Johnny Pacheo, the founder of the Fania record label in New York's Spanish Harlem and the Bronx, which brought together a range of different styles that combined and diversified before spreading widely across America and then Europe. The Lindy hop's roots, too, are firmly American and are found in the Charleston dances of the 1920s. Swing Dance UK, formed in 1986 by Simon Selmon and still in operation, claims to be the UK's first such society and covers a range of related styles, including Charleston and Balboa.[28] Argentine tango similarly saw renewed interest during the last decades of the twentieth century, first with performances and then with social dancing. All have their own detailed histories with many different versions. Disco even spawned its own couple dance, the disco fox or hustle, which originated in Germany.

The view that ballroom is restricted by its overly demanding technique and strict regulations in contrast to a more natural desire for individual expression forms the basis for the storyline in Baz Luhrmann's *Strictly Ballroom*. At the time of its release in 1992 it had become accepted to satirize the things we love, the less than sophisticated *Come Dancing*, often castigated for its tackiness or tastelessness along with other popular broadcasts such as the Eurovision Song Contest. Baz Luhrmann effortlessly transferred that to the big screen. *Strictly Ballroom* is unique in its depiction of the competitive ballroom dancing world. For all the characters in this film, dancing is a reality, not a fantasy; teachers, competitors, parents of competitors, pupils and adjudicators are all immersed in competition dancing. It very cleverly celebrates ballroom and Latin dancing while at the same time poking fun at it. Luhrmann, whose mother was a professional ballroom dancer, described the film as a 'celebration of kitsch'.[29] On release it was sidelined at Cannes and won the Youth prize; Luhrmann was thirty years old at the time.

The narrative has elements in common with both *Saturday Night Fever* and *Dirty Dancing*. First, it has an unlikely pairing of an expert dancer with a beginner that inevitably results in a romantic attachment and, second, it is the story of a younger generation's obstinacy and a refusal to conform to ballroom's expected norms. It also hints at the ethical questions surrounding the appropriation and codification of an imported national dance style by focusing on perhaps the most extreme example: the paso doble. In *Strictly Ballroom* Scott, the maverick, young and handsome dancer, risks his career by

Strictly Ballroom (1992) focuses on how the authentic Latin dances have been codified for the ballroom. In this scene the father, played by flamenco dancer Antonio Vargas, explains the paso doble to his daughter.

deciding to perform his own steps based on the authentic *sevillanas* or flamenco, and sets out to succeed with a new partner, Fran, the 'ugly duckling' student dancer. He learns the authentic version of the dance from Antonio Vargas, the real-life, internationally renowned flamenco dancer and choreographer cast as Fran's father. Vargas's expert and passionate demonstration is used to make clear the superiority of the authentic sevillanas compared with the codified version of the International Latin style paso doble.

Set in Australia, early adopters of the 'English style', the characters are exaggerated for comedic effect but are not far from the reality of the Latin American competitive world with its extremes of costumes, fake tans, dyed and lacquered hair and dancers' names such as Tina Sparkle. Invented names for figures such as the 'bogo pogo', the 'double ronde shuffle' and the 'reverse whip split' remind us just how baffling many of the real names, such as *botafogo*, 'double reverse' or 'whip', sound on first hearing. The spitefulness of the competitors is demonstrated by their criticism of Scott for not coming to a training session: 'He never showed up. With a guy like Scott it could be anything . . . sexuality, drugs, you know . . . He's obviously lost it, Sweetie.' *Strictly Ballroom* depicts competitors more as divas than committed athletes, where the central thrust of the narrative is that the authorities have decided there is only one way to do things. Terry says: 'That's why it's important that Scott is seen dancing the right steps with the right partner. Dancesport needs good young couples, Merv.' *Strictly Ballroom* has continued to be a very popular film and is cited by many as encouraging them to take up ballroom; perhaps due to its lighthearted and self-deprecating attitude, it paints a more encouraging picture of ballroom.

At the time when the various different forms of partner dancing were becoming popular, the ISTD and the IDTA were keen to include them and were developing a new syllabus. The competitive ballroom dancing organizations, on the other hand, were moving further away from social dancing, working hard to change its image in order to have it recognized as a sport. The Spencers and others had been lobbying for recognition of ballroom as a sport and for its inclusion in the Olympic Games since the early 1960s. In 1949 Alex Moore had welcomed the proposal to form the International Council of Ballroom Dancing: 'The English Style is now regarded as a serious competitive sport by the keen dancers and teachers of at least twenty countries . . . we shall have an International Council fully capable of controlling both the English and Latin-American styles of Dancing.'[30] It was not until 1990, however, that it was renamed Dancesport to distinguish it from social dancing, and in 1997 it achieved recognition by the International Olympic Committee (IOC). Dancesport joined the long list of recognized sports, and although it has not yet been included in the Olympics, it went on to debut at the World Games in 2005. The change of name and IOC recognition sparked discord within and between the principal organizations that now control Dancesport, and the World Dance Council (WDC) and the World DanceSport Federation (WDSF) ended their agreement (held since 1965) to separately support professional and amateur dancers respectively.[31] The decision of the WDSF to ban their members entering competitions run by other organizations led to the formation of Freedom to Dance, founded by Richard and Anne Gleave. When it was launched tentatively with a Facebook page in 2010, almost 1,000 people expressed interest in the first 24 hours. By 2019 it had grown to a membership of approximately 10,000 and holds events that have grown in size each year: 'The mantra of Freedom to Dance is simple – all couples from all Associations, Federations and Organisations are free to dance when and where they wish, without the threat of banning.'[32] Two other organizations – the World Dance Organisation, established first in 2019 as the World Dance Organisers to run amateur competitions in different countries around the world, and an affiliated group, the World Dance Competitors Commission, founded by Arunas Bizokas – see themselves as formed by dancers for dancers.[33]

Ballroom schools were still having difficulty attracting enough pupils, so some branched out to incorporate some of the other popular styles and other forms of partner dancing while continuing with their core syllabus; some felt threatened by a growing number of same-sex couples. The first dedicated same-sex London club had started following a chance visit to the London Lesbian and Gay Centre in 1989 by Ralf Schiller, an experienced competition dancer since the age of fifteen, and Tony Woszeck.[34] They were asked if they would teach the growing number of gay and lesbian couples who had experienced hostility dancing together at mainstream schools that refused to let men follow or women lead. Enthusiasm led to more and more people attending their classes, and after a move to the Bell pub in King's Cross at the invitation of veteran music presenter Jo Purvis, who had been running dances for the gay community since the 1940s, they regularly sought out other Saturday night dances. On their first visit to the Rivoli Ballroom after meeting up beforehand and arriving in a big group of around forty, they doubled the number of dancers on the floor. Some of the regulars complained about two men dancing together, but unlike some other venue managers who had asked that they leave, Bill Mannix was pleased to see so many enthusiastic younger dancers and encouraged them to return every Saturday night. Jacky Logan, one of the first female DJs, later agreed to run regular dance nights once a month for everyone, not only the gay community. She experienced more comments about introducing contemporary and alternative music than about the same-sex dancers. Since 1995 Jacky's Jukebox has become established as a regular monthly dance that continues today and hosts as many as three hundred dancers.

In 1996 Logan and Schiller started a new dance club, the Pink Jukebox, which made no distinction between the club dances and the ten International Ballroom and Latin dances; to celebrate the end of their first year in 1997, they organized a competition held at the Central Club Hotel in Great Russell Street. Called Dancerama, it included only single dance competitions. Only very few women took part. As Ralf says, 'In the regular (mainstream) dance scene I always danced with a woman; but a lot of the men were gay so when they heard about the same sex competitions, they could very quickly put a routine together and enter. The women it seemed were more likely to be beginners and as there were so few, everyone competed together.'[35]

This was just the beginning of same-sex dancing and a renewed interest in ballroom and Latin dancing as well as the club dances, which was to gather momentum in the first decades of the twenty-first century. According to Vernon Kemp, 'The Pink Jukebox trophy is reflective of our modern dance culture, which encourages anyone to have a go. There's no discrimination of any kind – age, sex, religion, nationality, experience. Everything must adapt to survive, and the same is true of ballroom. We have to embrace 21st century values.'[36] The importance of the other dancing styles had been accepted by the professional organizations and was reflected by the introduction of new branches or faculties for non-core subjects at the IDTA and at the ISTD: the Disco/Freestyle/Rock'n'roll faculty (DFR) in 1988 and an Alternative Rhythms faculty ten years later in 1999, the newest of the twelve ISTD faculties formed under the joint chairmanship of Anne Lingard and Nick Miles.

Vernon Kemp, founding chair of the UK Same Sex Dance Council (UKSSDC), who is passionate about dancing and all it brings, created the annual Fun Competition, 'an informal and fun practice competition for starter, beginner and improver same-sex and equality dancers', also run at the Rivoli. For Kemp 'It's [Ballroom and Latin] good for your health, it's creative, you learn something new, and you meet people doing it, rather than having the illuson of social interaction through Facebook or Twitter.'[37] His words will undoubtedly resonate among communities of competitors and social dancers worldwide.

John Church and Alex Levalle won the Over-35 Pre-champ Ballroom category at the Blackpool Champions of Tomorrow competition in January 2020 and have twice won the UK Closed Over-35 Pre-champ title in Bournemouth.

FOURTEEN

Twenty-First-Century Ballroom

It's very sociable, it's a great way to keep fit and it uses your brain as well as your body.

The Guardian, 1998[1]

For most, dancing solo has remained the norm, and social dancing at private events or clubs continues entirely separate from the world of Ballroom and Latin and its controlling authorities. However, as partner dancing of different kinds, such as the Argentine tango, Lindy hop, salsa and ceroc, have increased in popularity again, those choosing Ballroom and Latin have found other ways to challenge themselves with new kinds of competitions, and to enjoy their dancing through performance or display. The range is rich and varied: professional–amateur (pro–am) competitions where couples comprise a teacher and a student,[2] university competitions, wheelchair Dancesport, showdance teams, formation teams and a growing number of same-sex or equality dance competitions. Social dances and parties regularly include line dances, sequence dances, demonstrations and formation team and student–teacher performances. Whether we are all naturally competitive, or whether the framework for competition or performance gives us a goal to spur improvement, is difficult to know but the pro–celebrity version of ballroom competition on the BBC's *Strictly Come Dancing* has brought Ballroom and Latin to the attention of the public again.

The title *Strictly Come Dancing*, inspired by the success of *Strictly Ballroom* coupled with the original *Come Dancing* reinvented as a reality show, has a simple enough formula that sees one contestant voted out each week based on a dance performed with their professional partner. When it was launched in May 2004 just eight celebrities took part; but, witness to its popularity, by 2019 the number had almost doubled to fifteen. As a live broadcast including live musicians and singers and a studio audience, which is now a rarity in television, a different ambience is created in each episode and an element of risk is injected into the competition that could not be recreated in a recording. The format has changed little since the first series, although the dancing content has. The early series focused on the ten International Ballroom and Latin dances and followed their regulations such as a ban on lifts and a limited amount of time out of hold, but gradually the rules have become more relaxed and other dances – the 'alternative rhythms' or 'club dances' – have been introduced, such as the Charleston, salsa and Argentine tango. More recently, the addition of a 'couple's choice' perhaps echoes the 'off-beat' section introduced in *Come Dancing* to allow any form of dancing. The more technically difficult dances, in particular the rumba, are seen much less frequently, and the foxtrot is almost always an American smooth version, reminiscent of 1930s Hollywood films, to allow lifts and dancing out of hold. The less technically demanding 'club' dances make learning faster, allowing for more ambitious choreography, leading to potentially more entertaining routines for an uninformed broad audience. The more informed audience, though still pleased to see dancing on TV, is becoming frustrated with the increasing focus on performance or show dancing rather than the participatory essence of partner dancing. The amount of money used for the many distracting props and special effects in the more recent broadcasts have also been heavily criticized, and were perhaps not the best use of budget following rumoured reductions in the original flat fees paid to the celebrities. The continued high viewing figures are testament to the popularity of *Strictly Come Dancing* and a renewed public ownership of Ballroom and Latin. Perhaps because of the celebrity element – the themed content, which includes comic elements, or the public's identification with the learning process and its frequent surprises – the current version has not been satirized to the same extent as the original *Come Dancing*.

According to Fenia Vardanis, a BBC commissioner in 2003, her idea for the show was originally considered a big risk: 'At the time, I promise you, everybody thought it would be a horrendous flop so it was a risk – I mean ballroom dancing on a Saturday night?'[3] The idea was developed by producer Richard Hopkins, creative head of format entertainment at the BBC who had considerable experience in reality TV as executive producer on a range of competition programmes, such as *A Question of Sport*, *Mastermind*, *The Weakest Link* and his biggest hit, *Big Brother*. *Strictly Come Dancing* is, however, unique, offering more than the draw of reality shows; it not only offers 'contestants' an opportunity to learn a new skill, but provides them with a dedicated teacher who gives them their undivided personal attention daily and devises bespoke routines suited to their style and ability. The actors and other performers taking part may have some experience of that kind of attention being paid to them, but for the politicians, comedians, TV presenters, sportsmen and sportswomen, it is far from any previous experience. The equivalent of a dedicated full-time personal trainer is a luxury extremely few can enjoy. In addition, there are professional make-up artists and hair stylists, and the indulgence of made-to-measure clothes: the female dancers' dresses retail after the show for between £1,200 and £2,000. For many viewers the attention to physical appearance is as important as the dancing, which requires both participation and performance. The physical appearance of the dance, the couple and the costume together is an important part of the fantasy that says that with the right tuition, the right partner and the right costume, we could all achieve the same proficiency and perform.

The programme, together with its related gossip show on BBC2 and spin-off live touring shows, has provided new opportunities for many of the professional dancers taking part. The professionals and judges who take part in the show have acquired similar status as the celebrities they dance with, developing TV careers, publishing autobiographies and performing in associated stage shows. Most have been recruited from the ranks of the many recently retired competitive dancers who, by 35, are considered past their physical peak for major competitions and already categorized as 'seniors'. Lorna Lee-Stylianos was approached to take part as a judge but was not offered a role after having to miss the pilot; she was somewhat upset about it at the time, but in retrospect realizes that the time commitment required would have been too much.[4] Michael and Lorna have continued to be involved with the show, training several of the professional dancers and discussing technique with Shirley Ballas in her early days on the judging panel: 'It's been amazing for the industry in some ways. It lets people know that dancing exists, for middle aged people.'[5] Peggy Spencer too was approached to present the show but declined: 'She was of course thrilled at a proposal to put Ballroom on prime-time TV but considered that despite her extensive experience, the new version of *Come Dancing*, which was intended to attract a young and vibrant audience, would be better served by somebody younger. She was both delighted and amused when Bruce Forsyth was appointed to present the programme.'[6]

The producers of *Strictly Come Dancing* were not the first to identify the potential for viewers' interest – for both dancers and non-dancers alike. Since the earliest TV *Dancing Club*, which started in 1948, Victor Silvester pointed out that the performance of the thirty or so amateur couples 'provided the most essential ingredient in successful television – mass viewer identification'.[7] They danced well but their routines included only simple figures that the general dancer could imagine doing themselves, and it is likely that TV *Dancing Club* was responsible to an extent for a boom in dancing schools in the early 1950s. The increase in popularity was discussed at the ISTD, and the chairman at the time, Cyril Beaumont, was very supportive: 'Undoubtedly TV had made millions of people aware of the beauty and dignity of a ballroom, and of the grace and rhythm ordinary non-professional people can achieve with a little practice.'[8]

At the same time, Arthur Murray, who was perhaps as much an entrepreneur as a dancer, had seen the potential of the addition of a celebrity element in his American TV dancing competition. He had initially bought a series of five fifteen-minute slots on CBS for a weekly programme hosted by his wife, Katherine, before launching *The Arthur Murray Dance Party*, which was broadcast on all the major U.S. networks from 1950 to 1962. The programme was severely criticized in the early days mostly for its amateurism, but the decision to include star guests in a competitive element ensured its popularity. The first celebrity contestant was Helen Hayes, one of America's most famous actors, and, once she was booked, two of Hollywood's leading men, Melvyn Douglas and Don Ameche, and the journalist and TV host Sam Levenson were also persuaded to compete. Managing the celebrities that they continued to attract, along with their individually selected partners, was a challenge, particularly billing: no one wanted to be the 'opening act'; they all wanted top billing. Inducements to appear were usually large fees and even larger donations to their favourite charities.

The celebrity element was vital to the success of the programme. The attraction of watching 'stars' attempting to learn new skills and waiting for them to humiliate themselves was perhaps as strong as voting for their favourites. The celebrity element is clearly still of key importance, as demonstrated by BBC1's failed attempt at a reality dancing show without stars. *Strictly Dance Fever*, hosted by Graham Norton with a similar format to *Strictly Come Dancing* but dedicated to 'alternative rhythms', ran for only two seasons in 2005 and 2006. With no celebrity element, viewers were not interested in watching 'real world' amateur couples compete; nor were viewers interested in the group of wayward teenagers being taught discipline through dancing in the Channel 5 documentary *Bad Teen to Ballroom Queen* (2018).

Inspired partly by *Strictly Come Dancing*'s pro–celebrity format, pro–am dancing (or teacher–student for amateur competitive dancers) has increased considerably in the UK in the last few years. For those with enough cash, pro–am offers all the advantage of the pro–celebrity pairings seen on TV. Having a dedicated teacher who is also a partner for competitions makes learning to dance so much easier than trying to learn with another beginner. The downside is that while it goes on it is fine, but it is not necessarily easy to dance with others – if one becomes too accustomed to just one partner and a particular set of figures or routines, dancing with anyone else and improvising, either as leader or follower, can become difficult. In Britain it is seen largely as an American import; the WDC use the National Dance Council of America rules for competitions, where it developed much more quickly, as ballroom did not continue socially to the same extent. The increase in popularity in Britain has led to an increase in the numbers of competition events for all age groups and a pro–am show-dance category was introduced at the Blackpool Dance Festival in 2013. Some dancing schools also base their classes on a pro–am model with professional partners for all attendees. Dancing with a partner who knows what they are doing is undoubtedly a much faster way to learn, but compared with regular group classes, it is inevitably more expensive for the student and therefore limited to those with sufficient cash to spend on their dancing. Pro–am attracts those who like the certainty of a known partner and a known routine, and who also enjoy the challenge of higher standards and an element of performance.

While both male and female professional dancers take part, there is most often a female amateur and a male professional. The young men, often those who have come to the end of a competitive career and who are working on a freelance basis, are eager to earn more money direct from paying customers rather than taking the less-well-paid route to professional qualifications to teach in established schools.

As Silvester discovered in his early days as a dancer, there are plenty of wealthy women happy to pay a trained dancer to take them out at night, and for those who can afford to it may be preferable to having a weekly lesson in the studio. The arguments for and against are not very different today than they were a century ago. No one is concerned for the young women who may be taken advantage of or even if a young man is more gigolo than professional dancing partner. A discreet partnership is not noticeable, but at some studios the well-known gigolos – for want of a better term – have been asked not to attend. Their presence, especially in large numbers, can be seen to have a negative effect on the ambience if they refuse to dance with anyone other than their 'client' and sit out party dances, sequence and line dances, which are often part of the evening's programme. On the other hand, dance hosts or 'taxi' dancers, whether resident teachers or not, employed by the management to dance with anyone and everyone, are becoming an increasingly popular way to manage big events.

Luhrmann's *Strictly Ballroom* was also credited with inspiring a new generation of university ballroom dancing clubs. In 1998 *The Guardian* reported from Manchester University on the Northern Universities Dance Association (NUDA) end-of-year 'friendly' match. Manchester and Leeds universities both attract students on the basis of their nightlife, which is rarely associated with ballroom dancing, and both have clubs with membership of around five hundred students, making ballroom dancing one of the most popular of their societies. A student at Leeds thought that 'it's becoming cool in a retro sort of way,' citing both *Dirty Dancing* and *Strictly Ballroom* as an important influence and wanting 'that kind of glitz' plus claiming that it is not only glamorous, 'it's very sociable, it's a great way to keep fit and it uses your brain as well as your body.'[9]

The Intervarsity Dance Association (IVDA) had been set up in 1962 to promote Ballroom and Latin American dancing within universities and they continue to organize an annual Intervarsity Dance Competition (IVDC) and support university dancers who want to move on to the competitive circuit.[10] In 2019 they numbered approximately 10,000 student members at around 35 university dance clubs. The annual competition includes individual and team matches and has been held at Blackpool Empress Ballroom since 2007. Annual events that include competitions include the Sheffield Social; the Nottingham Varsity Event, which started in the 1980s and has around ten universities competing; and the Warwick Ball, which started in the late 1990s. Many of the competitions have popular team events, encouraging dances other than the usual ten Ballroom and Latin dances; the latest, a salsa formation competition, was introduced in 2019 and won by the Oxford University Mambo Team.

In the first two decades Liverpool and Leeds were frequent winners, but since the early 1980s the IVDC has been dominated by Oxbridge and Imperial College London.[11] Perhaps due to the inherently competitive nature of their students, the Oxford University Dancesport Club (OUDC, originally the Oxford University Ballroom Club) was one of the earliest, founded in 1968, and within ten years it had become the biggest membership club at the university.[12] Cambridge University Dancesport Team (CUDT) – its own branding is 'Slick, sexy and stamina building' – also runs a dance club aimed at social dancers for students and the local residents. An Oxford versus Cambridge ballroom competition, known as the Varsity Match and as competitive as the boat race, has been held annually since 1973, hosted alternately. A major achievement, as well as going on to dominate the IVDA competitions, was achieving recognition as a sports club, meaning more funding is available and with it the award of coveted Blues and Half Blues and the 'colours' recognizable since the boat race of 1836.[13] At Cambridge University in 1992, where the Dancers' Club was the largest sports club with 2,000 members, the 'sport' issue led to accusations of sexism from the male students. The all-female Blues committee had recognized ballroom dancing in 1991, but the all-male men's Blues club did not, stating, 'we just decided it simply isn't in the same category as things we regard as sport.'[14]

Recent years have also seen the expansion in same-sex dancing and the introduction of a growing number of same-sex competitions and events. The Pink Jukebox Trophy, the responsibility of Ralf Schiller and Jacky Logan, which was introduced in 1998 following the success of their Dancerama, is now the best known of the same-sex competitions, with international participation of up to ninety couples. In Logan's words, 'It is an annual opportunity for same-sex dancers to exhibit their talent and show how unique the style is within the wider ballroom and Latin dance world. It is an exciting and entertaining event and a chance to meet dancers from other countries who come from similar clubs all over the world.'[15] It has taken only a short time for same-sex competitions to become established. The Gay Games, which started in 1982 in the USA, was held for the first time in Europe in Amsterdam in 1998 when ballroom dancing was included for the first time, close enough to be attractive to British dancers. The next Gay Games, held in Sydney in 2002, were too far to travel for many, but British competitors then went to the 2004 Eurogames, which had been running since 1992. Organized by the European Gay and Lesbian Sport Federation (GLSF) and held in Munich, these had included Dancesport since 1996. The Gay Games are inclusive; there are no qualifying standards and they attract large numbers, overtaking the Olympics in 1994 with 10,864 competitors compared with 10,318 in the 1992 Barcelona Olympics.[16] A UK Same Sex Dance Council was formed in 2006 with founding members Vernon Kemp and Jacky Logan. It has now been renamed as the UK Equality Dance Council (UKEDC).[17]

As same-sex dancing has progressed, dancers have started to enter mainstream competitions, which has prompted controversy and disagreement among the governing bodies. The rules of the two principal organizations governing dancing competitions, the WDC and the WDSF, are both specific about the definition of a couple. The WDC states: 'As the WDC sanctions events in traditional dance styles, a "couple" in WDC dancing terms is strictly defined as comprising of

Latin dancers Lemington Ridley and Nejc Jus demonstrating at Elizabeth Anderson's Summer Ball at Southside Ballroom, London, in 2014.

[*sic*] two people, a man and a woman.'[18] The WDSF similarly states in its regulations: 'A couple consists of a male and a female partner.'[19] The British Dance Council rules included no such definition, but in 2014 proposed the introduction of a change to its regulations in order to include the definition of a 'couple' 'as one man and one lady . . . unless otherwise stated'. An article in the *Dancing Times* in July 2014 alerted dancers to the BDC's proposal, which seemed likely to lead to same-sex couples being unable to compete.[20]

In an interview in *The Guardian*, Bryan Allen, chairman of the BDC at the time, said more dancers were in support of the change than against and that he did not see the change as discriminatory; there would be separate categories for same-sex and mixed-sex couples.[21] The reason given was the obvious advantages an all-male couple would have as a result of their physical size and power. This ignored the fact that dancing is not judged on size and strength but on technique, style and musical expression and that many same-sex competitors are female. Same-sex dancing has made considerable progress in the last 25 years, but inevitably there remains an imbalance when compared to the mainstream competitions, which have been established and growing for a hundred years. For serious dancers who want to improve, the challenge of mainstream competitions with all that they can offer – competing against the best – is the obvious next step.

The proposal to make separate competitions for mixed-sex and same-sex couples was eventually considered to be discriminatory. Such a ruling would have had a disproportionate effect on women, as many more women than men take up dancing, and if for whatever reason they choose to dance together, they would be relegated to the far fewer number of same-sex championships.[22] As Heather Devine said in an interview with *The Times*, 'There were only two same-sex competitions in Britain compared with the hundreds organised under BDC's rules' and 'if this is about advantage for men, why are they banning women partnerships?'[23] Dancing competitions have long accepted two women dancing together, including holding competitions for girls, and many consider the proposed change was in fact aimed specifically at preventing two men dancing together.

In America there have been considerable efforts at inclusivity. In September 2019 the National Dance Council of America (NDCA) changed its rules to say that 'a "couple" will now be defined . . . as a leader and follower without regard to the sex or gender of the dancer' and 'Accordingly, beginning on September 23, 2019, same-sex/gender neutral couples will be able to compete with opposite-sex couples in all dance genres included in championships, competitions, and events sanctioned by the NDCA.'[24] At about the same time USA Dance set up a Gender Neutral Committee, stating that it plans to 'make a long overdue change – all their sanctioned competitions will be gender-neutral . . . The motion aims to change the definition of a couple from a "man" and a "woman" to "two athletes" to allow competitors of any gender configuration to compete, and to be able to represent their country at world championships.'[25] Approval is being sought from the WDSF and the proposed changes are still under discussion.

Regardless of any views on dancing and the definition of a couple, the BDC's proposal to refer to a female dancer as a 'lady' angered many; 'man and woman' or 'male and female' have long been accepted terms in favour of the outdated 'gentleman' and 'lady'. 'Ladies and gentlemen' might be just about acceptable when addressing a crowd, but otherwise ballroom technique books and competition regulations must be one of the very few instances where the term 'lady' is still in common usage. Dance schools are gradually catching up perhaps led by the European Same Sex Dancing Association (ESSDA), which supports the use of gender-neutral terminology: 'to work towards universal acceptance of "leader" and "follower" as teaching terms'.[26]

The first British Equality Open competition was held in Dorset in November 2019 with the ambitious aim of removing 'gender from the dance form and teaching everyone to both lead and follow as well as encourage beginners to the competitive scene at a very early stage'.[27] Couples can be any format, with the option to change the lead and follow at any time during the performance. The 2019 winners in the same-sex women's A (top) class were the world champions Caroline Privou and Petra Zimmermann from Germany, who started dancing together in 2001 and have been winning competitions since 2004, with their first gold medal at the 2006 Gay Games in Chicago. They won the first Same Sex Open at the Empress Ballroom in Blackpool in 2012, commenting, 'This competition lived up to the City's fine dance legacy, and we hope it's the start of a new tradition of great same-sex dancing in Blackpool.'[28]

For the 2020 series of *Strictly Come Dancing* the BBC finally decided to field a same-sex couple when Olympic champion boxer Nicola Adams agreed to take part on two conditions: that she wear trousers and that she could dance as leader with a female partner. Adams was surprised when complaints were received about her pairing with a woman as soon as the announcement was made and long before any dancing started: 'Just when you think 2020 can't surprise you anymore. Something else happens.'[29] During the 2019 series, when Johannes Radebe and Graziano Di Prima, two of the regular professional dancers, had danced together for only a few moments, the BBC received almost two hundred complaints. None of the complaints were upheld and interviews with the dancers were widely published. Di Prima's reponse, reported in the *Daily Express*, was straightforward: 'It is such a silly thing because dancing is for everyone. As long as you feel the energy that dance can give to you, you can dance with whoever you want.'[30] The BBC has been clear in its defence of the 2020 same-sex pairing: 'We have stated, in the past, that we are open to the prospect of including same sex pairings between our celebrities and professional dancers, should the opportunity arise. Nicola Adams requested an all-female pairing, which we are happy to facilitate. The show is first and foremost about dance, the sex of each partner within a coupling should have no bearing on their routine.'[31] For those familiar with same-sex dancing – Peggy Spencer held all-male tango competitions in the 1950s – it does seem to be a big fuss over nothing. Many dancers happily switch roles and every professional dancer knows both the leader's and follower's steps – it would be impossible to teach without that knowledge. George Lloyd recounts his experience with Elsa Wells when they were both waiting in Haylor's studio for a lesson and danced together: 'All was going well when suddenly without a word Elsa changed hold and took the lead. I was now the lady and she was the man. She stepped it up a notch or two. It was now relentless. Everything was syncopated, I was doing endless heel turns, same foot lunges, travelling contra checks, you name it she produced it!' At the end, of course, Wells repeated the age-old joke that next time he could try it in high heels.[32]

Strictly Come Dancing has definitely had a huge impact on the popularity of dancing. It also supports a second, daily TV show and brings glamour, appearing in the gossip columns for the duration of the competition, although the dancing itself is rarely discussed. *Strictly Come Dancing* is currently considered to be the most watched TV programme of all time and is so popular that the BBC has exported a facsimile, *Dancing with the Stars*, to sixty countries worldwide. Perhaps it has encouraged more people to take up dancing, and perhaps like the original *Come Dancing* something still remains of the tasteless, gently mocking self-deprecatory position – we are still looking for something to satirize. Pundits commenting on the 2020 series repeatedly told us that it was strange for Bill Bailey, or maybe just any man over fifty, to take dancing seriously and be good at it but without saying why. We all might guess that there was a casting error, that he was meant to be the comedy turn and be voted off after a few slapstick moments. Whatever the reason, it is odd that such blatantly ageist criticism was permitted, particularly when men and women of his age and much older can be seen on dance floors everywhere.

We can conclude that social Ballroom and Latin has seen something of a revival, although any useful statistics are hard to find. However, rather than existing only as a poor relation to the competitive version it is now identified within a much broader canvas of other

A recent Finals Day of the International Championships at the Royal Albert Hall, London. Spectators are invited to take to the floor during breaks between the different competitions.

kinds of social dancing: those that belong to the somewhat pejorative sounding 'alternative rhythms' at the ISTD or 'non-core' subjects at the IDTA. The mainstream competitive dancers may have secured a space for themselves as purists of a kind, sticking rigidly to the highly regulated approved ten International Ballroom and Latin dances and accepting the need to practise almost every day. They have achieved a separation from the social dancers who are undoubtedly from a much wider age range and probably include many, who are less athletic and engaged in other activities, and for whom dancing is a pleasurable pastime. Then there are the social dancers who are keen on technique, who take their 'hobby' seriously and enjoy the challenge of learning complex amalgamations and perfecting their technique.

As early as 1932 Josephine Bradley, writing in the *Dancing Times*, remarked: 'I have gleaned one big criticism of our style of dancing – it is too difficult for the general public.' She went on to say: 'We should divide our dancing into two classes, competition dancing for those interested in dancing as an art, and simplified dancing for the average dancer who wants to take his or her pleasure simply.'[33] But perhaps there are not just two classes but three or even more. Despite its demanding nature, there are many keen social dancers prepared to learn the ten Ballroom and Latin dances. Of course, it is likely that those who prefer the less challenging club dances would agree with Bradley's suggestion and with Baz Lurhmann's critique that ballroom dancing is hamstrung by its overly strict regulations, certainly for social dancers who are not prepared, or who simply do not have the time and/or money, to put in the months of effort required to achieve even a basic standard to enable them to dance with others. Today's dancers, rather than give up as earlier generations did, in collaboration with a new generation of teachers, studio owners and event promoters, have simply responded by reinventing partner dancing through their own style of competitions, their own ways to show off their skills, to challenge themselves with higher bars to jump. The IVDA includes salsa and team matches; same-sex dancers have always taken a more inclusive approach, with Ballroom and Latin part of a much broader landscape of other kinds of partner dancing – swing dancing, Argentine tango, modern jive, salsa, Lindy hop – together with line dances. Pro–am (and/or teacher–student) is growing bigger every year as more and more competition organizers add such events to their programmes, and sequence dancing, both old time and modern, has maintained its popularity since the 1940s.[34]

Despite Peggy Spencer's lament in the 1960s that UK competitive dancers should be treated like sports stars as they were in other European countries, the major Dancesport competitions are very rarely, if ever, reported in British newspapers' sports sections, and ballroom has still not been included in the Olympic Games.

Competition dancing goes from strength to strength but is largely unseen, and currently wrapped up in its own internal arguments over representation, enforcement of regulations, and definitions of professional and amateur status long abandoned by most other sports. The professional teaching associations do their best to encourage their pupils to learn the specifics of each dance and the correct technique, but for some the rigorous approach to technique is anathema – and always will be – to an enjoyment of music and spontaneity of movement. In the early days of the 1920s and '30s, the first generation of experts had the exciting task of inventing new steps and experimenting with new rhythms, but since the jive was added as the last of the Latin dances in 1968, very little in terms of technique has changed. As Richard Gleave says (describing modern): 'I think ballroom dancing is pretty much fixed . . . I can't see a lot of changes because the thing with ballroom dancing is it's unique because you dance together; there's no other form of dance where dancers dance together with contact that's required all the time.'[35] While dancers have become more athletic, more energetic and dynamic, and, noticeably, modern posture has changed for followers as their shoulders and upper body have moved further away from their leader, it is unlikely that much more will change. But while it may be unique as a form of dance where two people dance together as one, it is still frowned upon to want to dance one's own steps. Once again, *Strictly Ballroom* – focused on Latin dancing – expresses it perfectly. When Scott 'resorted to his own flashy, crowd-pleasing steps', Les the instructor explains: 'Well, to pick what was actually wrong with the steps . . . you'd have to be an experienced professional . . . like myself or Barry Fife, head of the Australian Federation.' Barry's response says it all: 'Well, of course, you can dance any steps you like. That doesn't mean you'll . . . win.'

Appendix

The Ten International Style Ballroom and Latin Dances

The following is a brief description of the International Style Ballroom and Latin dances codified in England between 1929 and 1968. Prescribed speeds vary; those listed here are from the BDC rule book, amended in December 2020. The approximate dates are from *The Laird Technique of Latin Dancing* (2009) and Lyndon Wainwright's *The Story of British Popular Dance* (1997).

International Ballroom

Dance and approximate dates	Time signature	Tempo (bars per minute)	Description
Waltz, 1927 as the Diagonal or Slow Waltz	3/4	28–30	Waltz timing is quite different from other styles in 3/4 time, with emphasis on the first beat and a flowing, smooth style. Basic figures have six steps, with a rotation of 270 degrees and a gentle rise and fall. More advanced figures incorporate sway, Contra Body Movement (CBM), syncopated rhythms and additional steps.
Foxtrot, 1927	4/4	28–30	Foxtrot has its roots in the ragtime music of America in the 1910s and was developed in England to suit the big band and swing music of the 1930s and '40s. Another graceful dance, it includes all the elements of the waltz but to 4/4 time.
Quickstep, 1927	4/4	48–50	Developed in England, the quickstep is danced to very fast and lively big band, swing-style syncopated music. Originally called the quicktime foxtrot, it incorporates both Charleston and foxtrot figures, with hops, runs, jumps and kicks.
Tango, 1936 and originally c. 1910	2/4	32–34	Traditionally tango music had the distinctive sound of the bandoneon, an instrument similar to an accordion. The ballroom tango has retained the dramatic intensity evolved from the Argentine tango, with staccato steps, no rise and fall, and a more compact hold than the other ballroom or 'swing' dances.
Viennese Waltz, 1775	3/4 or 6/8	56–60	The original fast rotary waltz that turns 360 degrees for every six steps. The International version has just three figures: natural (right or clockwise) and reverse (left) turns; the change step to change direction of the turns, which are travelling steps; and the fleckerl, which rotates on the spot.

International Latin

Dance and approximate dates	Time signature	Tempo (bars per minute)	Description
Cha-cha-cha, 1954	4/4	28–30	From Cuba, the cha-cha-cha is a very lively dance. Five steps are taken to four beats of music, with the emphasis on the second beat in the bar. The steps are compact and the feet stay close to the floor, allowing the movement of the hips to become more visible.
Samba, 1923 and 1913 as the Maxixe	2/4	50–52	Originally from Brazil and known as the party dance. It is a complex dance that demands continuous body movement, bounce and a range of different complex rhythm patterns.
Rumba, 1948 and 1931 as Square Rumba	4/4	25–27	The rumba is also a Cuban dance and has many similar figures to the cha-cha-cha. However, it is danced at a much slower pace. Three steps are taken to four beats of music, with the emphasis on the second beat in the bar.
Paso Doble, 1916	2/4	58–60	The style of this dance is often described as a representation of a matador circling in a bull ring. The complexity of the dance and exaggerated posturing make it fun to learn but difficult to lead and follow, which has in general limited it to competition and performance. It is rarely seen at social dances.
Jive, 1968 based on 1943	4/4	42–44	The jive, from America, is the most energetic of all the Latin dances and can include more gymnastic kicks, flicks and jumps. It is danced to any contemporary music at speed; the figures are easily adapted to slower speeds for more relaxed versions at social dances.

References

The epigraph to the book is taken from 'Sequins, Strict Tempo and Hard Slog', *Daily Mirror* (12 May 1971).

Introduction

1 See www.showtownblackpool.co.uk.

1 'A Flood of Splendour': Blackpool's New Ballrooms

1 Michael Bracewell, 'Blackpool Bossanova', *The Observer* (3 July 1994), p. D12.
2 Nikolaus Pevsner, *The Buildings of England: Lancashire – 2 The Rural North* (London, 1969), pp. 68–9.
3 Lynn F. Pearson, *The People's Palaces: The Story of the Seaside Pleasure Buildings of 1870–1914* (Buckingham, 1991), p. 21.
4 John K. Walton, *Blackpool* (Edinburgh, 1998), p. 87.
5 Ibid., p. 82.
6 Pearson, *The People's Palaces*, p. 67.
7 Louise Rogers, 'New Wave', *Architects' Journal* (14 February 1990), pp. 25–7, on the refurbishment of the Winter Gardens by David Quigley Architects.
8 Pearson, *The People's Palaces*, p. 12.
9 Ibid., p. 95.
10 'Selected Design for the Blackpool Eiffel Tower', *Building News* (3 July 1891), p. 29.
11 William E. Schmidt, 'Tacky, Wonderful Blackpool', *New York Times* (7 August 1994), pp. 8–10.
12 'Blackpool's New Palace: The Evolution of the Tower Ballroom', *Blackpool Times* (20 May 1899). Frank Matcham designed around ninety theatres between 1879 and 1912, including London's Hackney Empire and Victoria Palace.
13 Frank Matcham quoted ibid.
14 'Tower Ballroom: A Dream of Splendour', *Blackpool Gazette* (21 March 1913), p. 8.

15 'New Pavilion and Winter Garden, Blackpool', *Building News* (19 July 1878), p. 52.

2 Jazz, Ragtime and Tangoitis

1 'Serve Breakfast at the Dance Now: Odd Steps Are in Vogue', *New York Times* (30 December 1911), p. 11.
2 'Modern Dancing', *Hearth and Home*, XIV/359 (31 March 1898), p. 838.
3 'Our Dancing: "Savagery"', *The Observer* (18 March 1906), p. 4.
4 'Ballroom Fashions', *Manchester Guardian* (25 January 1911), p. 6.
5 Arthur Hopkins, 'Cleaning the Slate', *Punch*, CXXII/3198 (2 April 1902), p. 243.
6 Lewis Baumer, 'A Promising Partner', *Punch*, CXXVII/3320 (27 July 1904), p. 63.
7 Reginald Cleaver, 'Overheard at a Dance', *Punch*, CXXVI/3301 (23 March 1904), p. 211.
8 'From London', *Manchester Guardian* (13 October 1902), p. 6.
9 'Night-Club Dancing', *Manchester Guardian* (11 August 1926), p. 16.
10 'About Town Notes', *Dancing Times* (December 1923), p. 259.
11 Allen Dodworth (1822–c. 1910), *Dancing and Its Relations to Education and Social Life* (New York, 1900), p. 7.
12 Originally the Imperial Society of Dancing Teachers, now the Imperial Society of Teachers of Dancing, the ISTD or Imperial was 'Founded for the elevation and advancement of the art of dancing and the preservation of its ancient prestige and dignity and secondly for the fraternal co-operation of properly qualified teachers of dancing in the British Empire and foreign countries for the safeguarding of their mutual interests.' *The Observer* (26 July 1908), p. 5.
13 For a more detailed study of Crompton's (1845–1926) early efforts to professionalize dancing teaching, see Theresa J. Buckland, 'Crompton's Campaign: The Professionalisation of Dance Pedagogy in Late Victorian England', *Dance Research*, XXV/1 (2007), pp. 1–34.
14 'Miscellany', *Manchester Guardian* (26 July 1905), p. 6.
15 'Improved Dancing', *Daily Mail* (16 May 1906), p. 9.
16 'Coming Dances: How Hostesses Might Put Down Romping', *The Observer* (20 June 1909), p. 4.
17 'Next Season's Dances: No New "Squares" or "Figures"', *The Observer* (26 July 1908), p. 5.
18 'Coming Dances: How Hostesses Might Put Down Romping', p. 4.
19 'The Boston', *Manchester Guardian* (4 May 1909), p. 6.
20 'Slower Waltzing: New Music Induces More Graceful Measures', *The Observer* (24 July 1910), p. 6.
21 'La Maxixe', *Manchester Guardian* (6 November 1913), p. 6. According to Pierre's *Latin and American Dances for Students and Teachers* (1948), 'Before the 1914 war it (the Samba) was known as the

Brazilian Maxixe; in 1923/24 it was reintroduced in Paris as the modern Samba . . . the Samba is still very little known amongst the British dancing public, and rather than complicate matters by differentiating Samba, Carioca, and others it is better to include them all, as our North American friends are doing, under one heading the Samba.'

22 Horace Taylor, 'Modern Dancing', *Manchester Guardian* (12 February 1913), p. 14.

23 'Approve the Turkey Trot: Philadelphia Society Leaders Are Taking Lessons in Latest Dances', *New York Times* (22 December 1911), p. 13. 'Grizzly Bear Dance at Junior Cotillion', *New York Times* (6 December 1911), p. 13.

24 'Serve Breakfast at the Dance Now: Odd Steps Are in Vogue', p. 11.

25 'Dances for Working Girls', *Manchester Guardian* (26 February 1909), p. 6.

26 Irene Castle (née Foote, 1893–1969), *Castles in the Air as Told to Bob and Wanda Duncan* (New York, 1958), p. 85.

27 Lew Fields (1867–1941) had a successful career on stage before producing many musicals. He appeared with Castle in the musical *The Hen-Pecks* in 1911 and played himself in the film of the Castles' life made in 1939.

28 Castle, *Castles in the Air*, p. 54.

29 Elisabeth Marbury (1856–1933), *My Crystal Ball: Reminiscences* (London, 1924), p. 224.

30 Mr and Mrs Vernon Castle, *Modern Dancing* (New York, 1914), Foreword, p. 17. Vernon Castle (William Vernon Blythe, 1887–1918).

31 Ibid., Introduction, pp. 19–29.

32 Castle, *Castles in the Air*, p. 87.

33 Ibid., quoting Seldes.

34 Cecil Beaton, *The Book of Beauty* (London, 1930), p. 499.

35 Eve Golden, *Vernon and Irene Castle's Ragtime Revolution* (Lexington, KY, 2007), p. 104.

36 Maurice Mouvet (1889–1927) was known by his professional name Maurice.

37 Castle, *Castles in the Air*, p. 67.

38 Belle Harding (1866–1945) learned to dance at Camille de Rhynal's studio in Paris.

39 Gladys Beattie Crozier, *The Tango and How to Dance It* (London, 1913), p. 21.

40 Ibid., p. 141.

41 'Affairs in Berlin', *The Observer* (28 September 1913), p. 13.

42 'The Tango on the Defensive: A London Referendum', *Manchester Guardian* (6 January 1914), p. 8.

43 'The Real Tango', *Manchester Guardian* (4 November 1913), p. 8.

44 Evelyn Nesbit, 'How to Do the New Dances No. 1: The Roule Roule', *Washington Post* (4 October 1914), p. 62.

45 Margaret Hawkesworth, 'How to Do the New Dances No. 2: The Lulu-Fado', *Times Dispatch* (11 October 1914), p. 30.
46 Joan Sawyer (1887–1966), 'How to Do the New Dances No. 3: The Sawyer Maxixe', *Salt Lake Tribune* (25 October 1914), p. 37.
47 Margaret Hawkesworth, 'How to Dance the French Tango', *Washington Post* (25 October 1914), p. 62.
48 Joan Sawyer for Columbia Graphophone Company, *How to Dance the Foxtrot* (New York, 1914), p. 8.
49 'Dancing of Today: A Tribute from the Past to the Present', *Manchester Guardian* (23 May 1913), p. 4.
50 'Court and Society', *The Observer* (7 January 1913), p. 6.
51 'World Congress of Dance Masters', *The Observer* (26 July 1914), p. 12.
52 American National Association Masters of Dancing, *Description of Modern Dances as Standardized* (Pittsburgh, PA, 1915).
53 The *Ballroom Dancing Times* was created as a separate publication in 1958 when A. H. Franks took over as editor. It was relaunched in 2001 as *Dance Today* and since 2015 has been incorporated as part of *Dancing Times*.

3 The Democratization of Dancing

1 Sydney A. Moseley, 'Coronets and Jazz: Who's Who in the Dancing Peerage', *Sunday Express* (6 March 1921), p. 9.
2 'Entertaining in England', *Vogue* (New York) (15 April 1924), pp. 110, 116.
3 Moseley, 'Coronets and Jazz', p. 9.
4 'The Revival of the Waltz', *Manchester Guardian* (10 March 1919), p. 4.
5 'Revival of the Waltz: More Sociability in the Ballroom', *The Observer* (9 March 1919), p. 5.
6 The static figures, the natural and reverse fleckerls, were introduced later.
7 'The New Dances', *Manchester Guardian* (15 October 1919), p. 6.
8 'New Season's Dances: The Paso Doble and the Tango Valse', *Daily Mail* (14 October 1919), p. 5.
9 'Freak Dancing in the Ballroom', *The Observer* (2 May 1920), p. 8.
10 Philip J. S. Richardson (1875–1963), '15 Dancing Facts', *Daily Mail* (11 January 1921), p. 6.
11 Philip J. S. Richardson, *A History of English Ballroom Dancing (1910–1945)* (London, 1946), p. 149. 'Louis Bayo, a famous professional dancer, won first prize in the tango dancing with one of his amateur pupils, Mlle. Lemaire de Villars.'
12 Founded in 1958, the BDF aims to promote and support professional competitive ballroom dancers. The organization grew to prominence during the 1960s with Sonny Binnick as chair, Bob Burgess as vice chair and Walter Laird as honorary secretary. See www.bdfonline.co.uk.
13 Owing to the COVID-19 pandemic the 2020 festival was cancelled and the 2021 festival was held later in the year than usual, 24 August–3 September.
14 See Kit Hallewell's book *Blackpool, My Blackpool* (Birmingham, 1979) for

a year by year personal account of the events and the atmosphere of the standard competition in particular.

15 The amateur competition relied on district heats, but no reliable source has been found with detail of dates and numbers.

16 Josephine Bradley (1893–1985): 'Miss Bradley is one of the best known teachers of ballroom dancing in the metropolis . . . At the Knightsbridge Hotel where she holds her classes, she has established a very big reputation as a teacher of the best style of dancing – especially in the most popular of all dances, the foxtrot.' Advertisement, *Dancing Times* (December 1923), p. 244.

17 CBMP differs from Contra Body Movement (CBM), a body action which involves turning the opposite side of the body towards the moving foot, which is moving forwards or back, generally to initiate turn. CBM and Sway (where the entire body inclines from the vertical without breaking the sides) were not introduced until the early 1930s.

18 Arthur Murray (1895–1991): see *My Husband, Arthur Murray* (New York, 1960), written by his wife, Katherine, with Betty Hannah Hoffman, for details about his early life and career.

19 Ibid., p. 42.

20 Ibid., p. 45.

21 Arthur Murray, *How to Become a Good Dancer* (New York, 1922), postal version, p. 1, accessed at www.richardpowers.com, 2 January 2019.

22 Arthur Murray, *How to Become a Good Dancer* (New York, 1938).

23 Murray, *My Husband, Arthur Murray*, p. 16.

24 Arthur Murray, *The Modern Dances: An Introductory Course* (New York, 1922), p. 3.

25 Murray, *My Husband, Arthur Murray*, p. 9.

26 Arthur Murray, 'This Student Earns $15,000 a Year', *Forbes* magazine (17 April 1920), pp. 22 and 25.

27 Ibid.

28 Victor Silvester (1900–1978), *Dancing Is My Life* (London, 1958), p. 32.

29 Ibid., p. 41.

30 Pierre, or sometimes Monsieur Pierre, was the professional name used by Jean Philippe Zurcher-Margolle, a successful London-based French ballroom dancer and early tango enthusiast who went on to become best known as a Latin expert.

31 Lyndon Wainwright, *The Story of British Popular Dance* (Brighton, 1997), p. 15.

32 'Popular Dance Suppers', *Daily Express* (17 January 1923), p. 4.

33 'Dancing, Here and in Paris', *Daily Express* (13 October 1923), p. 4.

4 Basic Technique Takes Shape

1 Arthur Murray, *How to Become a Good Dancer* (New York, 1922), p. 4.

2 Philip J. S. Richardson, *A History of English Ballroom Dancing (1910–1945)* (London, 1946), p. 41.

3 'Ballroom "Bolshevism": Dancing Teachers' Steps to Abolish Dips and Splits', *Daily Mail* (13 May 1920), p. 3.

4 Others who addressed the conference include Madame Vandyck, Cecil Taylor, Edward Scott, Mr Hurndall, Charles d'Albert, Mr Latimer, Mr Bloodworth, Mrs Louis d'Egeville and Mr D. G. MacLennan.

5 'Middle of the Back Ruling', *Daily Mail* (26 July 1920), p. 5.

6 Richardson, *History of English Ballroom Dancing*, p. 44.

7 The committee members were Charles d'Albert, Edith Baird, Harry Bloodworth, Mrs Louis d'Egeville, George Fontana, Belle Harding, W. F. Hurndall, Maurice, Alec McKenzie, D. G. MacLennan, Muriel Simmons, Edward Scott, Miss Smurthwaite, Cecil Taylor and Madame Vandyck.

8 Richardson, *History of English Ballroom Dancing*, p. 47.

9 'The Tango Comes Back: A New Version of the Pre-War Dance', *The Observer* (5 March 1922), p. 9.

10 'The Tango and Its Chances: Will It Capture London?', *The Observer* (1 November 1925), p. 9.

11 The ISTD now has two main branches: Theatre, which covers all the dances for performance such as Imperial Classical Ballet, Tap, Modern Theatre Dance, National Dance and so on, and Dancesport, which has four faculties for Sequence, Modern Ballroom, Latin American and Disco/Freestyle/Rock'n'roll (DFR).

12 Richardson, *History of English Ballroom Dancing*, p. 59.

13 The *Dance Journal* was first published in 1907 and is now called DANCE. See www.istd.org.

14 Murray, *How to Become a Good Dancer*, p. 4.

15 'New Dances and Prospects: The American Influence, a New Musical Rhythm?' *The Observer* (15 July 1923), p. 9.

16 'The Five Step: A New Alternative to the Foxtrot', *The Observer* (13 April 1924), p. 9.

17 Alex Moore (1901–1991) was chair of the ISTD Ballroom Branch 1947–76 and the ICBD 1964–79. He started a letter service in 1932 and published technique books *Ballroom Dancing* in 1936 and *Revised Technique* in 1950. Phyllis Haylor (1904–1981), the 1925 World champion in the mixed category, was an established professional dancer, adjudicator and regular contributor to *Dancing Times*.

18 Zoe Tucker, 'A History of the Development of Ballroom Dancing in the UK, 1918–1939' (2019), quoting E. Romain in *Dance*, 74 (2005), www.wellingtonschoolofdance.co.uk, accessed 8 April 2019. Romain was a regular contributor to the *Ballroom Dancing Times* section on dancing figures and amalgamations.

19 Camille de Rhynal, 'Dances and Dancers', *Daily Express* (4 October 1924), p. 5.

20 'Charleston and Foxtrot: Changed Ballrooms in Coming Season', *The Observer* (28 February 1926), p. 19. Jack Hylton (1892–1965) was Britain's best known and most successful band leader of the 1920s and '30s and an arranger of early American jazz music, recorded for HMV, and is credited with bringing top

American musicians Louis Armstrong and Duke Ellington to Europe in the 1930s.

21 'Fast or Slow Foxtrot: The Charity Ball Season', *The Observer* (23 November 1924), p. 9.

22 'New Dance Tendencies', *The Observer* (19 April 1925), p. 9.

23 See https://dancemarathon.childrensmiraclenetworkhospitals.org, accessed 14 September 2021. The USA has seen a rebirth in recent years at university campuses across the whole country, raising money for charity. Contemporary marathons are generally limited to between 24 and 48 hours.

24 Peter B. Buckman, *Let's Dance: Social, Ballroom and Folk Dancing* (London, 1978), p. 187.

25 'New Dance Tendencies', *The Observer* (19 April 1925), p. 9.

26 Richardson, *History of English Ballroom Dancing*, p. 126.

27 Ibid., p. 127. The conference was held at the Hotel Cecil on 18 October 1926. Eighty people were present, including representatives of the dance hall managers.

28 'Dancing Here and in Paris', *Daily Express* (13 October 1923), p. 4.

29 Camille de Rhynal, 'Dancing as a Sport', *Daily Mail* (6 March 1924), p. 8.

30 'The Nations in the Ballroom', *Daily Express* (29 December 1924), p. 6.

31 'English Style in Dancing', *Manchester Guardian* (1 November 1924), p. 10.

32 'The Charleston', *Daily Mail* (6 April 1926), p. 8.

33 Ellin Mackay, 'The Charleston Takes the Floor', *Vogue* (New York), LXVII/4 (15 February 1926), pp. 72, 73, 140.

34 'Ballroom Dancing of Today', *The Times* (21 July 1925), p. 12.

35 'The Charleston: For and Against – Difficulties in Crowded Ballrooms', *The Observer* (2 May 1926), p. 13.

36 Victor Silvester, *Dancing Is My Life* (London, 1958), p. 88.

37 Ibid., p. 89.

38 Bemis Walker, *How to Charleston Correctly* (Minneapolis, MN, 1926), p. 4.

39 George Snowden (1904–1982), originator of the 'Shorty George' figure.

40 Silvester, *Dancing Is My Life*, p. 105.

41 'Have You Danced the Trebla?', *Daily Mail* (26 November 1926), p. 2.

42 'The Season's Dancing: The Java and the Paso Doble', *The Observer* (4 April 1926), p. 14.

43 Ibid.

44 The NATD was formed in 1906. In 1932 they initiated the medal test system for amateurs and in 1938 they initiated the juvenile and junior championships at the Blackpool Dance Festival, the first for children. See http://natd.hk.

45 Richardson, *History of English Ballroom Dancing*, p. 75.

46 The waltz steps described are the Viennese waltz.

47 Casani's *Dancing Times* full-page advertisements in the early 1930s included statements such as: 'I claim without boast or conceit, that by the aid of the Air, the Films, Personal Demonstrations and Newspaper Articles, the name of Santos Casani is by far wider known throughout the World than all Teachers put together.' Silvester's is more modest: 'The best and most thorough training in the country is given to those who wish to make Ballroom Dancing their Profession.'

48 The agreed tempos at that time were, in bars per minute: waltz 36–38, quickstep 54–56, foxtrot 38–42, blues 30–34 and tango 30–32.

49 Resolution 13 in Richardson, *History of English Ballroom Dancing*, p. 79.

50 Now the British Dance Council.

5 Dancing in Public

1 '1953 Official Guide to Hammersmith Palais de Danse'.

2 Frank and Peggy Spencer (Peggy: 1920–2016), *Come Dancing* (London, 1968), p. 16.

3 See *Architects Journal*, 10 March 1926. A London steelwork company, Francis Morton Junior and Co., patented the Valtor floor system in which the timber floor is laid on steel girders divided into short lengths pivoting on bolts through helical steel springs which are in turn bolted to stone or brick supports. The ends of the steel girders rest on cast iron rockers. A locking mechanism allows the floor to be stabilized when not in use for dancing.

4 'The Isle of Man', *Manchester Guardian* (7 June 1913), p. 11.

5 *Kebles General Advertiser* (undated, *c.* 1910s).

6 See www.historicengland.org.uk, accessed 1 November 2020. Designed by Ernest Borg (borough engineer) and Stanley C. Ramsey (architect).

7 'Dances of the Season: List of Fixtures', *The Times* (5 May 1919), p. 14.

8 'The Coming Season: Dancing and Dinners', *The Times* (19 January 1911), p. 10.

9 Arthur Murray, *The Modern Dances: Advanced Course* (New York, 1922), p. 22.

10 Linda Mizejewski, *Ziegfeld Girl: Image and Icon in Culture and Cinema* (Durham and London, 1999), p. 11.

11 At the Piccadilly Hotel, now the Dilly, the ballroom's resident dancing school is Inspiration2Dance.

12 *Dancing Times* (January 1923), p. 242.

13 'A Week under the Waves', advertisement in the *Pall Mall Gazette* (30 May 1923), p. 10.

14 Sir Charles T. Ruthen FRIBA, 'Increasing Prosperity', *The Times* (15 October 1923), p. 21.

15 'If Gossip We Must: Playtime at the Piccadilly', *The Bystander* (19 February 1930), p. 379.

16 'Ballroom Notes', *Dancing Times* (April 1931), pp. 24–7.

17 William Robert Crewe (1860–1937) is mostly known for his many theatres and his flamboyant neo-baroque style.

18 'Palais de Danse: Big Gathering at Hammersmith', *Fulham Chronicle* (31 October 1919), p. 6.

19 See Pat Kirkham, 'Dress, Dance, Dreams, and Desire: Fashion and Fantasy in Dance Hall', *Journal of Design History*, VIII/3 (1995), pp. 195–214.

20 C. B. Purdom, *The Building of Satellite Towns: A Contribution to the Study of Town Development and Regional Planning* (London, 1949), p. 128.

21 As reported in the *Citizen* (21 and 28 June and 12 July 1935).

22 Herman Darewski programme, 1934.
23 'How Herman Darewski Leapt into Fame', *Daily Mail Atlantic* (2 May 1930), p. 3.
24 See obituary in *The Times* (3 June 1947), p. 7.
25 Jo Clarke, reminiscences, 10 May 2021.

6 Nightlife and Private Clubs

1 'Summary', *Church Times* (17 October 1924), p. 415.
2 'Ballroom Dancing and How To Enjoy It', *Kingston Daily Gleaner* (26 February 1924), p. 5.
3 'Waltz Coming Back', *Daily Mail* (13 July 1931), p. 13.
4 'Act for the better preventing Thefts and Robberies and for Regulating Places of Public Entertainment and punishing persons keeping Disorderly Houses'.
5 'The Licensing Question: Temperance Reformers and Clubs', *Manchester Guardian* (19 November 1907), p. 9.
6 'Underground Homes of Tragedy', *Daily Mail* (11 March 1922), p. 5.
7 'Good and Bad Night Clubs', *Daily Mail* (13 March 1922), p. 8.
8 'Dance Club Scenes', *Daily Mail* (3 January 1924), p. 8.
9 The Brighter London Society included some powerful individuals: Members of Parliament, the entertainments promoter Sir Oswald Stoll, Sir Sidney Skinner, chairman of Barker and Co. department store, and Albert Voyce, chairman of the Variety Artistes Federation. 'Brighter London Campaign', *The Times* (5 May 1922), p. 12.
10 'Forty Acres of Fun', *Manchester Guardian* (9 April 1924), p. 4. The British Empire Exhibition ran from 23 April 1924 to 31 October 1925. 'The dance hall is one of the chief sights. Here there is to be non-stop dancing from May to October from ten in the morning to ten at night, and 2,000 people can dance at the same time. You pay a shilling for an hour's dancing. There will be three bands playing at once. Great experts will give exhibition dances here and possibly the various industries that are showing in the Exhibition.'
11 'Seaside Dance Licence', *Daily Mail* (3 June 1924), p. 7.
12 'Sunday Dances Protest', *Daily Mail* (15 December 1928), p. 9.
13 'Sunday Dancing', *Daily Mail* (13 April 1926), p. 7.
14 'Summary', *Church Times*, p. 415.
15 Ibid.
16 'Lost Arts of the Ballroom: Deportment Conspicuous by Its Absence: Teachers on Abuse of Licences', *Manchester Guardian* (28 June 1922), p. 7.
17 'Dancing Girls Not Wanted', *Daily Express* (21 February 1929), p. 3.
18 'LCC to investigate Dance Hostesses Scandal', *Daily Mail* (21 November 1931), p. 9.
19 'The Gayest Capital', *Daily Mail* (26 September 1929), p. 9.
20 Eduard Reeser, *The History of the Waltz* (Stockholm, 1949), p. 8.
21 T. A. Faulkner, *From the Ballroom to Hell: The Life Story of Bill Tansill* (Chicago, IL, 1892), Preface.

22 Ibid., p. 8.
23 Ibid., p. 13.
24 'After 151 Years, Dance Ban Ends at Baylor', *New York Times* (19 April 1996), p. B09.
25 'Dancing for Slimness', *Daily Express* (10 August 1928), p. 4.
26 'Dance – and Be Happy', *Daily Express* (17 February 1933), p. 8.
27 'Dancers and Dancing', *Daily Express* (8 November 1924), p. 5.
28 Irene Castle, *Castles in the Air as Told to Bob and Wanda Duncan* (New York, 1958), p. 90.

7 Hollywood Glamour

1 Ellen Spiegel, 'Fred and Ginger Meet Van Nest Polglase', *Velvet Light Trap* (Fall 1973), p. 17.
2 Amy Henderson and Dwight Blocker Bowers, *Red Hot and Blue: A Smithsonian Salute to the American Musical* (Washington, DC, and London, 1996), p. 3.
3 Fred Astaire (1899–1987) and Ginger Rogers (1911–1995): *Flying Down to Rio* (1933), *The Gay Divorcee* (1934), *Roberta* (1935), *Top Hat* (1935), *Follow the Fleet* (1936), *Swing Time* (1936), *Shall We Dance* (1937), *Carefree* (1938), *The Story of Vernon and Irene Castle* (1939).
4 Bevis Hillier, *Art Deco of the '20s and '30s* (London, 1986), p. 14.
5 Juan Antonio Ramirez, *Architecture for the Screen: A Critical Study of Set Design in Hollywood's Golden Age* (Jefferson, NC, and London, 2004), p. 161.
6 Cedric Gibbons, the art director at MGM, was one of the first to bring the new Art Deco style to film set design after visiting the Paris exhibition. His sets for *Our Dancing Daughters* (1928), *Grand Hotel* (1932) and *Gold Diggers of 1933* introduced the new style with lavish designs.
7 Donald Albrecht, *Designing Dreams: Modern Architecture in the Movies* (London, 1986), p. 45. The line-up of designers who collaborated on the sets, furniture and various accessories included all the well-known artists and designers of the time: Fernand Léger, Pierre Chareau, René Lalique, Jean Puiforcat and Jean Luce. Paul Poiret designed the costumes and Raymond Templier the jewellery. André Lurçat and the painters Robert and Sonia Delaunay collaborated on *Le Vertige* (1926).
8 Hans Drier, at Paramount from 1923 to 1950, had worked for the German government, and Jock Peters, designer of the Landmarked interiors at the Bullocks Wilshire department store in Los Angeles (1929) and employed by Famous Players-Lasky Corporation (pre-Paramount), had worked for pioneering German modern architect Peter Behrens; another set designer was Kem Weber, designer of the 'airliner chair', an early experiment in self-assembly, and architect for the Walt Disney Studios, Burbank.
9 Famous Players-Lasky's, the only backlot in New York, was built in 1920, close to Broadway. It is now the Kaufman Astoria Studios, was listed on

the National Register of Historic Places in 1978, and is still in use as a film and television studio.

10 Polglase (1898–1968) worked on many films and was nominated for six Oscars; among his credits are *Citizen Kane* (dir. Orson Welles, 1941) and *Gilda* (dir. Charles Vidor, 1946).

11 Arlene Croce, *The Fred Astaire and Ginger Rogers Book* (London, 1972), p. 75.

12 Ibid., p. 56.

13 'Fred Astaire's New Picture: Film Notes', *Dancing Times* (September 1935), p. 595.

14 It came to attention in the early 1970s at the height of the Art Deco revival when it was occupied by fashion designer Biba.

15 'Court and Society: Queen Mary's Engagements – Dancing on the Roof', *The Observer* (11 June 1939), p. 20.

16 Croce, *The Fred Astaire and Ginger Rogers Book*, p. 6.

17 Ginger Rogers won an Academy Award for *Kitty Foyle: The Natural History of a Woman* (dir. Sam Wood, 1940).

18 Damian Sutton, '"Let the Dance Floor Feel Your Leather": Dance and the Articulation of Audiences in RKO Radio's Astaire-Rogers Series', *Journal of Popular Film and Television*, XLIII/1 (2015), pp. 2–12.

8 Everyday Glamour

1 Josephine Bradley quoted in Roma Fairley, *Come Dancing Miss World* (London, 1966), p. 138.

2 Best known for his circus, Mills played a big part in control of entertainments. During the 1920s and '30s he was a member of the special committee of experts for the British Board of Film Censors, president of the Showmen's Guild of Great Britain and Ireland, chairman of the Entertainments Licensing Committee of London County Council, chairman of the Inspection of Films Sub-Committee and chairman of the Sunday Entertainment Sub-Committee.

3 Fairley, *Come Dancing Miss World*, p. 39.

4 Ibid., p. 51.

5 'A Night Out in the West End (s.w.16)', *Daily Mail* (31 March, 1939), p. 11.

6 Jenny Nicholson, 'War-Time Dance Hall', *Picture Post* (22 February 1944), pp. 14–17.

7 'Dancing Spoilt by Long Gowns', *Daily Mail* (8 January 1931), p. 7.

8 Santos Casani quoted in 'Dancing Spoilt by Long Gowns and Men Are So Lazy', *Daily Mail* (8 January 1931), p. 7.

9 In 1929 the chairman was P.J.S. Richardson; the board of directors comprised Josephine Bradley, Grace Cone, Ruby Peeler, Adela Roscoe, Muriel Simmons, Eve Tynegate-Smith, F. C. Barlow, H. Bloodworth, Santos Casani, Andy Cowan, H. Vivian Davies, Mr. Greenwell, F.W.C. Leslie, Alec Miller, Alex Moore, M. Pierre, St John Rumsay, Victor Silvester, Maxwell Stuart and Cecil Taylor. The OBBD changed its name to the British Dance Council (BDC)

in 1985. It was also instrumental in setting up the International Council of Ballroom Dancing (ICBD), now the World Dance Council (WDC).

10 'Waltz Coming Back', *Daily Mail* (13 July 1931), p. 13.

11 'Non-Stop Dance Folly', *Daily Mail* (22 July 1931), p. 4.

12 David Simmons, 'Black Rhythm and Roots', *Listener* (23 November 1978), pp. 692–3.

13 Eve Tynegate-Smith, *Textbook of Modern Ballroom Dancing* (London, 1933), p. 274.

14 'Rumba as Basis of New Dance Rhythm', *Daily Mail* (22 August 1932), p. 8.

15 'Fame Awaits You', *Daily Mail* (5 September 1932), p. 8.

16 In 1929 the BBC Dance Orchestra was featured in the first ever BBC television broadcast, with Jack Payne. Other publications besides *Melody Maker* that promoted jazz music include *Gramophone* (1923), *Rhythm* (1927) and *Swing Music and Hot News* (1935).

17 'Watching Them Dance', *Daily Mail* (8 November 1933), p. 4.

18 Victor Silvester, *Dancing Is My Life* (London, 1958), p. 107.

19 'How to Dance the Charleston "Blues"', *Daily Mail* (22 November 1933), p. 4.

20 'The Dance of This Season', *Daily Mail* (22 October 1935), p. 11.

21 'What Will You Dance This Winter', *Daily Mail* (22 September 1936), p. 16.

22 For a detailed study of the Lambeth Walk see Allison Abra, 'Doing the Lambeth Walk: Novelty Dances and the British Nation', *Twentieth Century British History*, XX/3 (2009), pp. 346–69.

23 Tom Harrison and Charles Madge, *Britain by Mass-Observation* [1939] (London et al., 1986), p. 139.

24 See 'New Dances for Everybody', 1938, https://britishpathe.com, accessed 19 March 2019.

25 Harrison and Madge, *Britain by Mass-Observation*, p. 161, quoting Adele England.

26 Ibid., p. 183.

27 The term 'shag' refers now to collegiate shag. The term was also used as a general term for all the fast swing dances like jitterbug or Lindy hop.

28 'Britain Will Dance "Yam" and "Cherry Hop"', *Daily Mail* (13 October 1938), p. 20.

29 Katherine Murray, with Betty Hannah Hoffman, *My Husband, Arthur Murray* (New York, 1960), p. 96.

30 '2 Partners at Once', *Daily Mail* (4 February 1933), p. 10.

31 Jack Hylton, 'I Must Think of the Average Man', *Daily Mail* (20 January 1930), p. 10.

9 Togetherness: Holiday Camps and Sequence Dancing

1 Butlin's Clacton Souvenir Brochure 1946, on the reopening after the war.

2 The impact of the paid holiday Act was not felt until the mid-1940s and the one week it legislated for was very soon replaced by longer periods. By 1951 some 62 per cent of manual labourers were entitled to two weeks' holiday with pay, and by 1955 this had increased to 96 per cent. Some workers could still

not afford a holiday away, and for those who could the 'all in' nature of holiday camps meant it was easier to budget.

3 Colin Ward and Dennis Hardy, *Goodnight Campers! The History of the British Holiday Camp* (Nottingham, 1986), p. 48.

4 Jill Drower, *Good Clean Fun: The Story of Britain's First Holiday Camp* (London, 1982), p. 52.

5 Holding founded the first camping club in 1901, the Association of Cycle Campers, which then merged with other clubs to become the National Camping Club in 1907. He wrote *The Camper's Handbook* in 1908.

6 The Cunningham Camp on the Isle of Man originated as an annual week away for young boys working in Liverpool's Toxteth area organized by the Sunday School in the late 1890s.

7 'Joys of Camp Holidays', *Daily Mail* (1 July 1938), p. 4.

8 Sandra Trudgen Dawson, 'Holiday Camps in Twentieth-Century Britain: Packaging Pleasure', *Cultural and Social History*, XI/1 (2014), pp. 150–54.

9 Ward and Hardy, *Goodnight Campers!*, p. 147.

10 George Orwell, 'Pleasure Spots', in *The Collected Essays, Journalism and Letters of George Orwell*, vol. IV: *In Front of Your Nose, 1945–1950*, ed. Sonia Orwell and Ian Angus (London, 1968), pp. 102–6.

11 Richard Hoggart, *The Uses of Literacy: Aspects of Working-Class Life* [1957] (London, 1991), p. 126.

12 Billy Butlin (1899–1980), *The Billy Butlin Story: A Showman to the End* (London, 1993), pp. 176–7.

13 Butlin's rebranded as Butlins Skyline Ltd.

14 For many critics such as Orwell (and Hoggart, see *The Uses of Literacy*) the holiday camp represented an imposition of mass culture, dumbing down and Americanization – an escape to a safe man-made environment that avoided serious thought and contact with the less predictable natural world.

15 Pradeep Bandyopadhyay, 'The Holiday Camp', in *Leisure and Society in Britain*, ed. Michael Smith, Stanley Parker and Cyril Smith (London, 1973), p. 245.

16 Butlin, *The Billy Butlin Story*, p. 120.

17 Charles Graves, 'I See Life', *Daily Mail* (12 May 1939), p. 10.

18 The amateur syllabus comprised the Valse, Boston Two-Step and Barn Dance for Bronze; the Valse, Veleta, Military Two-Step and Varsouviana for Silver; and the Valse, Veleta, Polka, Mazurka, Royal Empress Tango and a choice of La Rinka, Washington Post or Pride of Erin for Gold.

19 The International Sequence (Old Time) Dance Circle held their first annual festival in 1944 at the Empress Ballroom at Blackpool's Winter Gardens, and after a few years at holiday camps in Filey in Yorkshire, Prestatyn in Wales and on the Isle of Man until 1984. It grew to around 2,000 dancers for the week-long festival, which occupied two ballrooms, the Villa Marina and the Palace. Stuart Singleton (director of the ISDC 1975–2011), Audrey Singleton and daughter Jill continued to organize the festival at the Royal Hall, Bridlington, for 25 years from 1993 until the final one in 2018.

20 *Dancing Times* (January 1947), typical full-page advertisement, p. 210.

21 'International Sequence Dance Circles', *Dancing Times* (January 1947), p. 285.

22 Alex Moore started his monthly letter service in 1932 following a trip to South Africa in response to considerable demand for information on what was happening in the dancing world.

23 Wilfred Orange was chairman of the OBBD 1969–72, vice chairman of the Association of Ballrooms, and an accomplished competitive dancer. He worked as Entertainment Manager at various Butlin's camps from 1947 to 1957 and had particular responsibility for the Butlin's Dance Festival and the Butlin's annual reunions held at the Albert Hall.

24 Cecil Wilson, 'Time Dances Back', *Daily Mail* (21 April 1951), p. 2.

25 It Happens All the Time', *Daily Mail* (17 October 1956), p. 8.

26 A. J. Latimer, *A Bouquet of Old Time Dances* (London, 1948), Foreword.

27 Danceland was Mecca's publishing division.

28 See www.oldtimedance.co.uk, accessed 28 August 2019.

29 'New Glide Wins Old Time Dance Prize', *Daily Mail* (12 September 1950), p. 3.

30 See www.bblane.co.uk, accessed 6 November 2020. The Brockbank Lane Sequence Script Service run by Ron and Nichola Lane is the exclusive licensee to the BDC.

31 See www.englishnationaloldtimedancesociety.com, accessed 19 March 2019.

32 James Nott, *Going to the Palais: A Social and Cultural History of Dancing and Dance Halls in Britain, 1918–1960* (Oxford, 2015), p. 169.

33 'Old Time Dances Are so Tiring', *Daily Mail* (1 February 1949), p. 3.

34 Pickering was general manager at the Opera House and had worked for Mills for many years.

35 'I See Life', *Daily Mail* (20 December 1939), p. 6.

36 Butlin, *The Billy Butlin Story*, p. 177.

37 'Old Time Dances Kill Swing', *Daily Mail* (4 March 1946), p. 3.

38 'Ballroom Flashbacks No. 16: The Valeta', *Ballroom Dancing Times* (March 1958), p. 229. According to the *Ballroom Dancing Times*, the valeta was invented by Arthur Morris, dancing teacher and pianist, in 1900 and entered for the annual BATD competition. It did not win but was published with some modifications by Francis Day & Hunter. It was promoted by James Finnigan, then MC at the Empress Blackpool.

39 'Dancing at a Butlin Holiday Camp', *Dancing Times* (March 1947), pp. 315–17.

40 Ibid.

41 'Butlin's Filey Festival Reviewed by Alex Moore', *Ballroom Dancing Times* (October 1954), p. 43.

42 Martin Parr, *Our True Intent Is All for Your Delight: The John Hinde Butlin's Photographs* (London, 2002).

10 Jitterbug, Rock'n'Roll and Jive

1 Andrew H. Ward, 'Dancing in the Dark: Rationalism and the Neglected Social Dance', in *Dance, Gender and Culture*, ed. Helen Thomas (London, 1993), pp. 16–29.

2 'Sitter Out', *Ballroom Dancing Times* (March 1959), p. 238. 'Really strenuous efforts are being made to break the great Latin American deadlock. The latest move is for the Latin American Advisory Committee of the OBBD to meet with the Latin American Committee of the – Imperial Society . . . If only a little progress can be made in this round-the-table fashion perhaps greater progress will soon follow.'

3 At Blackpool in 1961, a British Amateur Latin American Tournament was held, and in 1962 a professional event. Both were upgraded to championship status in 1964. See www.blackpooldancefestival.com, accessed 26 January 2020.

4 From the oral history archive held at Stevenage Museum.

5 Jo Clarke, reminiscences, 10 May 2021.

6 'Will the War Change the "English Style"? The Jitterbug Menace', *Dancing Times* (March 1940), p. 357.

7 See 'Jive Dance 1943', www.britishpathe.com, accessed 19 March 2019.

8 'London's Dancing Halls Ban the Jitterbugs', *Daily Mail* (5 October 1943), p. 3.

9 From the oral history archive held at Stevenage Museum.

10 'Mr Katzman's Winning Formula: There's Money in Rock'n'Roll', *Manchester Guardian* (15 September 1956), p. 7.

11 'Law Takes Steps in the Spot Dance', *Daily Mail* (27 November 1953), p. 5.

12 'Sitter Out', *Dancing Times* (January 1940) p. 218.

13 'Sir, You May Dance 4 Days a Week', *Daily Mail* (14 August 1941), p. 3.

14 Peter Black, 'Slow, Slow, Quick, Quick Slow', *Daily Mail* (21 April 1956), p. 4.

15 'Rocking the Ballroom', *The Times* (27 December 1957), p. 7.

16 'Dance Hall Protest', *Daily Mail* (7 August 1950), p. 1.

17 'Hose Gang Soaks 3,000 Dancers', *Daily Mail* (31 July 1950), p. 1.

18 'Colour Bar by Dance Hall to Be Challenged', *The Observer* (15 June 1958), p. 13.

19 Katherine Murray, with Betty Hannah Hoffman, *My Husband, Arthur Murray* (New York, 1960), p. 59.

20 'The Value of Television', *Ballroom Dancing Times* (March 1958), p. 232.

21 Elsa Wells (1910–2002) won the Star Amateur Championship with her brother John Wells from 1929 to 1931. She received a Carl Alan award in 1965. She handed on the organization of the International to Bobby Short in 1976.

22 Brigitt Mayer-Karakis, *Ballroom Icons* (Düsseldorf, 2009), p. 28.

23 Ibid., p. 28, quoting Laurie Yates.

24 John Kimche, editor of the *Jewish Observer* and *Middle East Review*, sponsor of the Elsa Wells International Championships 1953, Catalogue, p. 12.

25 Denmark was one of the first to adopt the English Style and had developed a strong relationship with ballroom dancing and the Blackpool Festival since the 1930s.

26 Conversation with Richard Gleave, 25 February 2021.

27 From 2021 Dance News Ltd has handed on the presentation and organization of both the UK Championships and International Championships to Robin Short and Christopher Short Creative Productions Ltd.

28 See www.thebestcomps.net.

29 'Dancing Time: Glamour for Happiness', *The Guardian* (7 January 1960), p. 11.

11 Latin, the 1960s and Change

1 Pierre, *Latin and American Dances for Students and Teachers* (London, 1948), Preface.
2 'Where 60 Percent of Marriages Originate', *The Times* (5 December 1962), p. 7.
3 'Britain, a Land of Gardeners, Readers, Riders, Dancers', *The Times* (18 April 1964), p. 6.
4 'Sitter Out', *Ballroom Dancing Times* (February 1959), p. 183.
5 *Dancing Times* (January 1960) p. 13. Of the 5,113 members listed in the UK, 1,691 were in London and the Home Counties.
6 'Sitter Out', *Ballroom Dancing Times* (March 1959), p. 232.
7 Kitty Dixon, 'The Mer-eng-ay!', *Daily Express* (20 October 1959), p. 14.
8 'Where 60 Per Cent of Marriages Originate', *The Times* (5 December 1962), p. 7.
9 'Scots Business Men Take to Cha-Cha-Cha', *The Times* (10 January 1962), p. 6.
10 Only the paso doble and the samba have a number of travelling steps, but as the most technically challenging, they are danced less often at social events.
11 Juliet McMains, *Glamour Addiction: Inside the American Ballroom Dance Industry* (Middletown, CT, 2006), p. 12. And see 'Brownface: Representations of Latinness in Latin Dance', ibid., p. 109.
12 Leonard Morgan was chairman of the BDC from 1965 until 1968 and president from 1974 until 1989.
13 'Knocking the Rock', *Ballroom Dancing Times* (April 1957), p. 274.
14 'International Championships: Latin-American', *Ballroom Dancing Times* (Christmas 1957), p. 123.
15 Lyndon Wainwright, *The Story of British Popular Dance* (Brighton, 1997), p. 25.
16 Revised in 1960 and 1963 as *Latin-American Technique*.
17 See www.dancefund.org.uk. Gwenethe Walshe (1908–2006) founded the Gwenethe Walshe Dance Studio in 1938 after arriving in London from her native New Zealand. She studied with Alex Moore and was an adjudicator at the International from 1953 to 1989. The school was taken over in the late 1990s by her protégé, Vernon Kemp, as Central London Dance.
18 Brigitt Mayer-Karakis, *Ballroom Icons* (Düsseldorf, 2009), p. 94.
19 Arnell, with his partner, Jillian La Valette, was the Professional International Latin Champion 1955–9.
20 Now in its seventh edition (2014), it is used throughout the world.
21 Patrick Sergeant, 'The Twist Packs Them In', *Daily Mail* (9 December 1961), p. 11.
22 From the oral history archive held at Stevenage Museum.
23 Rank eventually bought Mecca in 1990. City editor, 'Mecca Reject Rank's £30M Bid', *The Times* (11 June 1964), p. 12.
24 'Mini-Ballrooms Plan in Mecca Deal', *The Times* (13 November 1964), p. 24.
25 See 'Rivoli Ballroom', www.historicengland.org.uk, accessed 1 November 2020.
26 'Going to the Dancing: From Strength to Strength in Glasgow', *Ballroom Dancing Times* (June 1959), p. 369.
27 William Cater, 'Silvester's Last Waltz – In Strict Tempo of Course!', *Daily Express* (18 March 1964), p. 5.

28 Mayer-Karakis, *Ballroom Icons*, p. 21.

29 'Ballroom Notes', *Ballroom Dancing Times* (October 1954), p. 36.

30 The letter service, which started in 1924, was taken over by Geoffrey Hearn and Peggy Spencer (then Hearn and Spencer Ltd), now DSI.

31 Marshall Pugh, 'It's Silly to Pick on the Dance Halls', *Daily Mail* (16 October 1956), p. 4.

32 Marshall Pugh 'The Palais Keeps Waltzing in Wealth . . . Always', *Daily Mail*, (15 October 1956), p. 4.

33 'Bingo Helps Mecca to 23 p.c. Spurt', *The Times* (18 May 1966), p. 19.

34 'Social Dancing or Anti-Social Dancing', *Ballroom Dancing Times* (October 1960), p. 30.

35 Mayer-Karakis, *Ballroom Icons*, p. 138.

36 Bill and Bobbie Irvine, *The Dancing Years* (Farnborough, 1970), p. 62.

37 Ibid., p. 77.

38 'Is Our Supremacy Ending? A Clear Cool Look at the International Scene', *Ballroom Dancing Times* (July 1966) pp. 508–9.

39 Now the British National Championships. In 1968 a Professional Invitation Ten Dance Team Match was introduced with just two teams from Britain and Germany; since then teams from Australia, Italy, Japan, Russia, Scandinavia and the USA have taken part.

40 'Sitter Out', *Ballroom Dancing Times* (March 1959), p. 233.

41 Victor Silvester, 'The English Teach the World to Dance', *Daily Mail* (9 January 1953), p. 4.

42 'A Nation of Dancers', *The Times* (6 August 1956), p. 10.

12 Television, Come Dancing and Peggy Spencer

1 Frank and Peggy Spencer, *Come Dancing* (London, 1968), p. 21.

2 Bob Lockyer, 'Dance on BBC Television: More Than Just Strictly', www.bbc.com, accessed 9 November 2021.

3 'Sitter Out', *Ballroom Dancing Times* (Christmas 1957), p. 98.

4 History of the BBC, 'Television Dancing Club 27 January 1948', from the introduction by Victor Silvester, www.bbc.com, accessed 17 January 2022.

5 John Warren was the son of the founder of Warren's School of Dancing in Glasgow. His father owned the Albert Ballroom, which opened in 1905. The building was sold in 1965. See www.danceclassesglasgow.co.uk, 4 March 2019.

6 John Gurney, 'Victor under Fire', *Daily Mail* (26 November 1959), p. 10.

7 Advertisement in *Daily Mail* (7 October 1958), p. 5.

8 Alex Warren was the winner, with Celia Bristoe, of the first Professional Scottish Championship.

9 'The World's Championships Reviewed by Hugh Carter', *Ballroom Dancing Times* (April 1959), p. 289.

10 Frank and Peggy Spencer received seven Carl Alan awards throughout their career and were presented with an MBE for thirty years' service to the dancing world in 1977.

11 Now DSI, the company (based in Croydon) provides everything dance related. Still hand-making in London, it has dress and tailoring departments, provides costumes for both stage and screen, and works closely with the *Strictly Come Dancing* costume designer. DSI TV streams live action from the major competitions.

12 Conversation with Peggy Spencer's daughter and formation team dancer, Helena Anderson, 29 July 2021.

13 Frank Spencer came second to Victor Silvester in the 1922 standard competition in Paris, dancing with Doris Nichols.

14 The origin of pattern or formation dancing is credited to Olive Ripman, founder of the Cone-Ripman School (1939), now ArtsEd.

15 'Butlin's Reunion', *Ballroom Dancing Times* (May 1957), p. 323.

16 Conversation with Angela Thurgood, 9 July 2021.

17 Conversation with Keith Gregory, 5 July 2021.

18 Conversation with Angela Thurgood, 9 July 2021.

19 Conversation with Frank Fronda, 5 July 2021.

20 Conversation with Angela Thurgood, 9 July 2021.

21 Pamela Coleman, 'Quick-Stepping to the Olympics?', *The Times* (14 October 1968), p. 7.

22 Conversation with Angela Thurgood, 9 July 2021.

23 Conversation with Helena Anderson, 29 July 2021.

24 Spencer, *Come Dancing*, p. 23.

25 Corrine Smither, reminiscences, April 2019.

26 Conversation with Francesca Canty, May 2020.

27 See www.pengeheritagetrail.org.uk, accessed 9 November 2021.

28 'Sitter Out', *Ballroom Dancing Times* (July 1976), p. 372.

29 James Kennedy, 'The International Style', *The Guardian* (15 May 1967), p. 5.

30 Recognition of the World DanceSport Federation (formerly the International DanceSport Federation) as the representative body for Dancesport was achieved in September 1997, but despite optimism from many quarters Dancesport has still not been included in any Olympic Games.

31 See 'Dancing Notes from 1964', https://archives.dance/2014/10/dancing-notes-1964-richard-gleave, accessed 9 September 2021.

13 The End of an Era

1 Jim Cane, 'Anatomy of a Dancer' (quoting Arlene Croce's 1973 reportage of the World's Championship in New York City in the *New Yorker*), *Dancer's Digest* (March–April 1979), p. 12.

2 Arlene Croce, 'Ballroom Britannia', *Ballroom Dancing Times* (February 1974), p. 191.

3 Donnie Burns has been president of the World Dance Council (WDC) since 2005.

4 'The Dance Report', American *Vogue*, CLVII/9 (May 1971), p. 192.

5 Dennis Johnson, 'Dance without Tears', *The Guardian* (19 September 1970), p. 11.

6 Ibid.

7 Franks was editor from 1958 to 1963. In 2015 the *Ballroom Dancing Times*, then called *Dance Today*, was reintegrated into the *Dancing Times*.

8 See Pat Kirkham, 'Dress, Dance, Dreams and Desire: Fashion and Fantasy in Dance Hall', *Journal of Design History*, VIII/3 (1995), pp. 195–214.

9 Irene Castle, *Castles in the Air as Told to Bob and Wanda Duncan* (New York, 1958), p. 244.

10 George Lloyd, *Ballroom Fever: A Strictly Love Affair* (London, 2020), p. 112.

11 Ibid., p. 114.

12 Lloyd, *Ballroom Fever*, p. 118.

13 Conversation with Michael Stylianos and Lorna Lee-Stylianos, 10 August 2021.

14 The team, together with Spencer and Lloyd, were Anne Lingard, Pat Thompson, Michael Stylianos and Dennis Drew.

15 Bryan Allen 'Blackpool, All Change: Part 1', *Ballroom Dancing Times* (July 1979), p. 374.

16 'Gwenethe Walshe, a Profile', *Ballroom Dancing Times* (July 1958), p. 411.

17 Christine Ajudua, 'A Temple for Night Life, Reborn', *New York Times* (25 June 2015), p. D6.

18 David Walsh, '*Saturday Night Fever*: An Ethnography of Disco Dancing', in *Dance, Gender and Culture*, ed. Helen Thomas (Basingstoke, 1993), pp. 112–18.

19 Paul Donovan, 'How Long Can *Come Dancing* Keep Out of Step?', *Daily Mail* (22 July 1978), p. 15. Quoting Bill Irvine.

20 Joseph Hone, 'Dancing and Fiddling', *Listener* (29 April 1976), p. 541.

21 Peter Fiddick, '*Come Dancing* Final on Television', *The Guardian* (29 April 1972), p. 8.

22 Alan Franks, 'Rumba Rhythm Is Out of Step with the Age', *The Times* (1 June 1984), p. 9.

23 Originally part of the 1951 Festival of Britain, and named the Festival Bikini-girl Competition, it was created by Eric Morley, then the PR officer at Mecca.

24 Angella Johnson, 'Rhythm and Hues Attract New Wave to Ballroom Dance Floor', *The Guardian* (14 August 1993), p. 6.

25 Conversation with Jacky Logan, 31 January 2020.

26 Walsh, '*Saturday Night Fever*', pp. 112–18.

27 Pierre, *Latin and American Dances for Students and Teachers* (Düsseldorf, 1948), preface.

28 Originally the London Swing Dance Society.

29 Michael Church, 'Stand By for Australia's Ballroom Blitz', *The Observer* (4 October 1992) p. 57.

30 Alex Moore, *Ballroom Dancing* [1936] (London, 1949), p. 12.

31 The first UK organization to support the teaching profession, the Official Board of Ballroom Dancing, was formed in 1929, then changed its name to the British Council of Ballroom Dancers (BCBD) before becoming the British Dance Council in 1996. The BDC's current president is Marcus Hilton

MBE. Professionals: the first international organization for professional dance teachers was founded in 1950 as the International Council of Ballroom Dancing (ICBD) with P.J.S. Richardson as chair and A. H. Franks as honorary secretary until Alex Moore took over as chair from 1964 until 1979. The name was changed in 1996 to World Dance and DanceSport Council (WDDSC) and again in 2006 to World Dance Council (WDC). Amateurs: following various earlier European incarnations, the World DanceSport Federation (WDSF) started life in 1957 as the International Council of Amateur Dancers (ICAD) with twelve countries as members. The name was changed in 1990 to International DanceSport Federation as part of the strategy to gain recognition as a sport, and in 1995 it became a member of the General Association of Sports Federations and the World Games Association. Importantly, the two organizations had reached an agreement in 1965 that ICAD (now WDSF) would control amateur championships and the ICBD (now the WDC) would control professional championships.

32 See www.freedomtodanceinternational.com, accessed 10 January 2021.

33 Arunas Bizokas and Katusha Demidova, undefeated Ballroom champions, retired in 2019. Dancing together since 2007, they have won ten World Championships, nine UK Open Championships and nine International Open Championships. See http://worldcompetitors.org, accessed 22 October 2019.

34 Schiller had been helping out at the Ballroom Club in Chiswick run by Heather Gladding and Glen Wright, both of whom had worked with TC Dance Club in Kensington. TC dance Club International launched the Arthur Murray franchise in Europe, opening studios in England, and continues offering services and licensing to dance schools in America, but no longer operates in Europe.

35 Conversation with Ralf Schiller, 27 October 2020.

36 Marianka Swain, 'Same Difference', *Dance Today* (April 2010).

37 Swain, 'Same Difference'. Vernon Kemp is a Fellow and Examiner in all ISTD Dancesport faculties and was formerly director of Central London Dance.

14 Twenty-First-Century Ballroom

1 Elaine Williams, 'From Cheek to Chic: Ballroom Is No Longer the Embarrassing Parent of Dancing', *The Guardian* (23 June 1998), p. vi.

2 Couples can be either pro–am (professional competitive dancer + student) or teacher–student (amateur competitive dancer + student).

3 Jack Shepherd, 'SCD Creator Paid Only £4,000 by BBC for Show', www.independent.co.uk, 6 July 2015.

4 Michael Stylianos and Lorna Lee-Stylianos are former seven times International Professional Latin Champions and three times UK and British Open Professional Champions. Since retiring they have held influential advisory roles at the ISTD, the BDF and the National Ice Skating Association, coach leading competitors and organize prestigious competitions.

5 Conversation with Michael Stylianos and Lorna Lee-Stylianos, 10 August 2021.

6 Conversation with Helena Anderson, 29 July 2021.

7 Victor Silvester, *Dancing Is My Life* (London, 1958), p. 224.

8 Ibid., p. 225.

9 Williams, 'From Cheek to Chic'.

10 See www.universitydancesport.com, accessed 19 March 2019.

11 The only other winners have been Lancaster (1981), Leeds (1988), Bristol (2005) and Cardiff in a three-way tie with Oxford and Cambridge in 2003.

12 See www.oudancesport.co.uk, accessed 20 October 2020.

13 Since 2019 Oxford women have Full Blue status and men discretionary Full Blue status. Full Blue usually means national-level success and Half Blue success at county or regional level.

14 'University Dancers Angry at Being Wrong-Footed by Sporting Rules', *The Guardian* (7 November 1992), p. 7.

15 Conversation with Jacky Logan, 31 January 2020.

16 Originally the Gay Olympics, they fought and lost a lawsuit against the IOC, which claimed exclusive rights to the name.

17 The UK SSDC, formed in 2006, has now changed its name to the UK Equality Dance Council (UKEDC); Malcolm Hill and Louise Hunt are chair and vice chair and Peter Meager is the publicity secretary. Meager, who is an active member of various sports organizations, also runs Out4Dance, which provides information on Equality Ballroom and Latin dance classes and social dance events in the UK and engages with dancers, teachers and social dance clubs to spread the word of gender-free dancing.

18 WDC competition rules, May 2020, p. 16.

19 WDSF competition rules, updated June 2021, p. 24.

20 Zoe Anderson, 'Potential Ban on Same-Sex Dance Partners at BDC Competitions', *Dancing Times* (11 July 2014).

21 Alexandra Topping, 'British Dance Council Bids to Ban Same-Sex Couples from the Ballroom', www.theguardian.com, 10 July 2014.

22 Marianka Swain, 'Opinion: Too Strictly? Battle in the Ballroom', https://theartsdesk.com, 18 July 2014.

23 David Brown, 'Strictly Heterosexual Ruling Sends Same-Sex Dancers into a Spin', *The Times* (11 July 2014), p. 3.

24 See www.ndca.org.

25 See www.usadance.org.

26 See http://essda.eu, accessed 17 March 2020.

27 See https://ukedc.org and http://essda.eu.

28 Marianka Swain, 'Stepping Out', *Dance Today* (December 2012), p. 45.

29 Cydney Yeates, 'Nicola Adams Speaks Out amid *Strictly Come Dancing* Same-Sex Pairing Complaints', https://metro.co.uk, 17 September 2020.

30 'Graziano Di Prima: Why Should I Care? Strictly Pro Speaks Out after BBC Show Complaints', www.express.co.uk, 3 January 2020.

31 'Nicola Adams Speaks Out'.

32 George Lloyd, *Ballroom Fever: A Strictly Love Affair* (London, 2020), p. 46.

33 Josephine Bradley, 'In Copenhagen', *Dancing Times* (January 1932), p. 36.

34 See www.sequencedanceuk.co.uk, accessed 24 January 2019.

35 Conversation with Richard Gleave, 25 February 2021.

Select Bibliography

To piece together such a broad and little-researched twentieth-century story, a wide range of sources has been consulted, from professional journals to popular magazine and newspaper articles, film and newsreel, personal anecdotes and contemporary reports, alongside a range of more conventional literature. Some information has been hard to trace and some was conflicting but every effort has been made to be accurate.

Key information was found at archives and libraries: Bishopsgate Institute; British Film Institute Reuben Library; Centre for Dance Research at the University of Roehampton; East Riding Archives; Hammersmith and Fulham Local Studies and Archives; History of Advertising Trust; The History Centre, Blackpool; ISTD Library; Letchworth Garden City Heritage Foundation; Margate Museum; RIBA Library; South East Archive of Seaside Photography; Stevenage Museum; Tyne and Wear Archives and Museums. Digital collections were also used: Richard Powers (www.richardpowers.com), Dance Archives (https://archives.dance) and The Frank and Peggy Spencer Penge Latin American Formation Teams Archive Site (www.pengeformationteams.com).

Abra, Allison, *Dancing in the English Style: Consumption, Americanisation and National Identity in Britain, 1918–50* (Manchester, 2017)

Albrecht, Donald, *Designing Dreams: Modern Architecture in the Movies* (London, 1986)

Allen, Bryan, ed., *The World of Phyllis Haylor and Ballroom Dancing* (London, 1984)

Beaton, Cecil, *The Book of Beauty* (London, 1930)

Buckland, Theresa Jill, *Society Dancing: Fashionable Bodies in England, 1870–1920* (Basingstoke, 2011)

Buckman, Peter, *Let's Dance: Social, Ballroom and Folk Dancing* (London, 1978)

Butlin, Billy, *The Billy Butlin Story: 'A Showman to the End'* (London, 1993)

Casani, Santos, *Casani's Self-Tutor of Ballroom Dancing* (London, 1927)

Casciani, Elizabeth, *Oh, How We Danced! The History of Ballroom Dancing in Scotland* (Edinburgh, 1994)

Castle, Irene, *Castles in the Air as Told to Bob and Wanda Duncan* (New York, 1958)

Castle, Vernon, Mr and Mrs, *Modern Dancing* (New York, 1914)

Croce, Arlene, *The Fred Astaire and Ginger Rogers Book* (London, 1972)

Crozier, Gladys Beattie, *The Tango and How to Dance It* (London, 1913)

Dannatt, Sylvia, *Down Memory Lane: Arthur Murray's Picture Story of Social Dancing* (New York, 1954)

Dodworth, Allen, *Dancing and Its Relations to Education and Social Life* (New York, 1900)

Drower, Jill, *Good Clean Fun: The Story of Britain's First Holiday Camp* (London, 1982)

Ericksen, Julia A., *Dance with Me: Ballroom Dancing and the Promise of Instant Intimacy* (New York and London, 2011)

Fairley, Roma, *Come Dancing Miss World* (London, 1966)

Franks, A. H., *Social Dance: A Short History* (London, 1963)

Golden, Eve, *Vernon and Irene Castle's Ragtime Revolution* (Lexington, KY, 2007)

Gwynne, Michael, *Old Time and Sequence Dancing* (London, 1950)

Hallewell, Kit, *Blackpool, My Blackpool* (Birmingham, 1979)

Harrison, Tom, and Charles Madge, *Britain by Mass-Observation* [1939] (London, 1986)

Hebdige, Dick, *Hiding in the Light: On Images and Things* [1988] (London and New York, 2002)

Henderson, Amy, and Dwight Blocker Bowers, *Red Hot and Blue: A Smithsonian Salute to the American Musical* (Washington, DC, and London, 1996)

Hillier, Bevis, *Art Deco of the '20s and '30s* (London, 1968)

Hoggart, Richard, *The Uses of Literacy: Aspects of Working-Class Life* [1957] (London, 1991)

Irvine, Bill and Bobbie, *The Dancing Years* (Farnborough, 1970)

Lamb, William, *How and What to Dance* (London, 1906)

Langdon, Claude, *Earl's Court* (London, 1953)

Latimer, A. J., *A Bouquet of Old Time Dances* (London, 1948)

Lloyd, George, *Ballroom Fever: A Strictly Love Affair* (London, 2020)

McMains, Juliet, *Glamour Addiction: Inside the American Ballroom Dance Industry* (Middletown, CT, 2006)

Marbury, Elisabeth, *My Crystal Ball: Reminiscences* (London, 1924)

Mayer-Karakis, Brigitt, *Ballroom Icons* (Düsseldorf, 2009)

Mizejewski, Linda, *Ziegfeld Girl: Image and Icon in Culture and Cinema* (Durham and London, 1999)

Moore, Alex, *Ballroom Dancing* [1936] (London, 1942)

—, *The Revised Technique of Ballroom Dancing* (Kingston, 1977)

Murray, Arthur, *How to Become a Good Dancer* [1938] (New York 1955)

Murray, Katherine, with Betty Hannah Hoffman, *My Husband, Arthur Murray* (New York, 1960)

Nott, James, *Going to the Palais: A Social and Cultural History of Dancing and Dance Halls in Britain, 1918–1960* (Oxford, 2015)

—, *Music for the People: Popular Music and Dance in Interwar Britain* (Oxford, 2002)

Orwell, Sonia, and Ian Angus, eds, *The Collected Essays, Journalism and Letters of George Orwell*, vol. IV: *In Front of Your Nose, 1945–1950* (London, 1968)

Osgood Wright, Mabel, *My New York* (New York, 1926)

Parr, Martin, *Our True Intent Is All for Your Delight: The John Hinde Butlin's Photographs* (London, 2002)

Pearson, Lynn F., *The People's Palaces: Britain's Seaside Pleasure Buildings* (Buckingham, 1991)

Pevsner, Nikolaus, *Buildings of England: Lancashire – 2 The Rural North* (London, 1969)

Pierre, *Latin and American Dances for Students and Teachers* (Hounslow, 1948)

Purdom, C. B., *The Building of Satellite Towns: A Contribution to the Study of Town Development and Regional Planning* (London, 1949)

Quirey, Belinda, with Steve Bradshaw and Ronald Smedley, *May I Have the Pleasure: The Story of Popular Dancing* (London, 1976)

Ramirez, Juan Antonio, *Architecture for the Screen: A Critical Study of Set Design in Hollywood's Golden Age* [1986] (Jefferson, NC, and London, 2004)

Reavely, Jack, *Magic Memories through My Eyes and Ears* (self-published, 2011)

Reeser, Eduard, *The History of the Waltz* (Stockholm, 1949)

Richardson, Philip J. S., *A History of English Ballroom Dancing (1910–1945)* (London, 1946)

Scott, Edward, *Dancing as an Art and Pastime* (London, 1892)

Silvester, Victor, *Dancing Is My Life* (London, 1958)

—, *Modern Ballroom Dancing* [1927] (London, 1942)

—, *Sequence Dancing* (London, 1950)

Spencer, Frank and Peggy, *Come Dancing* (London, 1968)

Spencer, Peggy, *The Joy of Dancing: The Next Steps; Ballroom Latin and Jive for Social Dancers of All Ages* (London, 1999)

Thomas, Helen, ed., *Dance, Gender and Culture* (London, 1993)

Thompson, Douglas, *Shall We Dance? The True Story of the Couple Who Taught the World to Dance* (London, 2014)

Toulmin, Vanessa, *Blackpool Tower* (Blackpool, 2011)

—, *Winter Gardens Blackpool* (Blackpool, 2009)

Tynegate-Smith, Eve, *Textbook of Modern Ballroom Dancing* (London, 1933)

Wainwright, Lyndon, *The Story of British Popular Dance* (Brighton, 1997)

Walton, John K., *Blackpool* (Edinburgh, 1998)

Ward, Colin, and Hardy Dennis, *Goodnight Campers! The History of the British Holiday Camp* (Nottingham, 1986)

Acknowledgements

There are many individuals I would like to thank for their help, encouragement and enthusiasm for a project that has taken a while to take shape and a long time to complete. Those with insider knowledge of dancing's professional associations, journalists and curators who helped with unravelling the complex histories of the organizations that run Dancesport, include Bryan Allen, Rebecca Antrobus, Michael Burton, Emma Heslewood, John Leach, Jack Reavely and Michael Williams. Colleagues at Bath Spa University Kerry Curtis, Beth Humphries and John Strachan, and friends Christine Guth and Penny Sparke who offered advice on early ideas and initial drafts. I'd also like to thank Vivian Constantinopoulos who commissioned the book at Reaktion, and extend thanks also to Susannah Jayes and Martha Jay.

Above all the task would have been impossible without the Ballroom and Latin dancers who shared their stories with me: social dancers, formation dancers, IVDA dance captains, and both amateur and professional competition dancers, especially those who provided access to their personal collections of photographs, catalogues and magazines. Helena Anderson, Paul Burbedge, Francesca Canty, Jo Clarke, Brian Dibnah, Frank Fronda, Janet Gleave, Richard Gleave, Keith Gregory, John Jackson, Lorna Lee-Stylianos, Jacky Logan, Peter Meager, Maddi Morelli-Batters, Georgiana Muja, Ted O'Higgins, James Oliver, Jean Picton Bentley, Hendrik Pröhl, Lemington Ridley, Ralf Schiller, Corinne Smither, Michael Stylianos, Angela Thurgood, Lynne Tolhurst (and the formation team dancers) and Viktoriya Wilton.

In particular I want to thank my local ballroom dancing studios, whose dancers and brilliant teachers inspired me to embark on this project: DanceLab Putney, Elizabeth Anderson Dance, Flow Dance and the Grafton Dance Centre.

Illustration Acknowledgements

The author and publishers wish to thank the organizations and individuals listed below for authorizing reproduction of their work:

AKG Images: pp. 185 (Ullstein Bild), 202 (Interfoto/Al Herb); Alamy: pp. 128 (AF Archive), 137 (Album), 138 (Entertainment Pictures), 141 (ClassicStock), 156 (Chronicle), 160 (ZUMA Press, Inc), 225 (Mauritius Images GmbH), 257 (AF Archive); American National Association Masters of Dancing, 1915: p. 53; *Architects' Journal*, 10 March 1926: p. 113; author's collection: pp. 183, 277; *Ballroom Dancing*, Alex Moore, 1942: p. 84; TP Bennett (courtesy of Henk Snoek/RIBA Collections): p. 207; Bishopsgate Institute: pp. 212, 217, 221, 235 (all courtesy of the Peggy Spencer Archive); Bishopsgate Institute: p. 223 (courtesy of the Peggy Spencer Archive and members of the Peggy and Frank Spencer Penge Formation Teams); postcard image courtesy of Bridlington Spa: p. 112; *Building News*, 31 July 1896: p. 24 bottom; from the Butlin's Heritage Collection at the History of Advertising Trust (HAT), by kind permission of Bourne Leisure: pp. 165 (B/3/1/2), 166 (B/2/1/1/2), 243 (B/5/1/8/4/1/35/C48-68); *Casani's Self-Tutor of Ballroom Dancing*, Santos Casani, 1927: p. 69; © Carole Edrich 2014: p. 272; *Fulham Chronicle*, 24 October 1919: p. 107; © Garden City Collection, Letchworth Garden City Heritage Foundation: p. 110 (100.249.138); Geeste-foto: p. 230; Getty Images: pp. 74 (photo © Hulton-Deutsch Collection/Corbis), 144 (photo by Atelier Jacobi/Ullstein Bild), 157 (Archive Photos), 180 (photo by Alex Dellow/*Picture Post*/ Hulton Archive), 245 (Bettmann); photograph courtesy of Keith Gregory: p. 222; Hammersmith and Fulham Local Studies and Archives: pp. 96, 108; © Historic England Archive: p. 227; *A History of English Ballroom Dancing*, Philip J. S. Richardson, 1946: p. 56; *How and What to Dance*, William Lamb, 1906: pp. 14, 35; *How to Become a Good Dancer*, Arthur Murray, 1922: p. 68; *How to Charleston Correctly*, Bemis Walker, 1926: pp. 88, 89; *How to Dance the Foxtrot*, Joan Sawyer, November 1914: p. 52; *Illustrated London News*: pp. 28 (27 June 1908), 45 (5 July 1913); reproduced by kind permission of The International Dance Teachers' Association: p. 94; JoTa Dance Photography (www.facebook.com/JoTaDancePhoto): p. 231; Library of Congress, Washington, DC: p. 116 (Underwood and Underwood photographer, 1930/LC-USZ62-35065); Mary Evans Picture Library: pp. 70, 104 and 126 (Jazz Age Club Collection), 171 (Photo Union Collection), 228 (The John Hinde Archive); *Modern Ballroom*

Index

Page numbers in *italics* indicate illustrations